DELIA'S
HOW TO COOK

This book is published to accompany the television series
Delia's How To Cook
which was produced for BBC Birmingham by Spire Films Ltd
Series Producer: David Willcock
Director: Philip Bonham Carter
Executive Producer for the BBC: Stephanie Silk

Published by BBC Worldwide Ltd,
Woodlands, 80 Wood Lane, London W12 0TT

First published in 1999

ISBN 0 563 38431 X

Edited for BBC Worldwide Ltd by New Crane Publishing Ltd
Printed and bound in Great Britain by Butler & Tanner Ltd, Frome, Somerset
Colour separation by Radstock Reproductions Ltd, Midsomer Norton
Jacket printed by Lawrence Allen Ltd, Weston-super-Mare

DELIA'S
HOW TO COOK

BOOK TWO

Photographs by Miki Duisterhof

Production Editor: Eirwen Oxley Green
Book and TV Series Coordinator: Tamsin Burnett-Hall

I would very much like to thank all the people who have helped me produce *How To Cook Book Two*. Thank you to Flo Bayley, Miki Duisterhof and Karen Hatch for design and photography. To Lindsey Greensted-Benech and Sarah Randell for their invaluable help during the filming. To Celia Stone and Pauline Curran for their assistance with recipe testing. To Linda Dwyer for equipment and Paula Pryke for the beautiful flowers. To my brilliant television crew, David Willcock, Philip Bonham Carter, Keith and Vivien Broome, Simon Wilson, Andy Bates, John Mills, Andy and Davina Young, Sheila Wilson, Beverley Russell, Julia Barclay, Linda Flanigan, Sally Coulthard, Bruce Law and Robert Alexander. Thanks also to Sara Raeburn, Lesley Drummond and Jeanette Farrier for make-up, hair and clothes.

A huge thank you to my life-saving team of Melanie Grocott, Amanda Clark, Tamsin Burnett-Hall and Eirwen Oxley Green.

Finally, my thanks to Kelly's in Essex for their help with the poultry chapter.

Conversion tables

All these are approximate conversions, which have either been rounded up or down. In a few recipes it has been necessary to modify them very slightly. Never mix metric and imperial measures in one recipe, stick to one system or the other. All spoon measurements used throughout this book are level unless specified otherwise; all butter is salted unless specified otherwise.

Weights

½ oz	10 g
¾	20
1	25
1½	40
2	50
2½	60
3	75
4	110
4½	125
5	150
6	175
7	200
8	225
9	250
10	275
12	350
1 lb	450
1 lb 8 oz	700
2	900
3	1.35 kg

Volume

2 fl oz	55 ml
3	75
5 (¼ pint)	150
10 (½ pint)	275
1 pint	570
1¼	725
1¾	1 litre
2	1.2
2½	1.5
4	2.25

Dimensions

⅛ inch	3 mm
¼	5 mm
½	1 cm
¾	2
1	2.5
1¼	3
1½	4
1¾	4.5
2	5
2½	6
3	7.5
3½	9
4	10
5	13
5¼	13.5
6	15
6½	16
7	18
7½	19
8	20
9	23
9½	24
10	25.5
11	28
12	30

Oven temperatures

Gas mark 1	275°F	140°C
2	300	150
3	325	170
4	350	180
5	375	190
6	400	200
7	425	220
8	450	230
9	475	240

Contents

My year in East Anglia: harvests, photographic sessions, football, and writing in the tree house, with a little help from Beau

Introduction

When Book One of *How To Cook* was completed and sent off to the publisher, there was, I suppose, a huge question mark hanging over the whole project, including the television programmes. Would a new look at basic cooking still be a useful thing for the 21st century? Given that there are now so many cookery books and television programmes, would going back to the beginning just seem boring?

Thankfully, as I now offer Book Two, there are no question marks this time round. I am happy to report there is a *great* deal of interest in the basic everyday skills of cooking, particularly amongst the young, whose letters, comments and general enthusiasm have been very encouraging. Here in Book Two we have moved on from the staple ingredients to see how beginners can approach the subjects of meat, fish, poultry and cheese. We examine how to get to grips with the rapidly increasing range of dairy products; we learn about preparing salads and dressings, cooking vegetables and fruits, and understanding how to deal with chocolate. Above all, the well-stocked store cupboard is, I feel, a mark of getting serious about wanting to enjoy a lifetime of cooking and good food.

I am as passionate as ever about wanting to communicate the techniques of good cooking to all who want to learn, and hopefully share with them the same lifetime of joy and pleasure that learning to cook has given – and still is – giving me.

Delia Smith

1

The serious cook's store cupboard

(or capers in the larder)

Why the curious sub-title, you're thinking. Nostalgia, really, because it dates back to the late-1970s, when I was a very coy, shy TV cook hardly daring to look up at the camera. I was trying to expound the virtues of capers as a useful cooking ingredient, and what I said was, 'I always have capers in my larder.' To which I received a very humorous letter from a gentleman curious to know just what kinds of capers I got up to in my larder!

What do I mean when I use the word serious? I suppose what I'm trying to say is that some people like to flirt with the subject of cooking – dip in and out, try a recipe here and there – but everyone knows the difference between a flirtation and a serious relationship: at some point flirtation stops and some kind of commitment begins. Cooking is absolutely like that. If I really, truly want to know how to cook well, then I certainly can, but somewhere along the line a decision has to be made – yes, I am now going to get serious, not just flirt with the idea, but really make a commitment to doing it properly so I can get the best out of eating and cooking for the rest of my life.

What does getting serious mean?

If you want to know how to cook then you need to begin by making life as easy as possible, and this means giving a little time and investment to, first, getting the right utensils and cooking equipment (something that has been emphasised all through *How To Cook*). Secondly, you need to have a well-stocked store cupboard.

Because I'm at the receiving end of a great deal of letters and comments, there is a familiar old carp that surfaces regularly amongst people who only flirt with cooking. 'Why do I have to go out and buy all those expensive ingredients just for one recipe?' Or, 'Can't I use curry paste in your recipe instead of all that tedious roasting and grinding?' First, if your kitchen cupboard is well stocked you won't often have to make special shopping trips and spend more money. Secondly, most storecupboard ingredients come in bottles or jars and have a long shelf life, so they cost very little over a period of time. And thirdly, dry-roasting and grinding spices in a pestle and mortar can all be done and dusted in 4 minutes at the outside. What that will then give you is twice or three times the depth of flavour.

Flavour is the most important word in cooking

If you're going to bother to cook, you need to get the very best flavour from all the ingredients you use. This doesn't mean that convenience ingredients don't have their place – obviously they do because there are always going to be days when we're simply not able to do much cooking. But on the days when we can, it's wonderful to have a stock of spices and flavouring ingredients within reach – a pinch of this, a splash of that – as and when we need them.

What about the cost?

For some reason, spending money on recipe ingredients and kitchen equipment is sometimes difficult and countless people just muddle along and make do. But think of it this way: if you want to learn to drive you have to pay for lessons, then you can enjoy a lifetime of driving, which will improve your quality of life. Same with cooking: a little investment at the beginning and you'll have years of pleasure in cooking and eating really well.

The well-stocked store cupboard

In the photograph on the previous page, you'll see what every serious cook should have on stand-by. You can use the list that follows in this chapter to have an annual check, which I always try to do in January. It's then that I throw out all stale ingredients and do one shop to replace them. I have learnt the hard way: I've been caught out so often in the past – just about to make a cake that needs mixed spice, for instance, only to find to my horror that mine is a year out of date and very un-spicy.

What you don't need

Certainly not all those foodie designer ingredients that you receive as gifts or buy in an unguarded moment. Be ruthless – you're never going to use that obscure fruit liqueur that Auntie brought back from Yalta, the pickled greengages that date back to the 1980s, or the gaudy-coloured fruit vinegar that looks like bath essence. They're like clothes you never wear, just taking up valuable space. So pack them off to the church bazaar and make room for something really useful.

The basics

What follows is what I think is a good basic list – not everything you're ever going to need, but what you should always have available.

Salt

The very best kind of salt for all cooking is, in my opinion, English sea salt from Maldon, in Essex. It's not a powdery pouring salt that contains chemicals to stop it getting damp and make it pour freely, but an absolutely pure salt that tastes of the sea. If you do a side-by-side tasting you'll find it is less sharp but somehow saltier (so you need to use less).

Maldon salt consists of very pretty, small white crystalline flakes that crush very easily between your fingers for cooking with. For the table, use it either in a good-quality salt mill or a small salt cellar. Crushed sea salt gives jacket potatoes a really crispy crust, and it's wonderful coarsely crushed over chips (or anything fried). I once discovered by accident, sitting at a restaurant table, that a fat, chunky chip wrapped in a rocket leaf, then dipped first in mayonnaise, then in sea salt, is a quite wickedly brilliant combination!

Peppercorns

You might be amused to know that when I first started writing a column for London's *Evening Standard* in 1972 I used to be unmercifully teased about my constant references to 'freshly milled black pepper'. Was that the precursor to the cranberries or liquid glucose of later years? No, I don't recall anyone actually selling out, but I quite definitely had a campaign going. I said I would always refer to pepper as freshly milled and black until I saw no more of the white, musty, dusty stuff that people sprinkle on their food. I'm still campaigning strongly because, even now, unbelievably, it continues to turn up in restaurants.

Black pepper

Black peppercorns are whole immature berries that are harvested while still green and dried in the sun till they turn black. The berries contain a white inner kernel – the hottest part of the berry, which is quite fiery when used on its own – and a black outer husk, which has all the aromatic fragrance that enhances the flavour of food. Thus if you use the whole berries you get a little bit of fire and a lot of aromatic fragrance.

White pepper

Here the berries are allowed to mature before harvesting, the husks are discarded and the white kernels dried to become white peppercorns. The dried berries, stored whole, will keep their aroma for a long time, but once they have been powdered to dust in a factory, hung about on the shelf and stagnated in a pepper pot, there is no surprise that the result is a million miles from the fragrance you can keep locked up in your pepper mill.

Sichuan pepper

Despite its name, this is not actually from the same family as black, white and green peppercorns, but comes from a type of ash tree. It's used in Oriental cooking and is an ingredient of Chinese five-spice powder.

Cayenne pepper

This is an absolute must in the kitchen. It's hot and fiery and needs to be used with extreme caution, but it is brilliant for that little sprinkling of piquancy. It's made from one of the hottest types of chilli, which is dried, then crushed to a powder including the seeds. I'm forever using a pinch here and there, and I love it sprinkled on smoked fish or prawn cocktail. Although spices, once ground, do not have a long shelf life, cayenne does seem to go on longer than most but still needs replacing fairly regularly.

Mustard

Yes, it's true – if you think about it, mustard is the one and only home-grown English spice, and for my money it's the best. I admit this is a personal thing: I like the ferocious kick of English mustard that makes its presence felt even when only very little is used. Although it comes in powdered form, it does have a good shelf life and can be made up as and when you require.

How to make mustard

The oils in mustard are what give it its pungency, but these are not developed in the whole seed or the dry milled powder. What is needed to release their flavour is the chemical reaction brought on by the addition of cold water (not hot, which causes a different reaction), just enough to make a thickish paste. Always make up your mustard in advance, as it needs a good 10-15 minutes for the flavour to develop fully. Mustard is also a good emulsifier: it can help to stabilise something like mayonnaise, and can provide a slight thickening to vinaigrette or Cumberland sauce.

Made-up mustards

There are three of these I would recommend, but first it should be noted that once they are exposed to the air, they deteriorate rapidly and lose much of their kick. This means the lid must be replaced firmly and quickly each time the mustard is used.

Dijon mustard

From Burgundy, in France, this is not as fiery as English mustard, tempered by the mixture of unripe grape juice (verjuice) or diluted wine vinegar. It is extremely good but it's very difficult to keep it fragranced once opened.

Wholegrain mustard

This is a mixture of mustard seeds, spices and wine vinegar, milder than straight made-up mustard but very good for the store cupboard as it not only adds flavour to dressings and sauces but also a lovely seedy texture. It keeps better than Dijon, but still replace the lid quickly to prevent the air from affecting it.

American mustard

You can't really have a barbecue without some of this famous mustard, which comes in squeezy bottles and is a mixture of mustard, turmeric, paprika and other spices. No decent frankfurter or sausage in a hot dog should ever be without it drizzled back and forth over the surface.

Mustard mayhem…

Like olive oils and wine vinegars, mustard suffers greatly from the designer effect, with every flavour, colour and texture under the sun creeping into the mustard jar. My advice is, don't bother. Even if you like the flavour of dill mustard or similar, once opened it will deteriorate very quickly. So don't make the mistakes I've made: one spoonful of some exotic mustard today and the whole lot thrown out several weeks later. If you want dill or tarragon or anything else in your mustard, it's best to add it yourself.

Clockwise from top: English mustard powder, Dijon mustard and wholegrain mustard

Bottled sauces

Worcestershire sauce

The very best-loved of English bottled sauces. I know an American foodie who has crates of the stuff sent over, because the American version never tastes as good. It's such a clever sauce because if you were asked (and didn't know) what the main ingredient was, you would never guess. It's anchovies, but only the finest anchovies from the Basque region of Spain, blended with shallots, onions and garlic and matured for three years. Worcestershire sauce is a flavour provider and enhancer, a real stalwart for jazzing up stocks, gravies and sauces, and for enlivening disappointing ready-meals. Even outside the kitchen it has another pride of place, and that's at every glitzy bar from Teesside to Thailand – because no Bloody Mary anywhere in the world could not include it.

Soy sauce

In this country we've been quite slow switching on to soy sauce, but now – wow! – soy sauce has landed. It is an ancient and crucially important ingredient in the Far East, used not just for seasoning but also for dipping, marinating, tenderising and at the same time purifying. What we need to concern ourselves with for the purposes of cooking is the enormous range in quality, and for cooks who care about quality the best soy sauce is made in Japan, where it is naturally fermented from wheat, soya beans, salt and water (the only ingredients that should appear on the label). Short-cut unnaturally fermented soy sauces are not in the same league, so if you stick to Japanese you'll be sure you're using the best.

Fish sauce (nam pla)

An even later arrival in this country, and in the beginning only available in specialist oriental food shops. Now it is much more widely distributed, and in supermarkets at last. You could almost say this is an Eastern version of Worcestershire sauce, not so much in flavour but in the way it gives the same kind of lift to other ingredients. As its name suggests, it is a fermentation of small, whole fish (sometimes shrimps) and is quite salty, so a little goes a long way. It's an essential ingredient in Vietnamese and Thai cooking, and because of the growing popularity of these cuisines (which I personally love), it has become a staple storecupboard ingredient.

Tabasco sauce

Hot liquid chillies in a bottle. Perfect if you want to perk something up with just a dash of heat, and also useful when you've added fresh chillies to a recipe and they haven't quite provided the heat you wanted – a few drops will supplement it beautifully. There are lots of chilli sauces around, but I find Tabasco has the best chilli flavour.

Organic tomato ketchup

This is simply in a different league to other tomato ketchups. It is totally true to the tomatoes it's made from, as their flavour has not been eclipsed by sugar or artificial sweetness. It's useful in cooking where you want to add true tomato flavour, and it's also great with fish and chips.

Redcurrant jelly

Redcurrant jelly is an invaluable ingredient for sauces, gravies or just to serve with lamb or game, but do make sure it's a good-quality one with a high fruit content, such as Tiptree: cheaper versions are far too sweet, which obliterates the real flavour of the redcurrants.

Cranberry jelly

I always keep cranberry jelly in my cupboard, too – it's good as an instant accompaniment to chicken or game, or can be used in sauces.

Mayonnaise

Home-made is preferable, but, it has to be said, not always practical, so a good-quality bottled mayonnaise should always be on hand. I find I don't use it often enough to buy it in large jars, so, because it stores better unopened, I find a couple of smaller jars are a better bet than having a third of a large jar lurking in the fridge waiting to be used.

Pure vanilla extract

As you'd expect, this is extracted from pure vanilla pods and not made synthetically (extract is the key word; essence is not the same thing). It's very useful for sauces, custards and a million and one sweet dishes or wherever a touch of vanilla flavour is required.

Greek or other types of honey

Personal preference reigns here. I love Greek mountain honey, which stretches as you lift it on the spoon – it never seems too sweet, but full of fragrance with caramel overtones. That said, whichever honey you prefer, it's a storecupboard must. For a quick snack, spread with good butter on freshly baked bread or spoon over thick Greek yoghurt. For recipes see pages 208 and 232.

Maple syrup

Once you get into the habit of pouring maple syrup over porridge or Greek yoghurt and using it in place of sugar to sweeten all kinds of things, you're sure to get addicted. And because Buttermilk Pancakes (Book One) are so quick and easy to make, having some maple syrup to hand means you're never short of an almost-instant dessert. Note: once opened it needs to be stored in the refrigerator and used within 3 months.

Gravy browning

Although, if I'm roasting meat (particularly beef), I often put an onion in to caramelise and colour the gravy, at other times it's useful to be able to add a spot of rich colour if a gravy looks too pale. Gravy browning is just dark caramelised sugar, so a couple of drops won't affect the flavour but will enrich the colour.

Tinned and bottled ingredients

Anchovies

Probably one of the most significant ingredients of all. Not only are they supremely good and highly prized in their own right, they are also very effective in enhancing the flavour of other ingredients. From my studies of 18th-century cooking in England I know that a barrel of anchovies was indispensable in many kitchens to enliven all sorts of recipes. 'But I don't like anchovies,' some of you are thinking. True, they are strong and gutsy – an acquired taste, you could say – but they do grow on you. So keep

trying a little here and a little there until you acquire it, and don't forget that most people who say they don't like anchovies do like Worcestershire sauce, in which anchovies are the main ingredient.

Anchovy essence

This is also a great flavour enhancer and is the British equivalent of the fish sauce of the Far East. As such, it can be used in oriental recipes when fish sauce is not available.

Storecupboard tomatoes

We are very fortunate to have instant tomatoes any time we want them – perhaps they are the most widely used storecupboard ingredient of all. First there's the tinned – chopped or whole – and sometimes in the winter months their flavour in cooking is superior to fresh, provided, of course, they're Italian, as these are way and above the best. Tomato purée and sun-dried tomato paste are also very useful, as are sun-dried tomatoes preserved in oil. But one new ingredient I've grown to love is mi-cuit tomatoes, which are half dried. The tomato flavour is concentrated but they are still quite squidgy and not as chewy as those that are totally dried.

Capers

These little Mediterranean berries – sometimes tiny, sometimes fat and squashy – are another acquired taste, but do persevere. Capers add a lively piquancy to all kinds of dishes, especially sauces and fish. Nobody likes their first alcoholic drink, but we've all experienced how soon *that* catches on, and it's the same with capers. You can buy them either preserved in salt (which I prefer) or in vinegar. Either way you need to place them in a sieve and rinse them under cold water first. Capers in vinegar will keep well once opened, provided the vinegar covers them completely. If it doesn't you'll need to do some topping up.

Cornichons

What we used to get were midget gherkins bottled in malt vinegar that seared your throat, but now, thankfully, we get the real thing, crunchy and fragrant. They are another must in the store cupboard, not just for eating with pâtés or served with drinks but as an important ingredient in tartare sauce (see page 50) and fish recipes.

Horseradish and wasabi

Horseradish is not just a good ingredient for accompanying roast beef or smoked fish, but also for adding flavour to sauces. It can be difficult to find a good creamed horseradish – what happens to the tear-inducing prickle of freshly grated horseradish once it's creamed and bottled is a mystery – but English Provender and Wiltshire Tracklements are the best. But now we can also buy Japanese wasabi. Ground from the cousin of our horseradish and called wasabi root in Japan, it is mixed with cold water just like mustard. Although its main use is as a condiment for sushi (delicious), it is also brilliant mixed into creamed horseradish to give it back its kick. Just use a ¼ teaspoon of wasabi powder to 2 tablespoons of creamed horseradish.

Opposite page, left to right: salted capers, caper berries and capers preserved in vinegar. Above: anchovy fillets

Below, from left: dried shrimps, rice noodles, Thai fish sauce and shrimp paste. Bottom: dried kaffir lime leaves

Olives

A must in every store cupboard, and although you can buy loose olives at deli counters (and it's good to buy small amounts to find which varieties you like), always have them tucked away in the larder in jars or tins as well. That means you can be spontaneous whenever you want to use olives in cooking. I like to have two kinds available: Greek calamata olives, which are quite large, and the tiny purple-brown Provençal ones, which are good for garnishes. Try to buy good-quality olives, and avoid the pitted ones, which are not the best. An olive pitter, *left*, will make removing the stones fairly easy.

Stem ginger in syrup

I always have a jar of this handy – it's lovely in cakes, it does wonders for rhubarb (see page 176), and can be used chopped as a garnish and sprinkled with its syrup over ice cream. It keeps for ages, so it doesn't matter if you're not using it often. My favourite ginger cake is made with this (see page 38).

Coconut milk

This is taken from fresh-grated coconut that has been soaked in water and squeezed to extract a creamy substance. It's great for instant use, as one of the wonderful things about Thai cooking is it can be spontaneous and quick, provided you have all the necessary ingredients in the cupboard.

Creamed coconut

This comes in block form and can be used to enrich curries and sauces. All you do here is grate it, then, using a whisk, blend it with boiling water to a creamy liquid.

Dried coconut powder

A great storecupboard stand-by, this is particularly good in Thai fishcakes (see the recipe on page 54).

Kaffir lime leaves

Fresh, these are very hard to track down, but now they come freeze-dried rather like bay leaves, but with that unmistakable oriental-Thai flavour. Use dried, pounded in a pestle and mortar or soaked in a little hot water, and they're almost as good as new. Fresh leaves can be kept in the freezer.

Shrimp paste

Another Thai ingredient, this is made from fermented salted shrimps that are pounded into a concentrated paste, but it must be cooked and not used in its raw state. Once opened, you need to store it in the fridge with a tight lid on and place it in a polythene bag, as it has quite a strong aroma. But that said, it helps to give a wonderfully authentic flavour to Thai recipes.

Dried shrimps

These have lots of concentrated shrimp flavour, unlike tired and tasteless frozen prawns, which have no value at all. They are available in oriental shops, but have only a short shelf life – about 4 weeks – so buy them in small quantities and, again, keep them refrigerated. They need to be soaked in hot water for 15 minutes before using.

Dried mushrooms

Without doubt one of the best ingredients to hit British food shops in the past century. However much we value them and are grateful for them, cultivated mushrooms will never have the flavour of mushrooms grown in the wild. But now that we can buy dried wild mushrooms, we can all enjoy that special flavour without having to search in country meadows, woods or Wimbledon Common at the break of dawn. Both the French and the Italians produce excellent dried mushrooms, and their native varieties, which include ceps and morels in France and porcini in Italy, are best of all. This means you can always add a touch of luxurious concentrated mushroom flavour whenever you are cooking with mushrooms.

Marigold Swiss vegetable bouillon powder

This is without doubt an ingredient that has revolutionised modern cooking. Before Marigold you had to either make your own stock or resort to the dreaded chemically flavoured cube. Fresh stock can now be bought in supermarkets, but it's expensive and not instantly available. Marigold is made with vegetables and has only pure vegetable flavour, meaning you can have instant stock any time. If there were good-ingredient awards, this would win first prize.

Gelatine

I always try to keep a stock of both powdered and leaf gelatine, and I use both regularly. The powdered variety is added and used in several different ways, which is explained fully in each recipe. Leaf gelatine is always used in the same way, and instructions and photographs are on page 186.

Unrefined sugars

These are made from pure unrefined sugar cane, and are pictured, *right*. This means the colour and flavour that is naturally present in sugar cane has not been refined out to make the sugar pure white. The most recent addition to this range is unrefined icing sugar. I love its flavour and pale-caramel colour when made into icing, and so would now not use white.

Golden syrup

A very British favourite, something that should always be available for sauces, puddings, butterscotch, sticky toffee sauce, treacle puddings or spread thickly on home-made bread with a generous amount of butter.

Molasses

This is the dark-ebony syrup that's left over after sugar has been refined – in unrefined sugars the molasses is included in different degrees. It's very concentrated, so only a little is needed. When I first started cooking you could buy dark (as opposed to golden) syrup. Now it's no longer available, but a little molasses added to golden syrup gives the same effect. One important point, though: now that molasses is widely available, always use it in place of black treacle in recipes – more expensive, but lots more rich, luscious flavour.

Unrefined sugars, clockwise from top right: molasses, golden granulated, dark muscovado (on spoon), light brown soft, golden icing sugar, dark brown soft, demerara, light muscovado and golden caster sugar

Alcohol for cooking

A most important section this one, because a touch of alcohol in any shape or form makes a significant difference to a wide variety of cooking: a splash of wine in a sauce or to deglaze a pan, or as a component in cakes, puddings and casseroles. The list is endless.

Beer and stout

These are good in slowly braised casseroles, particularly with beef or venison when they are subject to long, slow cooking. All the bitterness is cooked away, leaving a rich, mellow, dark sauce.

Strong dry cider

This is always available in my kitchen. It keeps longer than wine and can be used in any recipe that requires wine (making it less expensive). In some cases it is even better than wine, particularly with pork and apples (see page 86). If you have fried some pork sausages, remove them from the pan and keep warm, then deglaze by adding 5 fl oz (150 ml) of cider and a teaspoon of cider vinegar to the pan, let it bubble and reduce, scraping the base of the pan, until it becomes syrupy, then pour over the sausages before serving.

Wine

Using wine in your cooking can transform something quite ordinary into something extremely special, and now that you can buy quarter bottles with screw-tops you can always have some handy. If you have fried some pork chops or a steak, use white for the former, red for the latter, to deglaze the pan (see above) and provide a concentrated sauce to spoon over.

Fortified wines

These are absolute stars, both for drinking and in the kitchen, and over the 30 years I have been cooking I have used them in recipes time and time again. Basically, the ones I use most are dry manzanilla sherry, dry sercial Madeira, Marsala and, lastly, port, which seems to crop up around Christmas time a lot. They all keep well if sealed properly after use.

Spirits

When I first started writing recipes I was always terribly aware of the cost, and when a certain dish called for spirits I would always add the phrase 'available in miniatures'. Now I don't, because I have realised it is actually cheaper to buy the large bottle, the contents of which can be kept almost indefinitely. Here I would choose brandy, whisky, Calvados and rum as the four spirits most likely to be included in recipes.

Shaosing brown rice wine

This always adds that wonderfully authentic flavour and aroma to Chinese cooking. Dry sherry can be used instead, but it's worth hunting around oriental food shops for the real thing if you can.

Armagnac

This is the first cousin of Cognac but with its own special, distinctive flavour. It has a great affinity with prunes, so I have used it both in the brownies and the cake recipe on pages 243 and 244 respectively.

Spices

Always a tricky subject, because it is spices that come under the hammer most often from people who 'don't want to spend a fortune on one recipe'. I would suggest, however, that although the initial expense may seem large, if you think about it teaspoon by teaspoon in recipes over the course of a year, they represent a fraction of the overall cost. Having said that, though, what price is it worth for my very ordinary kitchen to be transformed by the alluring aromas of far-away exotic places? Once the spices are roasted and ground, I can close my eyes and be transported instantly to a Turkish bazaar, a Moroccan market, India, the Caribbean, Africa and the Far East – all are encapsulated in even the humblest collection of spices.

The case for whole spices

For cooks at home, there's no doubt that, for the most part, buying spices whole is best. First, and most importantly, spices, once ground, quickly lose much of their original pungency, whilst whole spices keep their exotic flavour and fragrance locked in for far longer. Then, when the spices are dry-roasted and subjected to heat, all those sublime flavours and aromas can be drawn out in a matter of moments.

Ready-ground spices

Without in any way detracting from what I've just said about whole spices, there are one or two exceptions: it is difficult, for example, to grind cloves or cinnamon, paprika is already ground from dried sweet peppers, cayenne from chilli peppers, and for baking it is easier to use a ready-made mixed spice mix. There is also a case for ground ginger in the kitchen, as it has different uses from fresh ginger. But I would repeat, these spices do not have a long shelf life, so replace them frequently. The best way to buy them is in refill packs, which are less expensive than the jars.

The *How To Cook* spice collection

Obviously whole books have been written about spices, but I will confine myself here to what I believe to be the essential list for every cook. It is hard to communicate in words their individual fragrances and flavours, but here is a little information about each one.

Allspice

This looks like a smooth peppercorn but larger, and it is so called because it is supposed to resemble in flavour a mixture of cloves, nutmeg and cinnamon. However, it is not really like any one of them but has a unique flavour of its own. It is sometimes called Jamaican pepper or pimento, and is used in marinades and pickles – you'll see the whole berries used in jars of commercial pickled herrings, and you can catch some of its flavour in the recipe for Tunisian Aubergine Salad on page 136.

Cardamom

This is an Eastern spice that comes encased in its own sun-dried pods, which are pale green or grey. Inside there is a treasure of tiny black, highly aromatic seeds. This is an important spice in curries, but it also turns up in sweet dishes – I once tasted a cardamom cake in which the flavour of the cardamom had permeated and mingled with the sweetness beautifully. I almost always throw in the pods as well to get every bit of flavour.

Cinnamon (whole and ground)

This is a popular spice that comes from the inner bark of a tree belonging to the laurel family. When whole, its design is exquisite: reddish-brown, brittle-layered curls that are hollow inside. Ground, it is used in home-baked puddings and desserts, and whole in fruit compotes, mulled wines and curries. In Greek cooking a little cinnamon finds its way into savoury dishes, such as the moussaka recipe in Book One. There is something evocative in the smell of home baking when cinnamon is involved, as it reminds me of small bakery shops from when I was a child.

Coriander (whole, never ground)

The leaves of coriander (like fresh limes) became the subject of Delia hype in the early 1990s. I'm unrepentant because attention was drawn to two very important ingredients. But here we are concerned not with the leaves but with the tiny beige-brown seeds, a magical spice that is said to have the flavour of roasted orange peel. Since I have been using the leaves I have come to discern the connection between the two, even though they're at the same time different. Coriander seeds are important in curries, Middle Eastern and Greek dishes.

Cloves

Cloves are like little dark-wooden nails, and can be used almost as such pressed into onions (for bread sauce) or oranges (mulled wine) or studded all over a piece of sugar-and-mustard-glazed gammon. They do have a very pungent aroma and flavour – people who were subjected to oil of cloves as a cure for toothache can't stand them, so strong was their impact – but used subtly cloves are one of my favourite spices and I still love them in apple pies and crumbles.

Cumin (whole)

These are tiny elongated brown-grey seeds, essential to curries, but also widely used in Mexican, Middle Eastern and Moroccan cooking. Roasted and ground, they have a warm, earthy flavour that is intensely fragrant. The combination of cumin and allspice in the Tunisian Aubergine Salad recipe on page 136 is a fine example of the role of spices in cooking.

Fenugreek (whole)

These are tiny, pale-coloured seeds to which I was introduced when a friend gave me a recipe for Sri Lankan curry (*Summer Collection*), a country where they are used widely, as indeed they are in Indian cooking. I have also used them in my Egg and Lentil Curry in Book One. Their

Opposite page, clockwise from top: cumin seeds, cardamom pods, juniper berries, coriander seeds, star anise, nutmeg and (centre) Sichuan peppercorns

flavour is strong, so little is needed, and they are usually used as part of a blend with other spices.

Juniper

A beautifully fragrant spice that is used to make gin, so think of gin and you've got juniper. The berries are purple-black, slightly wrinkled and grown wild in hill country. They ripen in autumn, so perhaps that is why juniper is often served with game and pork, wild boar and other autumnal recipes. It is quite pungent and a little goes a long way. When you place them in a mortar and begin to crush them, their deep fragrance and the anticipation of their flavour cannot fail to please.

Nutmeg and mace (whole)

Nutmeg is one of my favourite spices, one that we in this country have included in recipes throughout our history – think of a speckled brown custard tart, or the shiny nutmeg skin on a rice pudding (see Book One). It's curious how the French have ignored nutmeg, but the Italians and Spanish adore it as much as we do, using it in cheese dishes, pasta sauces and fillings, creamy béchamel and spinach. But a warning: you must never even think of buying nutmeg ready-ground, as it quickly loses all its charm. Instead always have some whole nutmeg and a grater, and grate it as and when you need it. Mace, as you can see in the photograph on page 11, is the outer casing of the nutmeg, resembling a thick meshed cage, which is dried and becomes brittle. It is sold in pieces (blades) and can be used in infusions, such as flavouring milk for a white sauce (see Book One). Ground mace has also been included in British recipes for potted meats, shrimps and fish pâtés. It is impossible to grind it at home, so this one has to be bought ready-ground and the date carefully watched.

Paprika (ground)

This is a spice that's ground from dried sweet red peppers – both mild and hot – and comes labelled as such. In this case hot does not really mean chilli-hot, but more piquant, so have no fear. It is made in Hungary and used extensively in Hungarian and Austrian dishes (in wonderful pepper-scented stews such as goulash or chicken paprika). The Spanish also produce paprika and it turns up in many of their recipes – the famous chorizo sausage is made with it. Recently Spain has been producing smoked paprika from dried smoked peppers, and this has added a whole new dimension to this particular spice. Once again, remember the rule: buy in small quantities and replace frequently.

Saffron

This is made from the dried stamens of a variety of purple crocus. It is therefore expensive, but the good news is you need only very little – the flavour is powerful and so is the colour (see Crunchy Roast Potatoes with Saffron in Book One). You can buy it ready-ground, but I find it best to buy the stamens whole and then pound them to a powder with a pestle and mortar. It can then be mixed with a little water before adding to a recipe, or the powder can be added directly. If, like me, you worry that your paella (see page 106) doesn't look quite as colourful as the one you had in Spain, fear not: you don't need more saffron – in Spain they sometimes cheat and add food colouring!

Star anise

Open a jar of star anise and you're immediately transported to the heart of Chinatown, where the shops seem to be permeated with its exotic aroma. The star shape is the pod and the tiny seeds nestle inside each star petal. It is usually used whole, like cardamom pods, and always looks very pretty. Its flavour faintly resembles aniseed but with warm, spicy overtones.

Turmeric

This is a root that belongs to the ginger family and in some oriental shops can be bought fresh, but the powdered version has been dried and pounded. It has a very fragrant aroma and a brilliant yellow-ochre colour, which is what makes Indian pilau rice that lovely pale yellow. It is also a major ingredient in our own beloved piccalilli. I always use a little in every curry mixture, as much for its fragrance as for its colour. Because it comes ready-ground, it doesn't have a long shelf life, so keep an eye on the date stamp.

Storecupboard extras

Obviously you'll need flour, pasta, rice and all the staples covered in Book One, but here is a list of other useful storecupboard ingredients that – as you begin to cook more and more – you might want to include. This, however, will depend very much on your own tastes and what you cook most often. Because the shelf life of these products is sometimes short, you might like to buy as and when you need them, as a two-year-old half-bag of almonds is only fit for the bird table, as I know to my cost.

Dried fruits: sour cherries, apricots, prunes and vine fruits – currants, raisins, sultanas and so on.

Nuts: unsalted pistachios (these actually keep well in the freezer), unblanched almonds, roasted unsalted peanuts, walnuts, pecans, brazils and pine nuts.

Coarse semolina for gnocchi (page 230).

Sweet oat biscuits and Grape-Nuts for cheesecake bases (page 232).

Chocolate and cocoa powder: unlike the items above, these should *always* be included, and notes on these are on pages 236 and 237.

The extended store cupboard

What I have included in this chapter is by no means an exhaustive list: there are literally hundreds of fascinating and useful storecupboard ingredients that I have not included but that you may want to use. What I have done is try to include what I use most of and what I feel is a good start for beginners.

Pad Thai
Noodles with
Shrimps

There's a long story attached to this recipe. I first ate it in a small street café in Ko Samui, an island off Thailand. It was so supremely good that my husband videoed it in close-up so that I could recreate the whole thing at home. I did, and here it is – every bit as good, I'm glad to say.

Serves 2 as a main course
4 oz (110 g) rice noodles (medium width, about ⅛ inch/3 mm thick)
2 tablespoons dried shrimps
6 oz (175 g) raw headless tiger prawns (if frozen, thoroughly defrosted)
3 tablespoons groundnut or other flavourless oil
2 cloves garlic, peeled and crushed
2 medium red chillies, deseeded and finely chopped
½ medium red onion, thinly sliced into half-moon shapes
2 tablespoons Thai fish sauce
juice 1 large lime (about 2 tablespoons)
2 large eggs, lightly beaten

For the garnish:
2 heaped tablespoons fresh coriander leaves
2 oz (50 g) natural roasted unsalted peanuts, roughly chopped or crushed in a pestle and mortar
2 spring onions, chopped, including the green parts

You will also need a deep frying pan with a diameter of 10 inches (25.5 cm), or a wok.

The way to tackle this is by having all the ingredients on the list prepared and assembled in front of you. First of all place the dried shrimps in a jug, cover with some boiling water and soak for 10 minutes, then do the same with the noodles, placing them in a bowl and making sure they're totally submerged in boiling water. After this time, drain the noodles in a colander and rinse them in cold water, then drain the shrimps. Now, to prepare the prawns, peel off and discard the shells, then you need to devein them. To do this, make a slit all along their backs using a small, sharp knife and remove any brownish-black thread, using the tip of the knife to lift it out. Now chop each prawn into 3.

When you're ready to start cooking, heat the oil in the frying pan or wok over a high heat until it is really hot. Then, first add the garlic, chilli and red onion and fry for 1-1½ minutes, or until the onion is tender, then, keeping the heat high, add the soaked dried shrimps and the prawns and fry for a further 2 minutes, or until the prawns have turned pink and are cooked. After that add the fish sauce and the lime juice, then stir this around for just a few seconds before adding the noodles. Now toss them around for 1-2 minutes, or until the noodles are heated through. Next add the beaten egg by pouring it slowly and evenly all over. Let it begin to set for about 1 minute, then stir briefly once more until the egg is cooked into little shreds. Then mix in half the garnish and give one final stir before serving absolutely immediately in hot bowls with the rest of the garnish handed round to be sprinkled over.

Anchoïade with Toasted Goats' Cheese Croutons

It's true that, because of overkill, everybody is tired of sun-dried tomatoes, but now we can buy semi-dried tomatoes, called mi-cuit or sun blush, which are more squashy and succulent, with lots of concentrated tomato flavour.

This is literally made in moments: all you do is place all the ingredients in a food processor, then briefly process until the mixture is chopped roughly. Store it in a bowl covered with clingfilm at room temperature till needed.

For the croutons, cut the baguettine into 12 slices on the diagonal (about ½ inch/1 cm thick), then spread very thinly with the goats' cheese and season with salt and pepper. Place on the baking tray and bake on the centre shelf of the oven for 20 minutes, until crisp and golden.

To serve, spread the anchoïade generously on to the baked croutons, garnish with the basil leaves and olives, and serve with something like a well-chilled Provençal rosé.

Instead of the croutons you could use the goats' cheese, onion and potato bread from Book One, toasted under the grill, as pictured below.

Serves 4

2 oz (50 g) anchovy fillets, drained
2 mi-cuit tomatoes
1 ripe tomato, skinned
1 heaped dessertspoon tomato purée
2 shallots, peeled
8 black olives, pitted
2 cloves garlic, peeled
1 teaspoon fresh oregano
1 tablespoon roughly chopped fresh basil
1 teaspoon white wine vinegar
freshly milled black pepper

For the croutons (makes 12):
1 oz (25 g) soft goats' cheese
1 baguettine
salt and freshly milled black pepper

To garnish:
basil leaves
black olives (preferably small Provençal ones)

You will also need a baking tray measuring 10 x 14 inches (25.5 x 35 cm).

Pre-heat the oven to gas mark 4, 350°F (180°C).

Linguine with Sardines, Chilli and Capers

Serves 2

8 oz (225 g) dried linguine
1 x 120 g tin sardines in olive oil, well drained and flaked into bite-sized pieces
1 tablespoon sardine oil, reserved from the tin
1 red chilli, deseeded and finely chopped
1 tablespoon salted capers, rinsed and drained
1 clove garlic, peeled and chopped
1 x 200 g tin Italian chopped tomatoes, well drained, or 4 ripe, medium-sized tomatoes, skinned and diced
a few fresh basil leaves, roughly torn, to garnish
salt and freshly milled black pepper

Good old tinned sardines are now becoming fashionable again and are an ideal storecupboard ingredient, great for serving on toast sprinkled with a little balsamic and lots of seasoning. This is also the perfect storecupboard meal for two, made in moments and great for students or anyone on a tight budget. I love the shape of linguine, but any pasta can be used.

First of all you need to cook the pasta. Always use a large cooking pot and make sure you have at least 4 pints (2.25 litres) of water for every 8 oz (225 g) of pasta and 1 level tablespoon of salt. Bring the water up to a good fierce boil before the pasta goes in and cook it for 8-12 minutes without a lid, until *al dente*.

Meanwhile, heat the tablespoon of sardine oil in a small frying pan, fry the garlic and chilli for about 4 minutes, until softened, then add the tomatoes, sardines and capers and gently heat them through, stirring occasionally. Taste and season with salt and freshly milled black pepper.

When the pasta is ready, drain it into a colander, then quickly return it to the saucepan. Add the sauce, toss it around thoroughly for 30 seconds or so, then serve in hot pasta bowls with the torn basil sprinkled over.

Mexican Guacamole

The first time I ever used Tabasco (hot chilli sauce) was when I made my first guacamole. This spicy Mexican purée, made with fresh avocados, chillies and ripe tomatoes, is still a great favourite. Serve it as a first course with good crusty bread or as a dip with raw vegetable strips. Don't make guacamole more than 3 hours ahead, though, or it will discolour.

First it's important to have ripe avocados. All you do is halve them, remove the stones, then cut them into quarters, remove the flesh from the skin and place it in the bowl of a food processor. Now, using a teaspoon, scrape away any green part of the avocado flesh that has adhered to the skin and add this, as this will help to give lots of green colour. Now skin the tomatoes by pouring boiling water over them, then leave them for exactly 1 minute before draining and slipping off their skins (protect your hands with a cloth). Then halve them and pop them in to join the avocado, followed by the garlic, onion and chillies, and then add the lime juice, a few drops of Tabasco and some salt and pepper. Now whiz it all to a smooth purée, pile it into a serving bowl and cover with clingfilm. Chill till you need it and serve it sprinkled with the fresh coriander leaves.

Serves 4

2 ripe avocados
2 large, red, ripe tomatoes
2 small cloves garlic, peeled and sliced
½ red onion, cut into quarters
2 small red chillies, halved and deseeded
juice 2 limes
a few drops Tabasco
2 tablespoons fresh coriander leaves, to garnish
salt and freshly milled black pepper

Marinated Pork with Jerk Seasoning and Grilled Pineapple Salsa

In the Caribbean, jerk seasoning comes either wet or dry. The latter is made with dried herbs, which I don't usually have available, so this is the wet version – great for a barbecue or just plain-grilled.

Serves 6

6 large British pork chops
1 large red chilli, deseeded
½ small red onion
½ tablespoon chopped fresh
flat-leaf parsley
1 clove garlic, peeled
¾ inch (2 cm) piece fresh root ginger,
peeled and sliced
½ teaspoon Maldon sea salt
½ teaspoon allspice berries, ground
¼ fresh nutmeg, grated
⅛ teaspoon ground cinnamon
⅛ teaspoon ground cloves
juice 1 lime
1 tablespoon Japanese soy sauce
1 tablespoon groundnut or other
flavourless oil
1 tablespoon molasses sugar
10 fl oz (275 ml) dry white wine
salt and freshly milled black pepper

For the pineapple salsa:

1 medium pineapple
1 tablespoon groundnut or other
flavourless oil
1 tablespoon runny honey
1 small red onion, peeled and very
finely chopped
½ medium red chilli, deseeded
and diced
juice 1 lime
2 tablespoons chopped fresh
coriander leaves
salt and freshly milled black pepper

You will also need a baking tray
measuring 11 x 16 inches (28 x 40 cm).

Start this way ahead of time: trim the fat off the chops and season them with salt and pepper, then place all the other ingredients, except the wine, in a food processor and mix to a thick paste. Next spread half the paste over the base of a shallow dish, place the pork chops on top, then spread the rest of the paste over the surface of each chop. Now cover the dish with clingfilm and leave for a few hours so the flavours can develop.

Meanwhile, make the salsa, and to do this you need to first pre-heat the grill to its highest setting, then mix the oil and honey with a good seasoning of salt and black pepper. Then, using a sharp knife, cut the top and bottom off the pineapple and, standing it upright on a chopping board, remove the skin using a large serrated knife, then dig out the 'eyes' using the tip of a potato peeler. Now cut the pineapple in half lengthways, then lay each half, cut-side down, on the surface and slice each into 6 long wedges. After that, trim off the inner core. (See the photographs on page 197.) Next brush each wedge with the honey mixture and place them on the baking tray, then pop them under the grill about 1½ inches (4 cm) from the heat and grill for 10-15 minutes, until they become nicely charred; you'll need to turn them halfway through the cooking time. After that, remove them from the grill and allow them to cool slightly before chopping roughly into ½ inch (1 cm) pieces and mixing them with the remaining salsa ingredients. Then set aside till needed.

When you're ready to cook the chops, pre-heat the grill to its highest setting for at least 10 minutes. Place the chops on the same baking tray, making sure their surface is completely covered with the marinade (reserve the marinade left in the dish), then grill them 3 inches (7.5 cm) from the heat for about 15 minutes. After that, turn them over, spread the surface with the rest of the marinade and grill for another 15 minutes, until the chops are cooked and the surface is nice and crisp. Remove the pork to a serving dish, then scrape any crusty bits and remaining marinade from the baking tray into a small saucepan. Add the dry white wine, let it bubble and reduce by about a third, and pour it over the pork before seasoning. Serve with the salsa.

Beef Curry Dopiaza

The word dopiaza means double onion, and because I really love thick, spicy onions, it's what I always order in Indian restaurants. My recipe is not authentic, but I feel it is as good as any I've had.

Serves 4

2 lb (900 g) chuck steak, chopped into
1 inch (2.5 cm) pieces
1 rounded teaspoon cumin seeds
1 rounded teaspoon coriander seeds
3 cardamom pods (whole)
1 teaspoon fennel seeds
1 teaspoon whole fenugreek
(alternatively, use powder)
3 tablespoons groundnut or other
flavourless oil
1 lb (450 g) onions, peeled and
sliced into half-moon shapes about
½ inch (1 cm) thick
3 cloves garlic, peeled and crushed
3 green chillies, deseeded and
finely chopped
1 tablespoon ground turmeric
1 tablespoon freshly grated peeled
root ginger
2 medium tomatoes, skinned
and chopped
3 oz (75 g) creamed coconut
10 fl oz (275 ml) boiling water
5 fl oz (150 ml) natural yoghurt
salt and freshly milled black pepper

To serve:
juice 1 lime
1 tablespoon chopped fresh
coriander leaves

You will also need a lidded flameproof
casserole with a capacity of 4 pints
(2.25 litres).

First of all you need to roast the whole spices, and to do this place them in a small frying pan or saucepan over a medium heat and stir and toss them around for 1-2 minutes, or until they begin to look toasted and start to jump in the pan. Now transfer them to a pestle and mortar and crush them to a powder.

Next place 2 tablespoons of the oil in the casserole over a high heat and, when it is really hot, brown the pieces of meat a few at a time. Remove them to a plate, then add the rest of the oil and, when that's really hot, too, fry the onions till well browned – about 10 minutes – then add the garlic and chilli and cook for a further 2 minutes.

Next return the meat to the pan, add the crushed spices, fenugreek powder (if you were unable to buy it whole), turmeric, ginger and tomatoes and stir everything around. Next grate the creamed coconut into a bowl and combine it with the boiling water using a whisk, then, when it has dissolved, pour it into the casserole, followed by the yoghurt and some seasoning. Now bring the mixture up to a slow simmer, put the lid on the casserole and simmer very gently for 2 hours. Just before serving, add the lime juice and sprinkle over the chopped fresh coriander. Serve with spiced basmati rice and Coriander Chutney (see Book One).

*Beef Curry Dopiaza served with
Basmati Rice, Coriander Chutney
and Mango Chutney*

Lambs' Kidneys with Two Mustards

This is a lovely light recipe for summer, when lambs' kidneys are at their plump best. I like to keep the mustard flavour quite subtle, but if you like it more pronounced, just add a little more mustard.

Serves 2-3

1 lb (450 g) lambs' kidneys
1 heaped teaspoon mustard powder
2 heaped teaspoons hot wholegrain mustard
½ oz (10 g) butter
1 dessertspoon groundnut or other flavourless oil
1 small onion, peeled, halved and thinly sliced into half-moons
4 oz (110 g) small open-cup mushrooms, cut into ¼ inch (5 mm) slices
3 fl oz (75 ml) dry white wine
7 fl oz (200 ml) crème fraîche
salt and freshly milled black pepper

You will also need a frying pan with a diameter of 10 inches (25.5 cm).

First prepare the kidneys: cut them in half horizontally and snip out the white cores with scissors – if you don't the kidneys will be tough – then peel off and discard the skins. Next place the frying pan over a high heat and heat the butter and oil together. When it's hot and foaming, add the kidneys and cook for 3 minutes, turning them over halfway through. Next remove them to a plate, then add the onion to the pan and, keeping the heat high, cook for 3-4 minutes, until softened and brown at the edges. Now add the mushrooms and cook for another 1-2 minutes, until the juices just start to run out, then add the white wine and let it bubble and reduce to half its original volume. Finally, add the crème fraîche and mustards. Now give everything a good seasoning, stir well and carry on reducing the liquid for 2-3 minutes. Finally, return the kidneys and their juices to the sauce and heat through for about 1 minute. Serve right away with plain basmati rice.

Oriental Pork Casserole with Stir-Fried Green Vegetables

This is quite an exotic recipe, a wonderful combination of flavours that develop and permeate the pork as it cooks very slowly. The surprising thing is the casserole takes only 6 minutes or so to prepare from start to finish. Serve it with Thai fragrant rice.

All you need to do is arrange the pork in a single layer in the base of a lidded flameproof casserole with a capacity of 4 pints (2.25 litres), then simply mix all the other ingredients (except the cinnamon and star anise) together, give them a good whisk and pour over the pork. Now tuck in the cinnamon sticks and star anise, place the casserole on the hob and bring everything up to a very gentle simmer. Put the lid on and simmer over the gentlest-possible heat for 45 minutes. At that point turn the pieces of pork over, replace the lid and simmer for 45 minutes more.

For the stir-fry, first prepare the vegetables: the cauliflower should be separated out and cut into tiny florets, and the same with the broccoli. Wash and trim the leeks, then halve and thinly slice them, while the spring onions should be sliced into matchsticks, as should the ginger. Finally, cut each head of pak choi into 6 wedges through the root.

When you're ready to cook, heat the oil over a high heat in a wok. Add the ginger and garlic and fry for 10 seconds, then add the cauliflower and broccoli and stir-fry for 1 minute. Next add the leeks and stir-fry for another minute. Add the spring onions and pak choi, toss everything together, then add the liquid and sugar. Reduce the heat to medium, put a lid on and cook for 4 minutes, stirring occasionally. Serve the pork and stir-fried greens with the spring onions and chilli sprinkled over each portion, remembering to remove the cinnamon sticks and star anise first. Note: if you like, spinach leaves can be used instead of pak choi.

Serves 4-6

2 lb (900 g) shoulder of British pork, chopped into 1 inch (2.5 cm) cubes
4 fl oz (120 ml) Japanese soy sauce
1 rounded tablespoon freshly grated peeled root ginger
1 dessertspoon molasses sugar
1 small onion, peeled and finely chopped
2 cloves garlic, peeled and crushed
2 medium red chillies, deseeded and finely chopped
4 fl oz (120 ml) Shaosing brown rice wine or dry sherry
2 x 3 inch (7.5 cm) cinnamon sticks
2 whole star anise

For the stir fried green vegetables:
4 oz (110 g) cauliflower
6 oz (175 g) broccoli
2 medium leeks
4 spring onions
2 inch (5 cm) piece root ginger, peeled
10 oz (275 g) pak choi
2 tablespoons groundnut or other flavourless oil
2 cloves garlic, peeled and thinly sliced
3 tablespoons Japanese soy sauce
3 fl oz (75 ml) Shaosing brown rice wine or dry sherry
3 fl oz (75 ml) water
1 dessertspoon golden caster sugar

To garnish:
2 spring onions, cut into fine shreds 1 inch (2.5 cm) long
½ medium red chilli, deseeded and cut into fine shreds

Preserved Ginger Cake with Lemon Icing

In all my years of cooking, this is, quite simply, my favourite cake. It's simple but absolute heaven. The spiciness of the ginger within the moist cake, coupled with the sharpness of the lemon icing, is such that it never fails to please all who eat it.

Makes 15 squares
5 pieces preserved stem ginger in syrup, chopped
2 tablespoons ginger syrup (from jar of stem ginger in syrup)
1 heaped teaspoon ground ginger
1 heaped teaspoon grated fresh root ginger
6 oz (175 g) butter, at room temperature, plus a little extra for greasing
6 oz (175 g) golden caster sugar
3 large eggs, at room temperature
1 tablespoon molasses syrup
8 oz (225 g) self-raising flour
1 tablespoon ground almonds
2 tablespoons milk

For the topping:
juice 1 lemon
8 oz (225 g) unrefined golden icing sugar
2 extra pieces preserved stem ginger in syrup

You will also need a non-stick cake tin measuring 6 x 10 inches (15 x 25.5 cm), 1 inch (2.5 cm) deep, and some silicone paper (parchment) measuring 10 x 14 inches (25.5 x 35 cm).

Pre-heat the oven to gas mark 3, 325°F (170°C).

First prepare the cake tin by greasing it lightly and lining it with the silicone paper: press it into the tin, folding the corners in to make it fit neatly (see Book One) – the paper should come up 1 inch (2.5 cm) above the edge.

To make the cake, take a large mixing bowl and cream the butter and sugar together until light and fluffy. Next break the eggs into a jug and beat them with a fork until fluffy, then gradually beat them into the mixture, a little at a time, until all the egg is incorporated. Next fold in the ginger syrup and molasses; the best way to add the molasses is to lightly grease a tablespoon, then take a tablespoon of molasses and just push it off the spoon with a rubber spatula into the mixture. Now sift the flour and ground ginger on to a plate, then gradually fold these in, about a tablespoon at a time. Next fold in the almonds, followed by the milk, and lastly the grated root ginger and pieces of stem ginger. Now spread the cake mixture evenly in the cake tin, then bake on the middle shelf of the oven for 45-50 minutes, or until the cake is risen, springy and firm to touch in the centre. Leave the cake to cool in the tin for 10 minutes, then turn it out on to a wire rack and make sure it is absolutely cold before you attempt to ice it.

For the icing, sift the icing sugar into a bowl and mix with enough of the lemon juice to make the consistency of thick cream – you might not need all the lemon juice. Now spread the icing over the top of the cake, and don't worry if it dribbles down the sides in places, as this looks quite attractive. Cut the remaining ginger into 15 chunks and place these in lines across the cake so that when you cut it you will have 15 squares, each with a piece of ginger in the centre. It's absolute heaven. If you'd like one or two of these cakes tucked away for a rainy day, they freeze beautifully – simply defrost and put the icing on half an hour before serving.

2

Fish without fear

Why is it that people are afraid to cook fish? Is it fear of the unknown, the unfamiliar, or are there now just too many varieties to choose from, making it difficult for a beginner to know where to start? Given that so many people love eating fish but so few want to cook it, I feel my task here is to reassure those of you who are afraid and try to provide a sort of simple introduction to the whole subject of fish cooking, which will hopefully persuade you to try.

It has to be said that fish is in the premier league as far as the 21st-century diet is concerned. Perhaps the singularly most important reason for this is speed – because for people who lead busy, pressured lives it's one of the few ingredients that can provide a main-course supper dish that's not only elegant, stylish and bang up-to-the-minute, but at the same time takes as little as 10 and rarely more than 30 minutes to prepare from start to finish.

But there's more. Nutritionally fish is not only rich in first-class protein, which is an essential part of our daily diet, but at the same time it happens to be, conveniently, low in fat (for the most part). Then, by some extra miracle of nature, the group known as oily fish (a bad description, because they actually contain a very small amount of fat) contains substances known as omega-3 fatty acids that are beneficial in preventing clogged arteries, which cause heart diseases and certain skin conditions. We should therefore all be eating and, more importantly, enjoying more fish. So here goes – I am going to have a big crack at persuading you. Let's first examine what the pitfalls might be.

The fear factor

Here, familiarity is the key – getting to know about fish and understanding it will automatically make you much more comfortable, so read on.

I don't know how to handle it

There's a bit of hand-me-down mythology here. Who says it necessarily needs handling? This is merely a kickback from the days when cooks had to deal with freshly landed fish that needed scaling, gutting, filleting and so on. With modern fishmongers, fish counters and chill cabinets, all this work is done for you. If you want to, you can now buy fish skinned, boned and ready to cook, which probably means less handling than trimming the average steak. Sometimes, as with jointing a chicken, some handling is needed, but only for those who choose it. Anyway, here all the handling you will ever need to know about will be explained to remove all the fear.

What about the bones?

Well, firstly, as explained above, there don't have to be any at all. However, if you really enjoy eating a wide variety of fish that is not always filleted, there's no bones about it (excuse the pun), provided you know how to handle and deal with them. This includes a few basic lessons, not just on preparation for cooking but also on how to actually eat the fish once it arrives on the plate (see the next point).

And the skin?

I used to be absolutely terrified of skinning a piece of fish because I simply didn't know how to do it, then I was taught and I've never looked back.

So, if I can teach you how to do it (see page 45), you, too, will no longer have any fears. But let me say that as a fish lover, I feel that leaving the skin on is sometimes preferable because it can give extra flavour to the dish (in which case it can simply be left on the side of the plate). However, it's now become fashionable in restaurants to sear the de-scaled skin of certain fish at very high temperatures so that it becomes so crisp that it resembles crackling, and this is, I have to say, quite delicious!

What about the smell?
There really shouldn't be any. If you have a reliable fishmonger and you buy fresh fish, it should not smell unpleasant; in fact the opposite is true – the smell of fresh fish sizzling in the pan can be quite appetising. As with all cooking, however, kitchens need to be well ventilated, with a window open or an extractor fan on. Kippers are perhaps the exception to this no-smell rule, but keep the window wide open as you cook them, or, if you get the chance, try cooking them outside on the barbecue: no smells to linger, and char-grilled they taste absolutely wonderful.

Where have all the fishmongers gone?
It has to be said that if you want to cook and enjoy eating fish, then your source is vital. Sadly, high-street food suppliers are victims of parking restrictions and I imagine we can put much of the blame for the demise of our fishmongers on those horrid yellow lines, making the free-parking offer of the supermarkets much more practical. However, there are still good fishmongers who need our support. What happens in supermarkets is that some fish counters, together with the pre-packed fish they sell, are of superb quality, others not so, but because this does vary enormously from store to store, the best guide is your nose. If, as you walk towards the fish counter, you can smell fish, don't approach it.

How much do I need?
I would say 7-8 oz (200-225 g) per person for boned white fish; on the bone (whole trout, plaice, mackerel and so on), 10-12 oz (275-350 g) each; and richer fish, such as salmon or tuna, 6-8 oz (175-225 g) would be right.

What kind of fish?
For a beginner I feel the best way forward is to get to know just a few varieties of fish and what to expect from them, so what I've tried to do here is firstly put them into groups to give you an initial guide.

Firm and flaky
This is essentially the cod family, which includes cod, haddock, hake and whiting. If you want a fairly firm, flaky flesh that is moist and succulent with a delicate flavour, this is what you'll get from this group.

Firm and meaty

This group, as these words imply, has more bite to it, and because it's more robust in texture, it can stand up to more vigorous cooking. Turbot and halibut are in this league, as are monkfish tails, and all have a fine flavour.

Delicate

This includes most of the group we call flat fish, and their texture varies. Skate, *left*, has sweet white flesh and an excellent texture; Dover sole has a fairly firm flesh with a fine flavour; lemon sole has a more delicate flesh and not such a good flavour; plaice is one of my own favourites, as it has a very fragile flesh and a lovely fragrant flavour of the sea, but only in the right season (June to November).

Lots of gutsy flavour

The oily fish group are for those who like real flavour, and herring, mackerel, sardines, sprats and whitebait all belong to this family – juicy and succulent, with tons of flavour. Here you are going to have to negotiate with bones, but it's worth it for the taste alone.

The king of fish

The salmon is definitely crowned king. Caught wild, it leaves the sea to enter the rivers, and it has just about everything: firm yet delicate flesh, and all the flavour of the sea. Farmed, it can be excellent or very poor. Thankfully it's easy to tell (*see left*) – too many white fat layers mean poor quality. The reason for this, believe it or not, is lack of exercise. The wild salmon negotiates strong currents, giving it a kind of 'aerobic' existence, and good farmed salmon comes from lochs and areas where strong currents exist.

Trout

Salmon trout – or sea trout, as it's sometimes called – looks like a small salmon, but though it has the appearance of salmon, it's less fatty and the flesh is more delicate. Trout proper is its small freshwater cousin that lives in lakes, rivers and streams. Wild it's called brown trout, is exceptionally special and only available if you know someone who goes fishing, but farmed it's called rainbow trout and is not so flavoursome.

Smoked fish

All the fish just mentioned can be smoked, and the flavour of the smoke and fish is an inspired combination. Finnan haddock is smoked on the bone, but is also sold as fillets, as is cod and whiting. Arbroath smokies are small young haddock or whiting that are smoked to a dark-bronze colour, which actually cooks them, so they only need re-heating. Smoked mackerel and kippers are similarly smoked, so no cooking is needed here, either; the grill or barbecue is enough to re-heat them.

There's nothing to be afraid of

Now you are embarking on a journey of learning how to cook fish, but although I have said everything can be prepared for you, I am including instructions on how to bone and skin fish – just in case you want to learn, or perhaps find yourself the lucky recipient of some freshly caught fish.

How to skin a fillet of fish

All you need is a flat surface and a sharp knife. First of all angle the knife at the thinner or tail end of the fillet, or, if it's all the same thickness, just start at one end. Cut a little bit of the flesh away from the skin – enough to get the knife angled in. Now, using your fingertips, hang on to the skin, clasping it as firmly as possible, then push the knife with your other hand, keeping the blade at an angle, *opposite, bottom left*. Push at the skin, not the flesh, remembering the skin is tough and the knife won't go through it. What's happening is the knife blade, as it slides between the skin and the flesh, is cutting the skin away. If you're not experienced, don't worry if you're left with a few patches of skin, you can just gently cut these away. Practice is all you need and you'll soon be able to feel when the angle of the knife is right.

How to bone a whole fish

This method applies to herring, mackerel and trout. First ask the fishmonger to scale and trim the fish, and if he will bone it for you, so much the better; if not, it really is dead simple. All you do is cut along the belly of the fish with scissors, snipping off the head, fins and, if you need to, the tail, then place it flesh side down on a flat surface. Now, using a rolling pin, give the fish a few sharp taps to flatten it out. Next press very firmly with your thumbs or the handle of a wooden spoon, *top right*, all along the back bone of the fish, which will loosen it. Now turn the fish skin-side down and, using a sharp knife and starting at the head end, gently ease the back bone away, *centre*: as it comes away, almost all the little bones will come away with it. Any that don't can be removed afterwards, and tweezers are helpful here. Finally, cut away the dark belly flaps using scissors, *bottom*.

How to cook fish

Set out over the next few pages are simple guidelines for various methods of cooking fish. Then, when you have tried the recipes, which each describe in detail how to cook the fish, you will have a fairly broad knowledge and, I hope, feel comfortable with fish cookery for the rest of your life. The timings that follow are guidelines, so just remember that thicker pieces of fish will need the longer times, thinner pieces the shorter.

Poaching

Poached smoked haddock, topped with a couple of fresh, lightly poached eggs and served with some brown bread and butter, is one of the quickest and best comfort meals I know. Poaching is fast, easy and no-fuss, and if you want to serve a sauce with the fish, then using the poaching liquid introduces the flavour of the fish itself. Thus the liquid from white fish poached in a mixture of half milk and half water can be used for a parsley sauce, and the cooking liquid from smoked fish fillets poached in the same way can be used to make a basic white sauce to which chopped hard-boiled eggs and chives can be added. Either sauce can be finished off beautifully with a tablespoon of cream or crème fraîche.

Rolled fish fillets, ie plaice or sole, can be poached in white wine or cider, which again will make a lovely sauce. Trout can be poached in a pan of water to which a glass of dry white wine or cider has been added, along with a few sprigs of fresh herbs, a couple of bay leaves, slices of lemon, thin onion slices and a few black peppercorns. Don't bother with fish kettles, which take up far too much storage space, as large, whole fish are better oven-baked in foil.

Poaching guidelines

Rolled fillets of sole and plaice will take 4-5 minutes, and the cooking liquid – dry white wine or cider – can be used to make a sauce. White or smoked fish fillets and fish steaks weighing 6-7 oz (175-200 g) will take 6-8 minutes, depending on their thickness. Whole trout weighing 10-12 oz (275-350 g) each will take 8-10 minutes – less for small fish. Use enough liquid to half-cover the fish and make sure the pan has a well-fitting lid.

Steaming

Steaming, like poaching, is great for calorie counters, as no fat is needed, so if you're cutting the fat in your diet, steaming fish is definitely for you. You can use either a traditional fan or bamboo steamer. I think steaming – as oriental cooks have discovered – is particularly good for rolled fillets of plaice, sole or trout, as they retain their shape perfectly and remain beautifully moist. Add about 2 inches (5 cm) of boiling water to the saucepan, then fit the steamer over, making sure it doesn't come into contact with the water, and cover with a tight-fitting lid.

Steaming guidelines

Whole Dover sole, lemon sole or plaice weighing 10-12 oz (275-350 g) will take 7-8 minutes; rolled fillets of the above, 7-8 minutes; trout fillets, rolled, will take 7-8 minutes; white or smoked fish, steaks and fillets weighing 6-7 oz (175-200 g), 8-10 minutes.

Shallow-frying

I have evocative memories of my grandmother shallow-frying skate wings, her favourite fish, which she first dipped in seasoned flour – they were golden and crisp at the edges and there were always special Victorian bone-handled fish knives and forks on the table. I think shallow-fried fish makes a simple but very tempting supper dish, but you need to follow a few basic rules to get it absolutely right. First the fish must be dried thoroughly with kitchen paper, and because the flesh of white fish is so delicate, there needs to be some kind of coating – seasoned flour, white or wholemeal, beaten egg and breadcrumbs.

The second rule is you must have the fat hot enough – olive oil or a mixture of groundnut or other flavourless oil and butter are my favourites. There should be enough to cover the pan and give a depth of about ⅛ inch (3 mm), and the most vital point is that it must be really hot. Watch the oil as it's heating and you will see a shimmering haze that will cue you as to when to add the fish. If in doubt, add a small cube of bread, which should sizzle quite fiercely; if it doesn't the oil is not hot enough. The idea is to seal the fish in the hot fat on both sides – it is only when the fat isn't hot enough that fried fish tastes oily. Always drain shallow-fried fish on crumpled greaseproof or absorbent kitchen paper before serving.

Shallow-frying guidelines

Whole Dover sole, lemon sole or plaice weighing 10-12 oz (275-350 g) each, 4-6 minutes each side; fillets of the above, 2-3 minutes each side; fish steaks and fillets weighing 6-7 oz (175-200 g), 5-6 minutes each side; skate wings, 4-5 minutes each side; whole herring or mackerel weighing 8-10 oz (225-275 g), 5-6 minutes each side; kippers weighing 9-10 oz (250-275 g), 4 minutes each side; sprats, 2-3 minutes each side.

Down with deep-frying

I have, I'm afraid, eliminated deep-frying from my own cooking repertoire. I think times have changed and we've all moved on from not only the bother of it but the 'write your name in it' layer of grease it leaves on the kitchen walls. Yes, there are deep-frying machines, but they're a bother to clean and take up too much space. I now prefer to use a high temperature oven-roasting for chips (see Book One), and fish I feel can be very successfully shallow-fried. Meanwhile, I can still enjoy deep-fried fish and chips from my local chippy and other deep-fried foods in restaurants and let *them* have the bother of cleaning the ceiling and walls.

Oven-baking

This and foil cookery (on the following page) is a trouble-free way of cooking certain fish because, as long as you put on a timer, you can pop the dish in the oven and forget all about it. Having said that, though, there are one or two things to be wary of. White fish, steaks and fillets on their own could end up being dry, so these are best brushed liberally with melted butter and protected with a buttered piece of foil lightly placed on top. However, if you use a topping to add moisture, the foil is not needed. Whole fish oven-bake beautifully if brushed liberally with butter or oil, and if a stuffing is added to the body cavity this will help keep the fish moist.

Oven-baking guidelines

Pre-heat the oven to gas mark 6, 400°F (200°C). For white fish or smoked fish fillets and steaks, brushed with butter and wrapped in buttered foil and weighing 6-7 oz (175-200 g), allow 15-20 minutes; whole mackerel, trout or herring weighing 10-12 oz (275-350 g) each, 25-30 minutes; tilapia weighing 12-14 oz (350-400 g), 15 minutes.

Oven-roasting

This is, in all the years I have been cooking, a breakthrough for me, as it cuts out a lot of shallow-frying and grilling. What happens is the oven is pre-heated to its highest setting (about gas mark 8, 450°F, 230°C), the fish then gets a real blast of heat, which cooks it quickly and retains all its moist juices. I hate standing watching grills or, equally, getting greasy from deep-frying; oven-roasting cuts down time and effort, and also, used instead of frying, cuts down the fat, which is always a good thing.

Foil-wrapped fish

You can, if you wish, foil-wrap fish and then cook it in a steamer, under the grill, on the barbecue or in the oven. The advantage is that all the flavours and juices are retained inside a sealed parcel. It's best to follow individual recipes for timings, but I have found that foil-wrapping is the best way to cook either a whole or large piece of salmon or a salmon trout. If, in the summer, you want to serve the fish cold, you can leave it inside its parcel until you're ready to serve it, which will keep it moist and juicy.

To cook salmon, I like the slow method, which very gently cooks the fish to absolute perfection. If you want to cook a whole salmon for a party, the fish can be cut in half, wrapped in two foil parcels, then, after baking and cooling, the two halves can be put back together once the skin has been removed and the join hidden by a band of cucumber slices. The oven temperature for this is gas mark ½ (S or E on some models), 250°F (120°C). Add 2-3 bay leaves to the body cavity and some sprigs of fresh tarragon, season with salt and pepper and tuck in 1-2 oz (25-50 g) of butter. Then wrap the whole thing in a double sheet of foil, loosely but sealing it tightly, place on a baking tray and bake in the pre-heated oven for the following cooking times. For a 1 lb 8 oz (700 g) salmon, 1 hour 10 minutes; 2 lb (900 g), 1 hour 30 minutes; 3 lb (1.35 kg), 2 hours; 4 lb (1.8 kg), 2 hours 30 minutes; 5 lb (2.25 kg), 3 hours.

Whole salmon trout or sea trout can be prepared as above and cooked with the same timings according to the weight. Salmon steaks weighing up to 8 oz (225 g) each need to be baked at a higher temperature than this: gas mark 4, 350°F (180°C). Wrap them – either individually or 4–6 at a time – in well-buttered foil, but first season them, adding torn bay leaves, sprigs of tarragon and 1 tablespoon of white wine per steak. Seal the edges of the foil securely and bake on a high shelf of the oven for 20 minutes. Salmon fillets weighing 5-6 oz (150-175 g) each will take 15-20 minutes.

Grilling and barbecuing

This is something of a minefield to give timings for, because domestic grills vary so much, as do shelf distances from the source of the heat, so bear this in mind when following these guidelines, especially with barbecues, where accurate degrees of heat cannot be measured. First remember to always line your grill pan with buttered foil, as this makes it easier to wash and prevents any fishy flavours from lingering in the pan. White fish needs to be brushed generously with melted butter and basted with more melted butter whilst cooking to prevent any dryness.

When using a barbecue have some melted butter handy to brush on the fish, and it's best to use one of the special fish grills, as this keeps the fish neatly intact without it breaking or sticking. Trout, mackerel and other small, whole fish all respond well to this cooking method, and you can add herbs and seasoning. For domestic grills always pre-heat them to their highest setting a good 10 minutes in advance.

Approximate grilling times

Whole Dover sole, lemon sole or plaice weighing 10-12 oz (275-350 g), 4-6 minutes each side; fillets of sole or plaice, 2-3 minutes each side; fish fillets and steaks weighing 6-8 oz (175-225 g), allow 5-6 minutes each side, flesh-side first, and have extra butter ready for basting during cooking; whole mackerel weighing 8-10 oz (225-275 g), make 3 diagonal scores on each side, and if you wish tuck in a slice of lemon or lime, brush with melted butter and grill for 6-7 minutes each side. Whole herring weighing 6-8 oz (175-225 g), score and butter as above and allow 4-5 minutes' grilling time each side; kippers weighing 9-10 oz (250-275 g), place a knob of butter on the flesh side and allow 4-5 minutes each side.

Microwaving

This is a tricky subject, and one that causes a great dilemma for the cookery writer. As microwave ovens are not standard and the power levels vary, it's difficult to give any kind of standard guidelines. The best course if you want to cook fish in the microwave is to follow the instructions in the individual manufacturer's handbook. But the danger with cooking fish in this way is that a few seconds more than it actually needs will render it overcooked and sometimes dry. For this reason I think cooking fish in a microwave is not at all easy for beginners and, because conventional cooking is quick and easy anyway, I would begin with this.

Fried Skate Wings with Very Quick Homemade Tartare Sauce

Serves 2

1 lb (450 g) skate wings (2 small, or
1 large and cut in half)
1 heaped tablespoon seasoned flour
2 tablespoons light olive oil

For the tartare sauce:

1 large egg
½ teaspoon Maldon sea salt
1 small clove garlic, peeled
½ teaspoon mustard powder
6 fl oz (175 ml) light olive oil
1 dessertspoon lemon juice
1 tablespoon fresh flat-leaf
parsley leaves
1 heaped tablespoon salted capers,
rinsed and drained
4 cornichons (baby gherkins)
freshly milled black pepper

To serve:

a few sprigs fresh flat-leaf parsley
1 lemon, sliced into wedges

You will also need a frying pan with a
diameter of 10 inches (25.5 cm).

People are scared of this, one of the finest and most delicious fish of all. But don't be: the flesh slides away from those ribby, gelatinous bones with simplicity and ease (see the photograph on page 44), so do give it a try. I love it simply plain with lemon squeezed over or with tartare sauce. This sauce has a mayonnaise base, which in this case is made by the quick method: that is, using a whole egg and a food processor or blender. This sauce will keep in a clean screw-top jar in the refrigerator for up to a week. It can also be served with any plain-grilled fish or with fishcakes.

Begin by making the tartare sauce. Break the egg into the bowl of the processor, add the salt, garlic and mustard powder, then switch the motor on and, through the feeder tube, add the oil in a thin, steady trickle, pouring it as slowly as you can (which even then takes only about 2 minutes). When the oil is in and the sauce has thickened, add some pepper and all the other ingredients. Now switch on the pulse button and pulse until the ingredients are chopped – as coarsely or as finely as you want. Lastly, taste to check the seasoning, then transfer to a serving bowl.

When you are ready to cook the skate wings, take the frying pan and put it over a gentle heat to warm up while you wipe the fish with kitchen paper and coat them with a light dusting of the seasoned flour. Now turn the heat up to high, add the oil to the pan and, as soon as it's really hot, add the skate wings. Reduce the heat to medium and fry them for 4-5 minutes on each side, depending on their size and thickness. To test if they are cooked, slide the tip of a sharp knife in and push to see if the flesh parts from the bone easily and looks creamy-white. When the fish is ready, remove it to warm serving plates, garnish with the parsley and serve with the tartare sauce and lemon wedges to squeeze over.
Note: for a change to the tartare sauce, replace lemon juice and parsley with lime juice and fresh coriander.

To make tartare sauce, simply place the egg, salt, garlic and mustard powder in the food processor, then add the oil in a thin, steady stream through the feeder tube. Once the sauce has thickened, add the remaining ingredients and pulse to the desired consistency, then season and transfer to a serving bowl

Roasted Fish with a Parmesan Crust

This works superbly well with plaice fillets, but sole would be excellent, or thicker fish fillets such as cod or haddock, in which case allow 5 minutes extra cooking time. I don't feel it needs a sauce, but a green salad with a lemony dressing would be a good accompaniment.

Serves 2

1 lb (450 g) plaice fillets (4 fillets)
3 oz (75 g) freshly grated Parmesan (Parmigiano Reggiano)
4 oz (110 g) white bread, slightly stale, cut into cubes
a handful of fresh curly parsley leaves
2 oz (50 g) melted butter, plus a little extra for brushing
salt and freshly milled black pepper

To garnish:

1 lemon, cut into quarters
a little fresh curly parsley

You will also need a baking tray measuring 11 x 16 inches (28 x 40 cm) and some kitchen foil.

Pre-heat the oven to gas mark 8, 450°F (230°C).

First of all prepare the baking tray by lining it with foil and brushing the foil generously with melted butter. Now wipe the fish with kitchen paper, then lay the fillets on the foil and season them with salt and black pepper. Next place the cubes of bread and parsley leaves in a food processor and switch on the motor to whiz it all to fine crumbs, then add the Parmesan, melted butter, ½ a teaspoon of salt and some pepper and pulse again to mix them in. Now spread the crumb mixture over the fish fillets, drizzle over a little more melted butter and then place the baking tray on a high shelf in the oven for 7-8 minutes, or until the crumbs have turned a golden brown. Serve with the lemon quarters to squeeze over and a sprig of parsley as a garnish.

Fried Herrings with Oatmeal and a Beetroot Relish

Why is it that fresh sardines are so highly thought of and yet herrings are largely ignored? Firstly they're very closely related, so their taste is similar; secondly, herrings don't have to be imported and therefore are fresh, plump and bright, and, being larger, they have more lovely, juicy flesh. Any leftover beetroot relish can be kept in the fridge for a couple of days.

Begin by making the beetroot relish, and to do this simply mix all the ingredients together and sprinkle with the chopped parsley.

Now wipe the herrings with kitchen paper, then place them, flesh-side up, on a plate and season well. Dip both sides into the seasoned flour, then dip the flesh-side only into first the beaten egg, then the oatmeal, pressing it down firmly into their flesh. Now heat the lard or oil in the frying pan over a high heat until it's shimmering hot, then fry the herrings flesh-side (oatmeal-side) down for 2-3 minutes, or until they look golden and crusty when you lift a little with a spatula. Now flip them over using a spatula and fork and let them cook for another 1-2 minutes, then transfer them to crumpled greaseproof or kitchen paper to drain before serving with the relish and some waxy potatoes. Garnish with the parsley and lime wedges.

Serves 2

2 medium-sized herrings weighing 10-12 oz (275-350 g) each when whole, boned (see page 45)
3 oz (75 g) pinhead oatmeal (coarse oatmeal)
2 heaped tablespoons seasoned plain flour
1 large egg, beaten
2 tablespoons lard or flavourless oil
salt and freshly milled black pepper

For the beetroot relish:

6 oz (175 g) cooked beetroot, chopped into ¼ inch (5 mm) dice
2 shallots, peeled and finely chopped
4 cornichons (baby gherkins), finely chopped
1 heaped tablespoon salted capers, rinsed and drained
1 dessertspoon red wine vinegar
1 dessertspoon good-quality mayonnaise
a little chopped fresh parsley, to serve
salt and freshly milled black pepper

To garnish:

a few sprigs fresh flat-leaf parsley
a few lime wedges

You will also need a frying pan with a diameter of 10 inches (25.5 cm).

Thai Fishcakes with Sesame and Lime Dipping Sauce

The ingredients list for these noble little Thai-inspired fishcakes looks very long but the good thing is they can be made and cooked with incredible speed. Serve them as a first or main course, or they're also good as canapés to serve with drinks, in which case make them smaller.

Serves 4 as a main course, 8 as a starter
1 lb (450 g) any white fish fillets, skinned and cut into chunks
1 stem lemon grass, roughly chopped
1 fat clove garlic, peeled
½ inch (1 cm) piece fresh root ginger, peeled and roughly chopped
3 tablespoons fresh coriander leaves, plus a few sprigs to garnish
2 kaffir lime leaves, roughly chopped (if unavailable leave them out)
zest 1 lime (the juice goes in the sauce)
1 medium red chilli, deseeded
½ small red pepper (use only ¼ if it's a large one), deseeded and roughly chopped
3 oz (75 g) dried coconut powder
2 tablespoons lightly seasoned plain flour
2-3 tablespoons groundnut or other flavourless oil, for frying
salt and freshly milled black pepper

For the dipping sauce:
1 teaspoon sesame seeds
1 tablespoon sesame oil
1 tablespoon lime juice
1 dessertspoon Thai fish sauce
1 tablespoon Japanese soy sauce
1 medium red chilli, deseeded and very finely chopped

You will also need a frying pan with a diameter of 10 inches (25.5 cm).

To make the fishcakes you first of all need to put the lemon grass, garlic, ginger, coriander leaves, kaffir lime leaves, lime zest, chilli and red pepper into a food processor, then turn the motor on and blend everything fairly finely. After that add the cubes of fish, process again briefly until the fish is blended in, then finally pour in the coconut powder through the feeder tube. Switch on the motor again but be careful at this stage not to overprocess – all you need to do is briefly blend it all for 2-3 seconds.

Then tip the mixture into a bowl, add some seasoning and shape the fishcakes into 24 fairly small, thin, flattish, round shapes about 2 inches (5 cm) in diameter. If you like you can make them ahead to this stage, but spread them out in a single layer, cover with clingfilm and keep them in the refrigerator till needed.

Meanwhile, make the dipping sauce. To do this, first of all begin by toasting the sesame seeds. Using a small, solid frying pan, pre-heat it over a medium heat, then add the sesame seeds and toast them, moving them around in the pan to brown them evenly. As soon as they begin to splutter and pop and turn golden, they're ready – this will take 1-2 minutes. Then remove them from the frying pan to a serving bowl and simply stir in the rest of the ingredients.

When you're ready to cook the fishcakes, first coat them in the seasoned flour, then heat 2 tablespoons of the oil in the frying pan over a high heat and, when it's really hot, turn the heat down to medium and fry the fishcakes briefly for about 30 seconds on each side to a pale golden colour. You will need to cook them in several batches, adding a little more oil if necessary. As they cook, transfer to a warm plate and keep warm. Serve with the dipping sauce, garnished with the remaining coriander.

Luxury Smoked-Fish Pie

I first introduced this in the 'Cookery Course', but this time round I've made it less of a family supper dish and into something more suitable for entertaining. Serve it with some sprigs of watercress for garnish, and I always think fish pie is lovely with fresh shelled peas.

Serves 6

8 oz (225 g) undyed smoked haddock fillet

2 Manx boneless kipper fillets

8 oz (225 g) Arbroath smokies

8 oz (225 g) smoked salmon or smoked salmon trimmings

15 fl oz (425 ml) whole milk

1 bay leaf

6 black peppercorns

a few stalks fresh parsley

2 oz (50 g) butter

2 oz (50 g) plain flour

5 fl oz (150 ml) single cream

3 tablespoons chopped fresh parsley

2 large eggs, hard-boiled and chopped

1 heaped tablespoon salted capers, rinsed and drained

4 cornichons (baby gherkins), chopped

1 tablespoon lemon juice

a few sprigs fresh watercress, to garnish

salt and freshly milled black pepper

For the topping:

2 lb (900 g) Desirée potatoes

2 oz (50 g) butter

2 tablespoons crème fraîche

1 oz (25 g) Gruyère, finely grated

1 tablespoon finely grated Parmesan (Parmigiano Reggiano)

salt and freshly milled black pepper

You will also need an ovenproof baking dish measuring 9 inches (23 cm) square and 2 inches (5 cm) deep, buttered.

Pre-heat the oven to gas mark 6, 400°F (200°C).

First of all arrange the haddock in a baking tin, pour over the milk and add the bay leaf, peppercorns and parsley stalks, then bake, uncovered, on a high shelf of the oven for 10 minutes. Meanwhile, remove the skin from the kipper fillets and skin and bone the Arbroath smokies – the flesh will come off very easily (see page 45). Then chop them into 2 inch (5 cm) pieces, along with the smoked salmon, if the slices are whole, then place all the prepared fish in a mixing bowl. Next, when the haddock is cooked, strain off the liquid and reserve it, discarding the bay leaf, parsley stalks and peppercorns. Then, when the haddock is cool enough to handle, remove the skin and flake the flesh into largish pieces, adding it to the bowl to join the rest of the fish.

Next make the sauce, and do this by melting the butter in the saucepan, stir in the flour and gradually add the fish liquid bit by bit, stirring continuously. When all the liquid is in, finish the sauce by gradually adding the single cream, then some seasoning, and simmer for 3-4 minutes, then stir in the chopped parsley. Now add the hard-boiled eggs, capers and cornichons to the fish, followed by the lemon juice and, finally, the sauce. Mix it all together gently and carefully so as not to break up the fish too much, then taste and check the seasoning and pour the mixture into the baking dish.

Now, to make the topping, peel and quarter the potatoes, put in a steamer fitted over a large saucepan of boiling water, sprinkle with a dessertspoon of salt, put a lid on and steam until they are absolutely tender – about 25 minutes. Then remove the potatoes from the steamer, drain off the water, return them to the saucepan and cover with a clean tea cloth to absorb some of the steam for about 5 minutes. Now add the butter and crème fraîche and, on the lowest speed, use an electric hand whisk to break the potatoes up, then increase the speed to high and whip them up to a smooth, creamy, fluffy mass. Taste, season well, then spread the potatoes all over the fish, making a ridged pattern with a palette knife. Now finally sprinkle over the grated cheeses and bake on a high shelf in the oven for 30-40 minutes, or until the top is nicely tinged brown. Serve each portion garnished with the watercress.

Roasted Butterflied Tiger Prawns in Garlic Butter

This is an amazingly good first course for garlic lovers and needs lots of really crusty baguette to mop up all the delicious juices. It is also delightfully simple and can be prepared well in advance.

Serves 4
20 raw, shell-on large tiger prawns (about 1lb 8 oz/700 g), thoroughly defrosted if frozen
4 cloves garlic, peeled and crushed
3 oz (75 g) butter, softened
1 heaped tablespoon chopped fresh parsley
grated zest and juice ½ lemon
salt and freshly milled black pepper

To serve:
1 dessertspoon chopped fresh parsley
1 lemon, quartered

You will also need 4 individual gratin dishes with a base diameter of 5 inches (13 cm), buttered, or a baking tray measuring 11 x 16 inches (28 x 40 cm), also buttered.

To butterfly the prawns, first of all pull off the heads and legs with your fingers, then simply peel away the shells, which come away very easily, but leave the tails still attached, as this makes them look prettier. Now turn each prawn on its back and, with the point of a sharp knife, make a cut down the centre of each prawn, *below left*, but do not cut through. Ease open with your thumb like a book and remove the brownish-black thread, *below centre*, scraping it away with the point of the knife – it should also come away easily. Next rinse the prawns and pat them dry with kitchen paper, then place them in the buttered gratin dishes or on the baking tray.

Next make the garlic butter, and all this involves is taking a large fork and combining the rest of the ingredients together in a small bowl. Now spread equal quantities of the garlic butter over the prawns. You can now cover the whole lot with clingfilm and chill in the fridge till needed.

To cook the prawns, pre-heat the oven to gas mark 8, 450°F (230°C), remove the clingfilm if you've made them in advance, and then place the dishes on the highest shelf of the oven and let them cook for 6-7 minutes (they will need only 5 minutes if you've used a baking tray). Serve sprinkled with the parsley and garnish with the lemon quarters.

Char-Grilled Tuna with Warm Coriander and Caper Vinaigrette

Because British domestic grills are so variable in their efficiency I think a ridged grill pan (see page 74) is a very good investment. It's particularly good for thick tuna steaks and gives those lovely charred stripes that look so attractive.

First of all brush the grill pan with a little of the olive oil, then place it over a very high heat and let it pre-heat till very hot – about 10 minutes. Meanwhile, wipe the fish steaks with kitchen paper, then place them on a plate, brush them with the remaining olive oil and season both sides with salt and pepper. When the grill pan is ready, place the tuna steaks on it and give them about 2 minutes on each side.

Meanwhile, make the vinaigrette by placing all the ingredients in a small saucepan and whisk them together over a gentle heat – no actual cooking is needed here, all this needs is to be warm.

When the tuna steaks are ready, remove them to warm serving plates, pour the vinaigrette all over and serve with steamed new potatoes.

Serves 2
2 tuna steaks weighing about 8 oz (225 g) each
1 tablespoon extra virgin olive oil
salt and freshly milled black pepper

For the vinaigrette:
1 heaped tablespoon roughly chopped fresh coriander leaves
1 heaped tablespoon salted capers, rinsed and drained
grated zest and juice 1 lime
1 tablespoon white wine vinegar
1 clove garlic, peeled and finely chopped
1 shallot, peeled and finely chopped
1 heaped teaspoon wholegrain mustard
2 tablespoons extra virgin olive oil
salt and freshly milled black pepper

You will also need a ridged grill pan.

Oven-Roasted Fish with Potatoes and Salsa Verde

This recipe is delightfully different and makes a complete meal for two to three people with perhaps a simple green salad with a lemony dressing as an accompaniment. Chunks of skinless cod fillet are good in this, but any firm, thick white fish could be used – chunks of monkfish tail would be particularly good for a special occasion.

Serves 2-3
1 lb (450 g) cod fillet, skinned
(see page 45)
1 lb 4 oz (570 g) Desirée or King
Edward potatoes
1 tablespoon olive oil
1 heaped tablespoon finely grated
Parmesan (Parmigiano Reggiano)
salt and freshly milled black pepper

For the salsa verde:
1 clove garlic, peeled
1 teaspoon Maldon sea salt
2 anchovy fillets, drained and chopped
1 teaspoon wholegrain mustard
1 tablespoon salted capers, rinsed,
drained and roughly chopped
1 heaped tablespoon finely chopped
fresh basil
1 heaped tablespoon finely chopped
fresh parsley
2 tablespoons olive oil
1½ tablespoons lemon juice
freshly milled black pepper

You will also need an ovenproof baking
dish measuring 7½ inches (19 cm)
square and 2 inches (5 cm) deep,
lightly buttered.

To begin this recipe you need to set to work preparing the salsa verde ingredients and have them lined up ready. Now crush the garlic with the salt using a pestle and mortar and, when it becomes a purée, simply add all the prepared ingredients and whisk well to blend them thoroughly.

Now turn the oven on at gas mark 6, 400°F (200°C). Next prepare the potatoes: put the kettle on, then peel and chop them into ¼ inch (5 mm) slices. Place them in a shallow saucepan, then add salt and just enough boiling water to barely cover them. Simmer, with a lid, for 7-8 minutes – they need to be almost cooked but not quite – then drain off the water and cover them with a cloth for 2-3 minutes to absorb the steam.

Now arrange half the potatoes over the base of the baking dish and season well, wipe the fish with kitchen paper, cut it into 1½ inch (4 cm) chunks and arrange it over the potatoes, seasoning again. Next spoon the salsa verde all over and arrange the rest of the potato slices over, overlapping them slightly. Then brush them lightly with the olive oil, season once more and sprinkle the cheese over. Now bake the whole lot on a high shelf of the oven for about 30 minutes, by which time the fish will be cooked and the potatoes golden brown.

Tiger Prawn Risotto with Lobster Sauce

Sounds rather grand, doesn't it? But it's not, because this in some ways is a cheat's recipe, as it's baked in the oven, which means no tiresome stirring, and the sauce is a ready-made lobster bisque – or you could use French fish soup – laced with dry sherry, then bubbled with Gruyère cheese under the grill.

First of all place the baking dish in the oven to pre-heat. Meanwhile, in the frying pan, melt the butter and, over a medium heat, sauté the onion for 7-8 minutes, until soft. Now stir the rice into the buttery juices so it gets a good coating, then pour in the lobster bisque (or soup) and sherry and season. Give it a good stir and bring it up to simmering point, then pour the whole lot into the baking dish and return it to the oven, uncovered, for 35 minutes.

Towards the end of the cooking time, pre-heat the grill to its highest setting. Take the risotto from the oven, taste to check the seasoning, then add the prawns. Next, scatter the cheese over the top and drizzle the cream over. Now place the dish under the grill for 2-3 minutes, until the cheese is brown and bubbling, then serve immediately, garnished with the watercress and the extra cheese sprinkled over.

Serves 2

6 oz (175 g) cooked peeled tiger prawns, defrosted if frozen
6 oz (175 g) risotto (arborio) rice
1 x 780 g jar lobster bisque or French fish soup
1½ oz (40 g) butter
1 medium onion, peeled and finely chopped
3 fl oz (75 ml) dry sherry
2 oz (50 g) Gruyère, finely grated, plus a little extra to serve
2 tablespoons whipping cream
a few sprigs fresh watercress, to garnish
salt and freshly milled black pepper

You will also need an ovenproof baking dish measuring 9 inches (23 cm) square and 2 inches (5 cm) deep, and a large frying pan.

Pre-heat the oven to gas mark 2, 300°F (150°C).

Roasted Salmon Fillets with a Crusted Pecorino and Pesto Topping

This recipe, invented by my good friend Lin Cooper, started life under the grill, but now, in my attempt to more or less eliminate the grill, I'm happy to say that it cooks very happily and easily in a high oven. One word of warning, though: it works much better with fresh pesto sauce from supermarkets than it does with the bottled kind.

Serves 2

2 x 5-6 oz (150-175 g) salmon fillets, about ¾ inch (2 cm) thick, skinned (see page 45)
1 rounded tablespoon finely grated Pecorino cheese
2 tablespoons fresh pesto sauce
squeeze lemon juice
2 tablespoons fresh breadcrumbs
salt and freshly milled black pepper

You will also need a baking tray measuring 10 x 14 inches (25.5 x 35 cm), covered in foil and lightly oiled.

Pre-heat the oven to gas mark 8, 450°F (230°C).

Begin by trimming the fillets if needed, and run your hand over the surface of the fish to check that there aren't any stray bones lurking. Now place the fish on the prepared baking tray and give each one a good squeeze of lemon juice and a seasoning of salt and pepper.

Next, give the pesto a good stir and measure 2 tablespoons into a small bowl, mix a third of the breadcrumbs with it to form a paste and spread this over both fish fillets. Then, mix half the cheese with the remaining breadcrumbs and scatter this over the pesto, then finish off with the remaining cheese.

Now place the baking tray on the middle shelf of the oven and cook for 10 minutes, by which time the top should be golden brown and crispy and the salmon just cooked and moist. Serve with steamed new potatoes.

3
How to cook meat

'Oh dear, oh dear, oh dear' was the oft-heard lament of Tony Hancock, a truly great comedian whom some of you may not be old enough to remember. No matter – those words for me are always so applicable when things go badly wrong, as, it has to be said, they did for the meat industry. Hopefully we are now recovering, lessons have been learnt and the quality of meat in this country is the best in the world, as it always has been.

I am personally a great lover of both fish and vegetarian food, but I am also a dedicated meat-eater.

I've always been a meat person. Pure and simple. I come from a long line of meat people. I well remember how my grandparents ate meat every day of their lives and at the same time enjoyed perfect health. And how my mother recovering from an operation and with a low blood count was prescribed lots and lots of red meat by her doctor.

There's absolutely no doubt in my mind that good meat is good for you. Everyone who lives, breathes and exists needs protein, and meat provides what is called first-class protein all by itself. Eating just 8 oz (225 g) in any one day gives an adult all they need without having to think about it.

In Britain, because the country's made up of a large presence of hill country where vegetables don't grow but there's lots of lush, green grazing, we're lucky to have what I believe to be the best meat in the world, and, from the earliest times throughout the centuries, all our cookery books contain lashings of meat recipes. William Cobbett, that great 19th-century chronicler of the English countryside, gave this advice to a young man looking for a wife: 'Never mind if she can embroider continents into a piece of cloth, watch carefully how she deals with a lamb chop!'

Thus the purpose of this chapter is to encourage you to enjoy eating and cooking good meat. We don't have to eat meat every day, and a healthy, interesting diet should be varied and include fish or vegetarian meals, but when we do cook meat what we need to know is how to get the very best out of it.

Roasting

Originally what the term roasting described was meat being placed near a fire, usually on a spit, with air circulating around it. Then, as the spit was turned, all sides of the meat were exposed to the fire and the whole was gradually and evenly cooked.

Nowadays we're not technically roasting in the true sense of the word any more. Thankfully, we don't have to fan flames and rake coals to get the required heat; all we have to do is simply switch on a domestic oven to absolutely any heat we require, which makes oven-roasting simple, efficient and very, very easy.

The only thing we need to learn from our hard-working ancestors is to take care. If we want the best results possible, it's well worth reading and absorbing some of the following notes. Then, once they're understood fully, and so long as the right kind of care is taken, roasting meat will always be successful and enjoyable.

What about the fat?

If you never learn any other lesson about meat cooking, please learn this one. If you want to enjoy meat at its most succulent and best you need to understand that fat is absolutely necessary. It doesn't have to be eaten (my husband never eats the fat), but it does need to be there. The fat in the meat contains a lot of the flavour and provides natural basting juices both from without and within. So don't choose meat that is too lean – let the fat do its wondrous work of enhancing flavour and succulence during cooking.

Ten guidelines when roasting meat

1) The cut

If you want to serve the roast meat of old England for a special occasion, it's best to get as large a joint as possible. The perfect roast includes a lovely crusty outside and lots of tender, succulent, juicy meat within. And while you're dreaming about that, consider how lovely it will be eaten cold or made into other dishes. A large joint, if you have some left over for other meals, can be quite economical, too.

The loin or the thick end of a leg of pork, the wing rib (three ribs) of beef or a leg of lamb will serve a large family, and these joints are all excellent for simple roasting at a high temperature. But what you also need to remember is that there are other cuts that are more suitable for lower-temperature roasting, which can be bought in smaller joints. If you try to cook a joint that's meant for slow-roasting at a high temperature, it will end up tough and dry.

2) Bone in or out?

When you cook meat on the bone, the bone inside provides an excellent conductor of heat – this means that the meat will be cooked more evenly with less loss of juices. I always prefer to cook meat on the bone as it definitely has more flavour and I think the meat cooked nearest the bone is the best part. However, the bones can be removed and the joint rolled neatly, making it much easier to carve, so it's just a matter of personal taste in the end.

3) Heat

For simple roasting of a prime joint, it is important to pre-heat the oven to a very high temperature. This gives the meat a very quick and efficient blast of heat so that the edges seize up and the precious juices inside are less likely to escape.

4) Added ingredients for roasting

I find that when roasting a joint of beef or pork, if you tuck a small halved onion underneath it at the edges, it caramelises during the roasting and provides both flavour and colour to the juices for the gravy. When cooking lamb, if you insert little slivers of garlic and rosemary leaves into the flesh, this imparts a lovely flavour and fragrance whilst roasting. You can insert garlic slivers and rosemary into a pork joint, too, if you want to give it a slightly different flavour.

Another tip: if you want to give an extra-crisp finish to the surface fat of a joint, lightly coat it with some flour, and for beef use some dry mustard along with the flour. Unless you're slow-roasting you won't need to add any fat to a joint specifically meant for roasting, as there will be sufficient natural fat within the joint itself.

5) Basting

Wise old cooks knew that to keep a joint really succulent while it was roasting it was important to baste it two or three times using a long-handled spoon. Use an oven glove to slide the roasting tin halfway out of the oven (or, if it's easier, take it out completely – but close the oven door to keep the heat in), then tilt the pan and thoroughly baste the joint with the fat and juices. The exception to this is pork, firstly because it has enough fat within it to provide a kind of internal basting and, secondly, if you spoon fat over the skin, you won't get good crackling.

6) When is it cooked?

If your oven is checked regularly and not faulty, the cooking times given in this chapter should serve you well. But the only way to really know if the meat is cooked to your liking is to first insert a flat skewer into the thickest part of the meat, then remove it and press the surface hard with the flat of the skewer and watch the colour of the juices that run out. If you like your meat rare (as in beef), the juices will still be faintly red; for medium the juices will still be faintly pink, and if you like it cooked all the way through, then the juices should run completely clear and not pink.

Remember, though, that meat continues to cook a little while it's relaxing, so if you like your beef rare, you'll need to take this into account.

7) All those precious juices

The reason roasting meat needs care and attention is that if it's badly cooked, it ends up dry. Careful cooking means doing all you can to keep those precious juices intact. The number-one rule is not to overcook; number two is to baste (see point 5); and number three is to always allow time for the meat to relax before you start to carve it.

What happens to meat during the cooking process is that it shrinks slightly, and juices, as they heat up, begin to bubble up to the surface. Some do escape (but not entirely, if you're making gravy). If you then carve the meat straight from the oven, all those surface juices will be lost, but if you allow the meat to relax for 30 minutes before carving, the surface juices will have time to gradually seep back down into the meat. There will still be a little coming out as you carve, so it's good to have a carving board with a little channel around the edge – then even these juices can be incorporated into the gravy.

8) Gravy

I never put meat on a roasting rack as I think the part that sits directly in the roasting tin provides lots of crusty sediment that improves the gravy. Gravy made with the meat juices ensures that every last drop of flavour and juice enhances the meat itself (see Book One).

9) Carving

A lot of people imagine that they can't carve very well, but the truth is probably that the knife they are using simply isn't sharp enough. What you really need to do is buy a good-quality carving knife and a sharpening steel and simply practise. I was taught by a butcher, who said knives should be sharpened little and often. I have also found the following advice good for anyone who wants to learn: hold the steel horizontally in front of you and the knife vertically, *right*, then slide the blade of the knife down, allowing the tip to touch the steel, first on one side of the steel and then on the other. If you really can't face it, there are knife sharpeners available.

10) Serving suggestions

Most of the traditional accompaniments to roast meat are already well known: horseradish or mustard with beef, savoury stuffing and apple sauce with pork, and mint sauce and redcurrant jelly with lamb.

How to roast beef

Choose sirloin or wing rib (three ribs) on the bone weighing about 6 lb (2.7 kg). Pre-heat the oven to gas mark 8, 450°F (230°C), season with salt and pepper and rub the fat with a dusting of flour and dry mustard. Roast at this temperature for 20 minutes, then reduce the temperature to gas mark 5, 375°C (190°C) and continue to roast – basting at least three times – for 15 minutes per lb (450 g) for rare, plus 15 minutes more for medium, and another 30 minutes for well done. Rest for 20-30 minutes before carving.

How to roast pork with crackling

Use a 5 lb (2.25 kg) loin of pork, on the bone but chined (this means the bone is loosened), and pre-heat the oven to gas mark 8, 450°F (230°C). Make sure the surface skin is really dry, then rub in Maldon sea salt and roast for 25 minutes, then lower the temperature to gas mark 5, 375°F (190°C) and allow 35 minutes per lb (450 g). Don't baste the pork, or the crackling won't be crisp. Relax for 20-30 minutes before carving.

How to roast lamb

For instructions on roasting lamb, turn to page 90.

Braising and pot-roasting

There's something about meat slowly braising in the oven in a casserole, filling the kitchen with sublime aromas and invoking pangs of hunger and anticipation of what's to come. I call it 'feel-good food' – comforting and soothing. It can rarely be done properly in busy restaurants that are short of oven space, so if you want to really spoil your friends as well as your family, choose something from this section for entertaining.

Fast food is all very well and has its place in busy lives, but slow cooking has in a way become a luxury, simply because of its rarity. 'But I don't have time for it,' you might be thinking. But I'm saying, yes, you do – just read on.

Ten guidelines when braising and pot-roasting

1) Dispelling the myth

The myth is that slow cooking is a lot of bother and takes too much time. The truth is that it doesn't in fact take any more time than other cooking; the only time taken up is whilst it sits happily all by itself in the oven, leaving the cook blissfully free to get on with other things.

2) Think slow

The principle to grasp here is that slow cooking really should be just that – too much bubble and boil always impairs the flavour and texture of the meat. What you want to aim for is this: the barest shimmer of movement with the occasional bubble just breaking the surface. Using a heavy flameproof casserole, you need to bring the mixture up to a gentle simmer, then put a close-fitting lid on and place it on the lowest shelf of a pre-heated oven at gas mark 1, 275°F (140°C). This gives just the right amount of heat and thus allows the very best flavours of the ingredients to be drawn out and married together.

3) Choosing the right cut

Without getting too technical, I think it's worth noting that in most cases forequarter meat (which comes from the front half of the animal) is best for slow cooking because this is the bit that works harder, stretching and pulling the rest along all the time (examples for beef include brisket joint, and braising and stewing beef). Muscle and tissue begin to build up as the animal matures, and this, together with a marbling of fat in-between the meat fibres, seems happily to be tailor-made for slow cooking.

What happens when the meat is subjected to a gentle heat over a long period of time is that this is all slowly rendered down and does a splendid job of permeating the meat fibres, keeping them succulent and at the same time adding body, substance and, most important of all, flavour. So for this reason, cuts such as rump, sirloin or fillet steaks should never be cooked slowly, as they do not contain the magic ingredients above!

4) What kind of cooking pot?

Old-fashioned cooks used earthenware cooking pots and sometimes, in order to seal them tightly, put a paste of flour and water on before the lid to give a perfect seal. Nowadays we have attractive flameproof casseroles so we can cook in them on top of the stove, in the oven and even bring them to the table. This would be my choice, because I think it's important to bring the ingredients up to simmering point on the hob before they go into a slow oven. If you prefer an earthenware cooking pot, then you must pre-heat it and make sure the ingredients are well up to simmering point before they're poured quickly into the pot and then put in the oven. Without this precaution the ingredients won't come up to simmering point for a very long time in a slow oven.

I have found that an approximately 4 pint (2.25 litre) capacity flameproof casserole is a good all-round family size and that a 6 pint (3.5 litre) casserole is a very useful size for entertaining. The modern way to seal the lid tightly is to use a double sheet of foil placed under the lid.

5) Browning meat

This is where care is really needed – and just a little patience. If the meat is seared around the edges, two things happen. Firstly, the crusty, rather charred surface provides flavour and colour and, secondly, as the edges of the meat seize up, this helps keep the juices in. What you need to remember is to only brown a few pieces of meat at a time. It's tempting to shove the whole lot in and cut corners, but if you crowd the pan, too much steam will be created and you will never, ever brown the meat.

Use a good, solid frying pan, get it really hot before adding oil or fat, then, as soon as the oil is smoking hot, add about six cubes (or one steak) at a time, browning them well on all sides and removing them before adding the next batch.

6) Adding liquid

Liquid has a very important role in slow meat cookery, because not only does it provide moisture but, as it mingles with the meat juices, it's what provides the finished sauce. Now, fortunately, we can all buy ready-prepared lamb and beef stock in supermarkets, which will help to enhance the flavour of both the meat and sauce. Another liquid that suits meat cookery very well is beer: both pale ale and stout are transformed into rich, fragrant sauces when subjected to long, slow cooking.

Wine – both red and white – is superb for sauces, and for a very special occasion Madeira wine makes one of the greatest sauces of all. If you want to add a touch of luxury that's really economical, the best thing to use is cider, either dry or medium – every kitchen should have some handy.

Fresh tomatoes, skinned and chopped, or tinned chopped tomatoes will also respond well to slow cooking and provide body to the sauce.

7) How much meat?

This depends largely on appetite. I found it very difficult when I did a book of recipes for one to balance portions that would suit a hungry student and a not-so-hungry pensioner. However, I think 6-8 oz (175-225 g) per person is a good guide. If a recipe says 'serves 4-6', it gives you the chance to size up the appetites and make your own judgement.

8) Skimming

Although meat can be trimmed of excess fat, the presence of some fat in braising cuts of meat is vital for flavour and succulence. In some cases, say with neck of lamb or oxtail, the excess fat will escape and bubble up to the surface, so if you're intending to serve this straight from the oven, tilt the casserole slightly and spoon off the fat, which will clearly separate from the juice. Any that you can't actually skim off with a spoon can be soaked up by lightly placing folded wodges of absorbent kitchen paper on the surface.

Finally, as most slow-cooked recipes taste better re-heated the next day, leaving the dish overnight means that the fat will completely solidify and can then be lifted off very easily before re-heating.

9) Thickening

If you're making a casserole, the easiest way to thicken the sauce is to add some flour to the ready-browned meat, onions and so on, stir it in to soak up all the excess juice, then gradually add all the liquid, a little at a time, stirring and mixing well after each addition. With pot-roasting it's best to add the thickening later. This can be done by straining the liquid into a saucepan, then reducing it slightly by fast-boiling, which concentrates the flavour, and adding a mixture of butter and flour or olive oil and flour (1½ tablespoons of flour to 1 oz/25 g of butter or 1 tablespoon of olive oil to thicken about 15 fl oz/425 ml of liquid). Arrowroot is another thickening agent that gives a fine glaze and a smooth-textured sauce, and it's very easy to use – just blend with a little cold water before adding to the liquid.

10) Freezing and re-heating

Casseroles and braised dishes often improve in flavour if they're made a day ahead, cooled, refrigerated and re-heated, in which case pre-heat the oven to gas mark 4, 350°F (180°C) and give it 35-45 minutes altogether. It's very important that the casserole reaches a gentle simmer. Casseroles and braised dishes also freeze very well in foil containers, but make sure they're thoroughly defrosted before re-heating. Discard the cardboard lids, cover with a double sheet of foil and re-heat as above.

Grilling, frying and baking

In contrast to cuts of meat for braising, the meat that comes from the hind quarter of the animal is, for the most part, more tender, and for this reason has the advantage of being more suitable for fast cooking. If you're looking for a meal in a hurry, the quick-cooking grilling or frying cuts are the ones to go for. Some of these can also be used for oven-baking with other ingredients or with a sauce.

Ten guidelines when grilling, frying and baking

1) Choosing the right cuts for grilling or frying

Beef steaks, pork steaks, pork escalopes (good for frying), lamb cutlets and chops are ideal – and if you're in a real hurry there's something called 'flash-fry' steaks, which cook in 1 minute flat. Most of these can now be bought ready trimmed and cut into strips for the fastest of all cooking – stir-frying.

2) The healthy option

If you want – or have been told – to cut the fat in your diet, grilling is for you, as it enables you to enjoy lean meat with the minimum of fat. If you place the meat on a grill rack with a tray underneath, you'll find a percentage of fat within the meat will run out during the cooking. The secret here is not to overcook, otherwise the meat will be dry.

3) Grilling meat

What grilling should achieve is a lovely seared, faintly charred outside edge with the rest of the meat very tender and juicy within – this is the closest thing to cooking on an open fire, as, when the meat is placed on a rack, the air circulates and this gives the grilled meat its unique flavour.

If you're using a domestic grill, what you need to do is pre-heat it to its highest setting at least 10 minutes before you want to start cooking, and remember to try and position the meat 2-3 inches (5-7.5 cm) from the heat, turning the meat over halfway through to grill the other side. Timings vary because the thickness of meat differs, so you need to use a skewer or the blade of a small knife inserted in the thickest part to test if the juices are the right colour. Approximate timings are as follows.

For a steak 1 inch (2.5 cm) thick (ie sirloin or rump), 1½-2 minutes on each side for rare; medium, 3 minutes on each side; and well done, about 4 minutes on each side.

For a fillet steak 1½ inches (4 cm) thick, give it 5 minutes on each side for medium; 1 minute less each side for rare; and 1 minute more for well done.

Pork chops will need approximately 10 minutes on each side, and pork steaks slightly less. Lamb chops would need about 10 minutes each side, and cutlets about 5 minutes each side.

Never season meat before grilling, frying or browning, as salt draws out the precious juices you're trying to keep in (but do remember to season before serving).

A ridged grill pan, *left*, is a very efficient way of grilling meat, as well as other foods – just smear the pan with very little oil, pre-heat it for about 10 minutes and use the timings just listed.

4) Frying meat

Whether you choose to grill or fry meat is, to a certain extent, personal choice. Grilling, as we've already discussed, gives special flavour to meat, but you do lose some of the juices. Frying, on the other hand, means that all the escaped juices are there in the frying pan and can be spooned over the meat or used with reduced wine to make a sauce.

5) Hot as you dare

It's very important when you're frying meat to have the heat as high as possible, so the frying pan has to be one with a thick, solid base to conduct the heat properly. What you need to do is place the pan over direct heat turned to high and let the pan become very hot before you add the smallest amount of oil or fat, just to cover the pan surface. Then, as soon as the fat itself is smoking hot, holding the piece of meat in both hands, drop it directly down so that the whole of the surface hits the heat at the same moment. What this does is sear the meat, sealing the edges and encouraging the juices to stay inside.

For steaks (rump and sirloin), give them 1 minute's searing each side, then turn the heat down to medium and cook them for no more time at all if you like them really rare ('blue'), otherwise, for medium-rare give them 2-3 more minutes on each side; medium, 3-4 more minutes on each side; and well done, 4-5 more minutes on each side.

For fillet steak 1½ inches (4 cm) thick, after the initial searing you'll need another 6 minutes' cooking time, turning it over halfway through; give it 2 minutes less for rare and 2 minutes more for well done. Once again, all these timings are approximate because the thickness of the meat will vary.

6) Adding fats and oils

If you're cutting down on fat, then grill without fat or oil; however, if that is not your priority, it is better to brush very lean meat such as pork steaks with a little melted butter, and fillet steaks with a little oil before grilling. If you're frying steaks, then use a little oil or a small piece of beef dripping, which will withstand the very high temperatures.

If you're frying pork, the best thing to use is a little butter and oil mixed together so that you get the flavour of the butter, and the oil stops it from burning.

7) Marinating

This really does enhance the flavour of meat for grilling. If you marinate cubed lamb (from leg steaks), use the juice of a lemon and 6 tablespoons of oil to 1 lb 8 oz (700 g) of meat, adding a dessertspoon of chopped oregano and some slivers of onion. Leave them in the marinade overnight, turning a couple of times, then thread the cubes of meat and slivers of onion on to flat skewers. You can make delicious kebabs and grill them for 15-20 minutes, basting with some of the marinade as you cook them. You can also do exactly the same with cubed pork, only this time using a dessertspoon of crushed rosemary leaves and giving them 5 minutes' more grilling time.

8) Glazing

One interesting way of grilling meat is to add a glaze to it before it goes under the grill. The best and probably the simplest one I've come across is to spread a thin layer of English mustard over the meat and then dip it in demerara sugar. Once this coating hits the heat, it gives a lovely shiny barbecue-flavoured crust. I like it best with lamb cutlets, but you could always use it with pork ribs. Either way, give them 5 minutes' grilling on each side.

9) Stir-frying

If you cook with gas, then a classic rounded wok is perfect for a stir-fry, but if you're using electricity you need to have a wok with a special flat base. If you don't have a wok, don't worry – you can still stir-fry with a large, roomy frying pan. Either way, remember that speed is what it's all about. Heat the wok or pan until it's very hot indeed, then add oil and, as it sizzles, add the meat and constantly stir it around so that it comes into constant contact with the heat on all sides (the meat should be half-cooked before the vegetables are added).

10) Oven-baking

There is a method of cooking meat that comes somewhere in-between fast- and slow-cooking, and that is oven-baking. One of the best things about it is that it leaves you free to do other things.

You can oven-bake pork or lamb chops in a shallow tin by seasoning them and tucking chopped onion in around them and baking them at gas mark 6, 400°F (200°C) for 30-40 minutes, depending on the size and thickness of the chops. After that, you can deglaze the roasting tin with wine, cider or stock to make a gravy with the juices.

Shepherd's Pie with Cheese-Crusted Leeks

This recipe can be made either with fresh minced lamb (shepherd's pie), fresh minced beef (cottage pie) or minced leftover beef or lamb from a cooked joint (in which case cut the initial cooking time to 15 minutes). In the following recipe we're using fresh minced lamb, and what puts this dish in the five-star category is the delicious crust of cheese and leeks.

Serves 4

1 lb (450 g) minced lamb
1 tablespoon olive oil
2 medium onions, peeled and chopped
3 oz (75 g) carrot, peeled and chopped very small
3 oz (75 g) swede, peeled and chopped very small
½ teaspoon ground cinnamon
1 teaspoon chopped fresh thyme
1 tablespoon chopped fresh parsley
1 tablespoon plain flour
10 fl oz (275 ml) fresh lamb stock
1 tablespoon tomato purée
salt and freshly milled black pepper

For the topping:

2 oz (50 g) mature Cheddar, coarsely grated
2 medium leeks, cleaned and cut into ½ inch (1 cm) slices
2 lb (900 g) Desirée or King Edward potatoes
2 oz (50 g) butter
salt and freshly milled black pepper

You will also need a large lidded frying pan or saucepan, and a 7½ inch (19 cm) square baking dish, 2 inches (5 cm) deep, well buttered.

Begin by taking the frying pan or saucepan and, over a medium flame, gently heat the olive oil. Now fry the onions in the hot oil until they are tinged brown at the edges – about 5 minutes. Add the chopped carrot and swede and cook for 5 minutes or so, then remove the vegetables and put them to one side. Now turn the heat up and brown the meat in batches, tossing it around to get it all nicely browned. You may find a wooden fork helpful here, as it helps to break up the mince. After that, give the meat a good seasoning of salt and pepper, then add the cooked vegetables, cinnamon, thyme and parsley. Next stir in the flour, which will soak up the juice, then gradually add the stock to the meat mixture until it is all incorporated. Finally, stir in the tomato purée. Now turn the heat right down, put the lid on the pan and let it cook gently for about 30 minutes.

While the meat is cooking you can make the topping. Peel the potatoes, cut them into even-sized pieces and place in a steamer fitted over a large pan of boiling water, sprinkle with some salt, put a lid on and steam until they're completely tender – about 25 minutes. While this is happening, pre-heat the oven to gas mark 6, 400°F (200°C).

When the potatoes are done, drain off the water, return them to the saucepan, cover with a clean tea cloth to absorb the steam and leave them for about 5 minutes. Next add the butter and mash them to a purée – the best way to do this is with an electric hand whisk. Don't be tempted to add any milk here, because the mashed potato on top of the pie needs to be firm. Taste and add more salt and pepper if necessary. When the meat is ready, spoon it into the baking dish and level it out with the back of the spoon. After that, spread the mashed potato evenly all over. Now sprinkle the leeks on top of the potato, scatter the cheese over the leeks and bake the whole thing on a high shelf of the oven for about 25 minutes, or until the top is crusty and golden.

Entrecôte Hongroise

As I've said before, I prefer to cook steak in a frying pan because, as some of the precious juices are bound to escape, they can be incorporated into the sauce to give extra body and flavour.

Serves 2

2 entrecôte or sirloin steaks weighing about 8 oz (225 g) each, removed from the fridge about 1 hour before you need them
1 tablespoon light olive oil
3 shallots, peeled and finely chopped
1 small red pepper, deseeded and finely diced
6 fl oz (175 ml) red wine
1 tablespoon half-fat crème fraîche
¼ teaspoon paprika
a few sprigs fresh watercress, to garnish
salt and freshly milled black pepper

You will also need a solid frying pan with a diameter of 10 inches (25.5 cm).

First of all heat half the oil in the frying pan over a high heat, then fry the chopped shallots and pepper until they're softened and tinged dark brown at the edges – about 6 minutes – and remove them to a plate. Now add the remaining oil to the pan and, keeping the heat high – the pan should be as hot as you dare – season the steaks with coarsely milled black pepper, but no salt yet, as this encourages the juices to come out. Now add the steaks to the hot pan and press them gently with a spoon so that the underneath is seared and becomes crusty. Cook the steaks for about 3 minutes each side for medium, 2 for rare and 4 for well done. Then, about 2 minutes before the end of the cooking time, return the shallots and peppers to the pan, pour the wine around the steaks and, still keeping the heat high, boil until reduced and syrupy. Then add the crème fraîche and stir it into the sauce, then season with salt and sprinkle in the paprika. Serve the steaks on hot plates with the sauce spooned over and garnish with watercress. They're lovely served with jacket potatoes and a salad.

Entrecôte Marchand de Vin

This classic French recipe has the simplest-possible sauce for a fried steak. The red wine bubbles down and deglazes the pan so that all the lovely flavours of the steak are incorporated into the sauce.

First of all heat half the oil in the frying pan over a high heat, then fry the chopped onion until it's softened and tinged dark brown at the edges – about 6 minutes – and remove to a plate. Now add the remaining oil to the pan and, keeping the heat high – the pan should be as hot as you dare – season the steaks with coarsely milled black pepper, but no salt, as this encourages the juices to come out. Now add the steaks to the hot pan and press them gently with a spoon so that the underneath is seared and becomes crusty. Cook the steaks for about 3 minutes each side for medium, 2 for rare and 4 for well done. Then, about 2 minutes before the end of the cooking time, return the onion to the pan, pour the wine around the steaks and, keeping the heat high, boil until reduced and syrupy. Serve the steaks on hot plates with the sauce spooned over. Chunky Chips (Book One) and a green salad would be very good with this.

Serves 2

2 entrecôte or sirloin steaks weighing about 8 oz (225 g) each, removed from the fridge about 1 hour before you need them
1 tablespoon light olive oil
1 small onion, peeled and finely chopped
6 fl oz (175 ml) red wine
freshly milled black pepper

You will also need a solid frying pan with a diameter of 10 inches (25.5 cm).

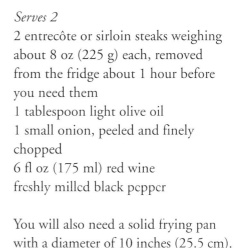

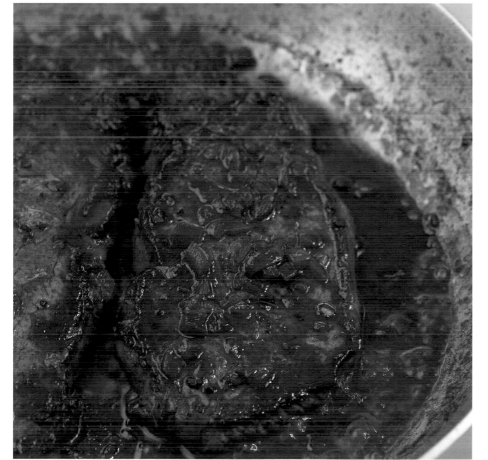

Individual Steak, Mushroom and Kidney Pies

Steak and kidney is one of the most wonderful combinations of flavours I know, provided ox kidney and no other is used. If it's cut really small, most people who think they don't like kidney will enjoy the rich, luscious flavour without even noticing it's there.

Serves 6

2 lb (900 g) chuck steak or blade, cut into 1 inch (2.5 cm) cubes
8 oz (225 g) dark-gilled mushrooms, quartered
8 oz (225 g) ox kidney, trimmed and cut into very small cubes
2 tablespoons beef dripping
8 oz (225 g) onions, peeled and thickly sliced
2 tablespoons plain flour
2 tablespoons Worcestershire sauce
½ teaspoon finely chopped fresh thyme
1 pint (570 ml) beef stock
salt and freshly milled black pepper

For the pastry:

12 oz (350 g) plain flour, plus a little extra for rolling
pinch of salt
3 oz (75 g) lard, at room temperature
3 oz (75 g) butter, at room temperature
about 1½ tablespoons cold water
a little beaten egg, to glaze

You will also need 6 x 15 fl oz (425 ml) pie dishes or ovenproof soup bowls with top diameters of 5 inches (13 cm) or an ovenproof pie dish with a diameter of 9 inches (23 cm), and a lidded flameproof casserole with a capacity of 6 pints (3.5 litres).

Pre-heat the oven to gas mark 1, 275°F (140°C).

I think the flavour of steak and kidney is improved enormously if you take a bit of time and trouble over initially browning the meat. What you need to do is melt 1 tablespoon of the beef dripping in a large, solid frying pan. When the fat is really hot, pat the cubes of meat with kitchen paper and add them a few at a time, but don't crowd the pan; if you put too much in at once, this creates a steamy atmosphere and the meat won't brown, so brown the pieces on all sides in batches, adding them to the casserole as you go.

Once the meat is browned, add the rest of the dripping to the frying pan and do exactly the same with the kidney. When these have joined the meat, keep the heat high and brown the onions in the frying pan, turning and moving them until they are nicely browned at the edges – 6-7 minutes. Then, using a draining spoon, transfer the onions to the casserole, place it over a direct heat for 2 minutes before seasoning, then add the flour and stir with a wooden spoon until it's been absorbed into the meat juices. It doesn't look very nice at this stage, but that's not a problem. All you do next is add the Worcestershire sauce, thyme and mushrooms, followed by the stock and seasoning. Stir well, bring everything up to a gentle simmer, put the lid on the casserole and place in the pre-heated oven, on the centre shelf, and leave it there for about 2 hours, or until the meat is tender.

Meanwhile, make the pastry. First of all sift the flour with the pinch of salt into a large bowl, holding the sieve up high to give it a good airing. Then add the lard and butter and, using only your fingertips, lightly and gently rub the fat into the flour, again lifting the mixture up high all the time to give it a good airing. When everything is crumbly, sprinkle in the cold water. Start to mix the pastry with a knife and then finish off with your hands, adding more drops of water till you have a smooth dough that leaves the bowl clean. Then pop the pastry in a polythene bag and let it rest in the refrigerator for 30 minutes.

Once the meat is ready, transfer the cooked meat and its gravy to the dishes (or dish) and allow it to cool.

When you are ready to make the pies, pre-heat the oven to gas mark 7, 425°F (220°C), then roll out the pastry on a floured surface. Take a small saucer (about 5½ inches/14 cm in diameter) and cut out 6 rounds – you may have to re-roll the pastry to get all 6. Then, using the trimmings, roll out a strip about 3 x 14 inches (7.5 x 35 cm) and cut it into 6 to make borders for the pies. First dampen the edges of each dish with water and place a strip of pastry around the rim of each one, pressing down well. Next dampen the pastry strips, then place one pastry round on top of each dish and seal carefully. Now use the blunt side of a knife to knock up the edges, then flute them using your thumb to push out and your forefinger to pull in again (see the photos). For the large pie, cut out a 10 inch (25.5 cm) circle of pastry, using the trimmings to make strips for the border.

Now make a hole in the centre of each pastry lid to let the steam out during baking, and brush the surface with the beaten egg. Place on a large baking sheet, then cook in the oven on the centre shelf for 25-30 minutes for the small pies, or 35-40 minutes for the large one, by which time the pastry should be golden brown and crusty.

Note: the pies can be filled and topped the day before, covered and chilled, then just brushed with egg and popped in the oven when you need them – by the time the pastry is cooked the steak and kidney will be bubbling hot.

Latin American Beef Stew with Marinated Red-Onion Salad

This is very colourful and has lots of great flavours and textures – ideal for entertaining because all the vegetables are already in it, so all it needs is some plain rice.

Serves 4-6
2 lb (900 g) braising steak, cut into
1 inch (2.5 cm) cubes
1 rounded tablespoon cumin seeds
1 rounded tablespoon coriander seeds
2 tablespoons olive oil
2 medium red onions, peeled and
roughly chopped
3 medium red chillies, deseeded and
finely chopped
6 cloves garlic, peeled and crushed
1 heaped tablespoon plain flour
1 x 220 g tin chopped tomatoes
16 fl oz (450 ml) brown ale
5 fl oz (150 ml) red wine
12 oz (350 g) butternut squash,
peeled, deseeded and cut into 1 inch
(2.5 cm) cubes
8 oz (225 g) fresh sweetcorn (about
2 cobs), or frozen and thoroughly
defrosted
1 red pepper, deseeded and roughly
chopped into 1½ inch (4 cm) pieces
salt and freshly milled black pepper

For the red-onion salad:
1 medium red onion, peeled and
thinly sliced into half-moon shapes
grated zest 1 lime and juice 2 limes
3 tablespoons chopped fresh
coriander leaves

You will also need a lidded flameproof
casserole with capacity of 6 pints
(3.5 litres).

Pre-heat the oven to gas mark 2,
300°F (150°C).

First of all you need to roast the spices, and to do this place them in a small frying pan or saucepan over a medium heat and stir and toss them around for 1-2 minutes, or until they begin to look toasted and start to jump in the pan. Now transfer them to a pestle and mortar and crush them to a powder.

Next pat the cubed meat with kitchen paper, then place the casserole over a high heat. Add 1 tablespoon of the oil and, as soon as it's really hot, brown the meat about 6 cubes at a time, till it's well browned and crusty. As the cubes cook, remove them to a plate and brown the rest in batches. Then heat the other tablespoon of oil and fry the onions, chilli and garlic until they're nicely tinged brown at the edges. Now add the flour and stir this in to soak up the juices. Next add the spices and return the meat to the casserole, then add the tomatoes, ale and wine, season and stir well, then bring it up to simmering point, put the lid on the casserole and place in the centre of the oven for 2 hours.

After that add the squash, sweetcorn and red pepper, stir again and return the casserole to the oven for a further 40-45 minutes. Meanwhile, to make the salad, mix the red onion with the lime zest, juice and coriander in a small bowl and set aside to marinate for at least 15 minutes before serving, then hand it round separately as a garnish.

Mini Boeufs en Croûte

Serves 4

4 x 6 oz (175 g) fillet steaks, cut from the middle of the fillet so they're nice and thick
9 oz (250 g) bought puff pastry
1 teaspoon beef dripping
a little brandy
1 large egg, beaten
6 fl oz (175 ml) red wine
salt and freshly milled black pepper

For the filling:
½ oz (10 g) dried porcini mushrooms
1 large onion, peeled
8 oz (225 g) dark-gilled open-cap mushrooms
1 oz (25 g) butter
freshly grated nutmeg
salt and freshly milled black pepper

You will also need a solid baking sheet, well buttered, and a solid frying pan.

If you want luxury, think fillet steak, and if you want to turn a 6 oz (175 g) fillet into a man-sized portion, encase it with a wild-mushroom stuffing in the very thinnest-possible layer of puff pastry. What you'll then have is a delectable combination of juicy steak, concentrated mushrooms and a very crisp crust. Good news, too, if you're entertaining: these can be prepared several hours ahead and just popped in the oven when you're ready for them.

Begin by making the filling well ahead, as it needs to be chilled before you use it. Start off by soaking the porcini in boiling water for 20 minutes, and while that's happening the onion and open-cap mushrooms will need to be chopped as finely as possible. If you have a food processor you can do this in moments; if not, use a very sharp knife and chop them minutely small. When the porcini have had 20 minutes, squeeze out all the excess liquid, then chop them small as well. Now, in a medium saucepan, melt the butter and stir in the onions and mushrooms to get a good buttery coating, then season well with salt, pepper and a few gratings of fresh nutmeg.

What you need to do now is turn the heat to its lowest setting and cook, uncovered, allowing the juices from the mushrooms to evaporate slowly. This will take about 35 minutes altogether – stir it from time to time and what you should end up with is a lovely concentrated mixture with no liquid left. Spoon the mixture into a bowl, cool and chill in the fridge.

A few hours before you want to serve the steaks, heat the beef dripping in the frying pan until it's smoking hot, or, as the chef who taught me to cook said, 'Hot as you dare!' Now place the steaks 2 at a time in the pan and give them 30 seconds on each side – what you're trying to achieve here is a dark, seared surface without cooking the steaks – then remove them to a plate. Turn the heat off under the pan, but don't wash it, because you're going to need it again later.

While the steaks are cooling, cut the pastry into 4 pieces and roll each one out thinly to about a 7½ inch (19 cm) square; trim the edges to get a neat square and reserve the trimmings. As soon as the steaks are cold, brush them with a little brandy, season with salt and pepper, then lightly brush the surface of each pastry square with the beaten egg. Reserve 1 tablespoon of the mushroom mixture for the sauce, then place about an eighth of the remaining mixture in the middle of each square of pastry, then top with a steak. Now place the same amount of mushroom mixture on top of each steak, then bring 2 opposite corners of pastry up to overlap in the centre, tucking in the sides as if you were wrapping a parcel, brush the pastry all over with more beaten egg and bring the 2 remaining corners up to overlap each other. Be careful to seal the pastry only gently, because if you wrap it too tightly it tends to burst open in the oven. If you like you can use the reserved trimmings to make leaves for decoration.

Then, using a fish slice, gently lift the parcels on to the baking sheet, cover with a clean tea cloth and chill for at least 30 minutes, or until you're ready to cook them. When you are, pre-heat the oven to gas mark 7, 425°F (220°C), pop them in the oven on a high shelf and cook for 25 minutes, which will give you medium-rare steaks. If you want them well done, give them 5 minutes more; if you want them rare, give them 5 minutes less.

While they're cooking, pour the wine and reserved mushroom mixture into the frying pan. Let it all bubble and reduce by about a third – this will deglaze the pan and you can then spoon a little of the reduction around each portion before it goes to the table. One word of warning: you must have your guests seated and ready before this is served, because if the steaks wait around, they go on cooking inside the pastry.

Fast Roast Pork with Rosemary and Caramelised Apples

It's hard to believe that you can serve a roast for six people in about 40 minutes flat from start to finish, but you can, and here it is. It's also outstandingly good, dead simple, can be prepared in advance and, once tried, I'm sure you'll want to make it again and again.

Serves 6
2 thick British pork tenderloins
(weighing 12 oz/350 g each after trimming)
1 rounded tablespoon fresh rosemary leaves
3 Granny Smith apples, skins left on, cored and cut into 6 wedges each
2 cloves garlic, peeled and cut into thin slices
1½ oz (40 g) butter
1½ tablespoons cider vinegar
1 small onion, peeled and finely chopped
1 tablespoon demerara sugar
8 fl oz (225 ml) strong dry cider
2 heaped tablespoons half-fat crème fraîche
salt and freshly milled black pepper

You will also need a flameproof baking tray measuring 11 x 16 inches (28 x 40 cm), lightly buttered.

Pre-heat the oven to gas mark 8, 450°F (230°C).

First of all, using a small, sharp knife, make little slits all over the pork and push the slivers of garlic into them, turning the fillet over so the garlic is in on both sides. Next place the rosemary leaves in a mortar and bruise them with a pestle to release their fragrant oil, then chop them very finely.

Now melt the butter and combine it with the cider vinegar, then brush the meat with some of this mixture, sprinkle with half the rosemary and season with salt and pepper. Scatter the onions over the buttered baking tray and place the pork on top. All this can be prepared in advance, then covered with clingfilm.

When you want to cook the roast, prepare the apples by tossing them with the remaining cider vinegar and butter mixture, then arrange them all around the pork on the baking tray and sprinkle with the sugar and the rest of the rosemary. Place the baking tray in the oven on a high shelf and roast for 25-30 minutes (this will depend on the thickness of the pork), until the pork is cooked and there are no pink juices.

After that remove the baking tray from the oven and transfer the pork and apples to a hot serving dish, cover with foil and keep warm. Meanwhile, pour a little of the cider on to the tray, over the heat, to loosen the onions and juices from it, then pour into a saucepan over a medium heat, add the rest of the cider and let it bubble and reduce by about a third – this will take about 5 minutes. Then whisk in the crème fraîche, let it bubble a bit more and add some seasoning.

After the pork has rested for about 10 minutes, transfer it to a board and carve it into thick slices, then return them to the serving plate to rejoin the apples. Pour the sauce over and serve as soon as possible. Roast potatoes and braised red cabbage are particularly good with this.

Spanish Braised Pork with Potatoes and Olives

This is a brand new version of a recipe originally published in the 'Cookery Course' – the pork slowly braises in tomatoes and red wine, absorbing the flavour of the olives. Because I now cook potatoes in with it, all it needs is a green vegetable or a salad for a complete meal. I started off stoning the olives, but I now prefer them whole, as they look far nicer.

Serves 4-6

2 lb (900 g) shoulder of British pork, trimmed and cut into bite-sized pieces
1 lb (450 g) salad potatoes, halved if large
1½ oz (40 g) black olives
1½ oz (40 g) green olives
1 lb (450 g) ripe red tomatoes
2 tablespoons olive oil
2 medium onions, peeled and sliced into half-moon shapes
1 large red pepper, deseeded and sliced into 1¼ inch (3 cm) strips
2 cloves garlic, peeled and chopped
1 heaped teaspoon chopped fresh thyme, plus a few small sprigs
10 fl oz (275 ml) red wine
2 bay leaves
salt and freshly milled black pepper

You will also need a lidded flameproof casserole with a capacity of 6 pints (3.5 litres).

Pre-heat the oven to gas mark 1, 275°F (140°C).

First skin the tomatoes: pour boiling water over them and leave them for exactly 1 minute before draining and slipping off their skins, then roughly chop them. Now heat 1 tablespoon of the oil in the casserole over a high heat, pat the cubes of pork with kitchen paper and brown them on all sides, about 6 pieces at a time, removing them to a plate as they're browned. Then, keeping the heat high, add the rest of the oil, then the onions and pepper, and brown them a little at the edges – about 6 minutes.

Now add the garlic, stir that around for about 1 minute, then return the browned meat to the casserole and add all the thyme, tomatoes, red wine, olives and bay leaves. Bring everything up to a gentle simmer, seasoning well, then put the lid on and transfer the casserole to the middle shelf of the oven for 1¼ hours. After that add the potatoes, cover the pan again and cook for a further 45 minutes, or until the potatoes are tender.

Pork Chops with a Confit of Prunes, Apples and Shallots

This is a great recipe. The confit goes equally well with crispy roast duck, and is brilliant served with a rough pork-based pâté.

You can make the confit at any time – the day before, even. All you do is cut the apple into quarters, remove the core, then cut the quarters into ½ inch (1 cm) slices, leaving the skin on. Then just place all the ingredients together in a medium-sized saucepan, bring everything up to a gentle simmer, then let it cook as gently as possible, without a lid, for 45 minutes to an hour – you'll need to stir it from time to time – until all the liquid has reduced to a lovely sticky glaze.

When you're ready to cook the pork chops, dip them lightly in the seasoned flour, shaking off any surplus. Now heat the oil in the frying pan and, when it's really hot, add the butter. As soon as it foams, add the chops and brown them on both sides, keeping the heat fairly high. Then lower the heat and continue to cook the chops gently for about 25 minutes in total, turning them once. While they are cooking, warm the confit, either in a saucepan or in a dish covered with foil in a low oven, while you warm the plates; the confit shouldn't be hot – just warm. After that, increase the heat under the frying pan, then pour in the cider for the glaze and let it bubble briskly and reduce to half its original volume, which should take about 5 minutes. Serve the chops on the warmed plates, with the cider glaze spooned over and some confit on the side.

Serves 4
4 thick British pork chops
1 heaped tablespoon seasoned flour
1 tablespoon groundnut or other flavourless oil
½ oz (10 g) butter

For the confit:
5 oz (150 g) pitted pruneaux d'Agen
1 good-sized Granny Smith apple
4 shallots, peeled and cut into 6 wedges through the root
10 fl oz (275 ml) strong dry cider
2 fl oz (55 ml) cider vinegar
1 tablespoon dark brown soft sugar
2 good pinches powdered cloves
⅛ teaspoon powdered mace

For the cider glaze:
8 fl oz (225 ml) strong dry cider

You will also need a solid frying pan with a diameter of 10 inches (25.5 cm).

Roast Leg of Lamb with Shrewsbury Sauce

This is one of my favourite ways of cooking lamb, particularly in winter – plainly roasted with lots of basting to keep it juicy and succulent, then incorporating all the meat juices and crusty bits into what is truly one of the best sauces ever created. It's sweet and sharp at the same time and complements the lamb perfectly.

Serves 6-8
5 lb (2.25 kg) leg of lamb
1 small onion, peeled and sliced
a few sprigs fresh rosemary, to garnish
salt and freshly milled black pepper

For the Shrewsbury sauce:
2 tablespoons plain flour
1 heaped teaspoon mustard powder
1 pint (570 ml) beaujolais or other
light red wine
5 rounded tablespoons good-quality
redcurrant jelly, such as Tiptree
3 tablespoons Worcestershire sauce
juice 1 lemon
salt and freshly milled black pepper

You will also need a solid-based,
flameproof roasting tin.

Pre-heat the oven to gas mark 5,
375°F (190°C).

First of all place the meat in the roasting tin, tucking the slices of onion beneath it. Season the surface with salt and freshly milled black pepper, then place it, uncovered, in the pre-heated oven on the middle shelf. Roast for 30 minutes per lb (450 g) – for a 5lb (2.25 kg) leg this will be 2½ hours. Make sure that you baste the lamb at least 3 times while it is cooking, as this will help keep it juicy and succulent. If you like to serve your lamb quite pink, give it 30 minutes less cooking time. To tell if the lamb is cooked to your liking, insert a skewer into the centre, remove it, then press the flat of the skewer against the meat: as the juice runs out, you will see to what degree the meat is cooked – the pinker the juice, the rarer the meat. When it is cooked as you like it, remove it to a carving board and keep it in a warm place to rest for 30 minutes.

Now, to make the sauce, spoon off any surplus fat from the roasting tin, tipping it to one side and allowing the fat to separate from the juices; you need to leave about 2 tablespoons of fat behind. Now place the tin over a direct heat turned to low and stir in the flour and mustard powder until you have a smooth paste that has soaked up all the fat and juices. Next add the wine, a little at a time, mixing with a wooden spoon after each addition. Halfway through, switch from the spoon to a whisk and continue to whisk until all the wine has been incorporated. Now simply add the redcurrant jelly, Worcestershire sauce, lemon juice and seasoning, then whisk again until the jelly has dissolved.

Now turn the heat to its lowest setting and let the sauce gently bubble and reduce for about 15 minutes, then pour it into a warm serving jug. Carve the lamb, garnish with the rosemary, pour a little of the sauce over and hand the rest round separately.

4

Chicken and other birds

If you sometimes feel depressed or let down, if you're suffering from the pressures of life, or simply having a plain old grey day, my advice is to roast a chicken. I'm not precisely sure why, but there is, and always has been, some magical 'cure-all' involved in the whole process. Sometimes you need to turn your back on the complications of life, give yourself some space and become homespun and happy for just a couple of hours. It really does act as a kind of therapy.

For starters, just imagine the smell of it: even when you wander past some fast-food rotisserie it hits you with that evocative come-hither aroma – and multiply that 10 times over when you have one roasting in your own kitchen. And what about the sound of it? All those juices sizzling and spluttering; and finally the vision of it – plump, bronzed and shining as it emerges from the oven! It doesn't have to be complicated, either. A simple roast chicken can be served just as it is, with chunky chips or crusty bread and a salad. And really good roast chicken is just as much of a treat when it's cold. But then it *can* be all kinds of other things, too: very smart and special, stuffed with herbs, served with sauces... Can there be anyone on earth who doesn't long to eat roast chicken? (Except vegetarians, of course!) There's one proviso, of course, and that is that the chicken has to be a really good one to start with, one traditionally and naturally reared for the table to provide the best eating quality.

First catch your chicken

Seventy-five years ago chickens were slowly reared and fattened for the table. They were fine birds: strong and plump, with lots of succulent, juicy flesh and luscious, concentrated chicken flavour. A whole family could dine on a roast chicken and still have some left over. Roast chicken was very special – not an everyday thing, but something to be anticipated, savoured and looked forward to. The sad thing is there are young (and not-so-young) people who have never actually tasted the real thing. The reason? Progress. Now I'm not against progress – far from it – but it can sometimes run away with us, forcing us to rein in a bit and try to get back on track.

What's gone wrong?

Mass production means masses of cheap chickens. We have created new breeds of fast-growing chickens that can be reared very intensively, which means limited living space in a computer-controlled environment and feed containing antibiotics and growth promoters. The average life span of one of these hens is less than 50 days. At the end of this short, uncomfortable life the chicken is then plunged into scalding-hot water, after which a mechanical process removes its feathers. During this process it is absorbing water – up to 7.4 per cent of its own body weight – and then it's likely to be frozen, water and all. The result is coarse-grained, watery, limp chicken that has no flavour at all.

How can we put it right?

For the most part we can't, because a large section of the community wants cheap chicken and doesn't care about flavour. OK, everyone is free to choose, but ironically, up until now, that has not been the case. People who really do care about flavour have been very limited in their choice, and tracking down a real, naturally reared old-fashioned chicken has not been easy. This has to change, and I am reminded of how often I've been told, when attempting to improve the quality of ingredients, that there's no demand for it. But here I am campaigning again and, hopefully, creating a demand that will ultimately provide us all with a real choice.

What is a proper old-fashioned chicken?

1) The first thing we need to be concerned with is breeding. The bird has to be slow-growing, or rather it has to grow naturally, as nature intended. It must have a reasonable life span – not less than 81 days.

2) It needs (to use a modern phrase) to have its own space and not live in overcrowded conditions.

3) It has to be truly free range. There is, in this country, a bit of a free-range fantasy that has been put about. If you buy a chicken that is labelled 'free range', what that can mean is 'sort-of free range'. We have a kind of cockeyed labelling law that includes three types of 'free-range' chickens. Without going into details, my advice is to forget the words 'free range' on their own, which don't indicate the best-flavoured chicken, and look for the words Traditional Free Range or, in some cases, Free Range Total Freedom.

The best type of chicken is truly free to *range*, to have 24-hour access to the outdoors, to breath fresh air, to have access to a large meadow, field or orchard to peck and scratch about, and to have a truly natural existence; to be protected from foxes and other vermin by an electric security fence, to have shelter from the weather when needed, to have a place to roost and a plentiful supply of grain and fresh water.

4) The next question to ask is has it been dry-plucked? Real chicken does not get dunked into hot water. For the flavour to be at its best, dry-plucking is the optimum process.

5) A little age adds a lot of flavour! This old adage was never more true. If you hang a chicken with its guts intact in a controlled temperature it will, like cheese, mature naturally, which will concentrate the flavour.

I repeat, I'm all for progress, but I've never wanted good food to be only for the privileged few who are in the know. What I've observed is that the very best food producers in the world today are those who use traditional skills and methods alongside the latest technology.

Where can you buy real chicken?

Let's begin with what's most widely available. If you want a small (what I would call an everyday) chicken weighing about 3 lb (1.35 kg) and suitable for very fast roasting (see page 102), then the best-flavoured chickens I've found that are widely available are French and called Label Rouge, and the label may also state either 'raised in the open air' or 'raised in total freedom'. This type of chicken is also great in casseroles and so on. If you want chicken joints, these are also available as Label Rouge. Finally, the crowned king of free-range chickens is Old Fashioned Original Chicken.

The method of producing this chicken, which fulfils all the criteria just mentioned, has been pioneered by Paul and Derek Kelly of Danbury in Essex, and is now being adopted by other suppliers around the country. See page 251 for a list of recommended suppliers of chicken.

How to roast a chicken

I want to give two options here: one is for a traditional Sunday home-roast chicken and the other a fast-roast chicken that can be adapted in various ways with different sauces and flavours. But first a few points to remember.

Does it need to be trussed?

No. The original idea of trussing was merely to make the bird look neater, but I find it's easier to cook if it hangs loose. So cut away and discard any trussing strings if they are present.

Which way up should I roast it?

On its back is my favoured way, sitting it directly in the roasting tin. Why? Because I have found that the more robust meat of the chicken is sitting next to the direct heat this way, and this, in the end, provides lovely crispy bits to a) serve and eat, and b) be scraped up into the sauce or gravy, giving it an extra dimension. Some cooks say you should begin by roasting a chicken upside down, then on its side, then on its back, but I don't think the breast part, which is the most delicate, should be in direct contact with the heat of the roasting tin. Also, turning very hot, slithery chicken over on its side, breast and so on during cooking is not a good idea. I tend not to use a rack for chicken for the reason outlined above, but I do use one for duck (see page 101).

Will it be dry?

No, I promise it won't, as long as you are careful, follow the guidelines given and don't overcook it. With the slower, traditional roasting, fat, streaky bacon placed on the breast provides protection as well as a gradual slow-basting of the breast, and the pork in the stuffing provides the same internally, so all this – and the chicken's natural juices – keeps it moist. Don't forget that the better the quality of chicken, the moister and easier it will be to cook. In the case of fast-roast chicken, because the bird is in the oven for a much shorter time, less evaporation occurs and the chicken stays beautifully moist.

When is it cooked?

Obviously if you stick to the timings for slow-roasting given on page 108 you shouldn't go far wrong, but there are two tests: one is to insert a thin skewer into the thickest part of the leg, remove it and press it flat against the flesh to see if the juices run clear; the second one is to give the leg a tug – if it has some give in it and is not too resistant, that indicates the chicken is cooked. If you are in real doubt, cut a bit of the leg away and look at the area of meat where the thigh joins the body – there should be no visible pink juices.

Fast- or slow-roasting?

I have, after a number of experiments, come up with a method of roasting a smaller chicken at the highest temperature in the oven, and I have to say it's absolutely ace. With a bigger bird, slow-roasting is recommended: here you have a more melting, tender, finished texture, whereas with fast-roasting the flesh is firmer but still tender, as the chicken is younger. What's good is to have a choice – the slower method for leisurely family meals at weekends and the fast for the midweek, after-work scenario.

Why does it need to rest before carving?

When a chicken is cooked, the heat in the oven causes all the internal juices to bubble up to the surface just under the skin – sometimes you can see the skin almost flapping with the amount of juice inside it. Because of this you should always allow the bird to rest for at least 15 minutes before carving it, so that all these wonderful juices travel back from whence they came and keep everything lovely and moist. The fibres of the chicken will also relax, and this will make carving easier.

How do I carve a chicken?

Very easily, provided you have a sharp knife (see page 69) and follow the instructions given below.

To carve a chicken, insert the knife between the leg and body and remove the thigh and drumstick in one piece

Remove the wing on the same side, then slice the breast. Repeat this on the other side of the bird

Finally, divide the drumstick and thigh, cutting through the joint so you have two leg portions

Jointing chicken

1) Using a very sharp knife, begin by cutting through the parson's nose, then stand the chicken in a vertical position

2) Now insert the knife into the cut you've just made and cut straight down the back of the chicken

3) Place the chicken skin-side down, open it out flat like a book and cut right through the breastbone

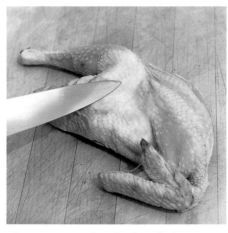

4) Now turn the chicken halves over, stretch out the leg and cut through the line dividing the leg from the breast

5) For six portions, turn the legs over, find the thin white line at the centre of the joint and cut through it

6) If you need eight portions, simply cut the breast portion in half

Chicken Cacciatora

This is my version of the famous Italian classic – best made in the autumn when there's a glut of red, ripe, full-flavoured tomatoes, but it's still good in winter, as there are now some well-flavoured varieties available. Either way, the tomatoes need to be very red and ripe.

First of all heat the oil in the casserole over a high heat and season the chicken joints with salt and pepper. Then, when the oil gets really hot and begins to shimmer, fry the chicken – in 2 batches – to brown it well on all sides: remove the first batch to a plate while you tackle the second; each joint needs to be a lovely golden-brown colour all over. When the second batch is ready, remove it to join the rest. Now add the onions to the casserole, turn the heat down to medium and cook for 8-10 minutes, or until they are softened and nicely browned at the edges.

Meanwhile, skin the tomatoes. To do this, pour boiling water over them and leave them for exactly 1 minute before draining and slipping off their skins (protect your hands with a cloth if they are too hot), then chop them quite small.

When the onions are browned, add the garlic to the casserole, let this cook for about 1 minute, then add the tomatoes, tomato purée, rosemary, bay leaf, white wine and white wine vinegar. Now add some seasoning and bring it up to the boil, then let it bubble and reduce (without covering) to about half its original volume, which will take about 20 minutes. Now add the chicken pieces, stir them around a bit, then put the lid on and allow to simmer gently for 40 minutes, until the chicken joints are cooked through. This is good served with green tagliatelle, noodles, rice or a simple vegetable.

Serves 4

1 x 3 lb (1.35 kg) Traditional Free Range chicken, jointed into 8 pieces (see opposite page)
1 tablespoon olive oil
2 largish onions, peeled and thickly sliced
1 lb 8 oz (700 g) ripe red tomatoes
2 large cloves garlic, peeled and crushed
1 tablespoon tomato purée
1 tablespoon fresh rosemary leaves, bruised and finely chopped
1 bay leaf
10 fl oz (275 ml) dry white wine
1 tablespoon white wine vinegar
salt and freshly milled black pepper

You will also need a lidded flameproof casserole with a capacity of 6 pints (3.5 litres).

Other birds

These are simply those birds, besides chicken, that are specifically bred for the table – what used to be known as domestic poultry. In this chapter I have included guinea fowl, quail and farmed duck.

Guinea fowl

Guinea fowl is unusual in that it is neither totally wild nor truly domesticated. It has been reared for the table in this country since Elizabethan times. Its flavour is somewhere between pheasant and chicken and, though it isn't as plump as chicken (one will really only serve two people), it does have an extra-gamey flavour. You can use it for any chicken recipe, but if you want to make something like coq au vin, where the bird needs to be jointed, ask the butcher to do it, as it's quite difficult.

Quail

These are completely domesticated game birds, bred in this country for the table. Don't be taken in by their tiny appearance, which is, in fact, quite deceptive – they are surprisingly plump and the flesh is delicious. Serve two quail per person and, apart from the very special recipe for Roast Quail Wrapped in Pancetta and Vine Leaves with Grape Confit on page 110, another good way to serve them is to place a sage leaf on the breast of each bird, wrap each one in bacon, them place them on a bed of previously softened onions and mushrooms, along with 5 fl oz (150 ml) of dry white wine, cider or Madeira. Then braise them in a medium oven – gas mark 4, 350°F (180°C) – and give them 40-45 minutes.

Duck

Ducks – or, if they are under two months old, ducklings – come in a variety of sizes, anything from 2 lb (900 g), to 7 lb (3.2 kg) at Easter and Christmas. Everyone associates Aylesbury with ducks, which is where production in this country used to be centred, but now most commercial ducks come from Lincolnshire and Norfolk and are very distant descendants of the original Aylesbury breed. The majority come oven-ready, weighing 4-5 lb (1.8-2.25 kg), and will feed four people.

Barbary ducks, a French breed, are fairly widely available in this country. They are usually three months old and can be anything from 3 to 7 lb (1.35 to 3.2 kg), depending on whether they're male or female (the males are much bigger). They are less fatty than other birds and quite meaty.

In my opinion the very best type of duck available at the moment is a relatively new breed developed in England called Gressingham, and it's a cross between Pekin and the wild mallard. The result is a bird with a rich, gamey flavour and, although sometimes smaller (3 lb-5 lb 8oz/ 1.35-2.45 kg), it has a lighter frame and therefore has as much meat on it as a conventional bird twice its weight.

Roast duck at last!

In over 30 years of cooking and writing recipes, duck has posed some problems. It is a magnificent bird – rich and succulent, with bags of flavour; it has masses of fat, which is not a problem, because it all comes out in the cooking; but what the cook has to aim for is that elusive, really crunchy, almost crackling-like skin, with moist, tender flesh beneath. I used to belong to what I call the semi-Chinese school, which meant vastly overcooking it to get it really crisp but losing much of the succulent flesh in the process. I've also tried the complicated Chinese method of boiling it first, then drying and roasting it. Both methods were never quite right. Now, after all these years, I've cracked it – fast-roasting is the answer (see the recipe on page 104): perfect roast duck every time without a worry.

Because so much fat comes out of the duck as it's cooking, it needs to sit either on a roasting rack, *right*, or on some crumpled kitchen foil to allow the fat to drain away from the bird, making the skin really crisp.

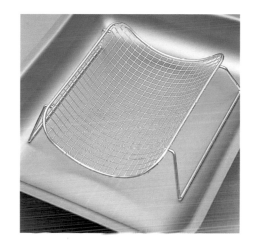

Carving

It has to be said that this is another 'at last', after years of cutting a roast duck into rather inelegant quarters. I have now discovered the correct way to carve the whole thing into eight perfect portions to serve four people. This is thanks to my friend and poultry specialist Bill Curran, and below we have photographed his ingenious method.

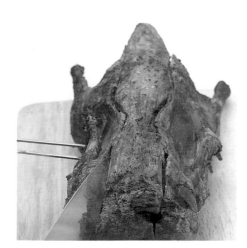

Turn the bird on to its breast and cut down through the meat along the full length of the back bone on either side, then turn the duck on to its back

Next, cut the meat away from the carcass, keeping the knife close to the bone. When you reach the base of the bird, carefully cut through the leg joint

Cut each half of the duck between the leg and the breast, then cut the leg into two pieces at the joint. Finally, divide the breast into two

Fast-Roast Chicken with Lemon and Tarragon

Here it is, as promised earlier: a revolution in the best way to roast a small chicken. The flavourings can vary in any way you like – crushed chopped rosemary leaves, sage leaves or thyme can be used, or a mixture of herbs, and you could replace the garlic with a couple of finely chopped shallots. It's a great recipe for adapting to whatever you have handy.

Serves 4

1 x 3 lb (1.35 kg) French Traditional
Free Range chicken
½ small lemon, thinly sliced and the
slices halved, plus the juice of the
remaining lemon
2½ tablespoons chopped fresh
tarragon leaves
2 cloves garlic, peeled and crushed
½ oz (10 g) softened butter
1 dessertspoon olive oil
10 fl oz (275 ml) dry white wine
salt and freshly milled black pepper

You will also need a solid-based,
flameproof roasting tin measuring
9 x 11 inches (23 x 28 cm), 2 inches
(5 cm) deep.

Pre-heat the oven to gas mark 8,
450°F (230°C).

Begin by taking the chicken from the fridge about an hour before you intend to cook it (obviously if it's a hot day give it about 30 minutes only), and remove the string that holds the legs of the bird together so that the joints are loose – this will take the chill off the bird and help it to cook in the shorter time.

Now make a garlic and herb butter by placing the garlic, 2 tablespoons of the chopped tarragon leaves and the butter in a bowl and combine them with a fork, adding some salt and pepper. Then place the herb butter inside the body cavity of the bird, along with the halved lemon slices. Smear a little of the olive oil over the base of the roasting tin, place the chicken in it, then smear the rest of the olive oil all over the skin of the bird. Lastly, season well with salt and black pepper and then pop the roasting tin into the lower third of the oven. Now let it roast for 45 minutes without opening the oven door. When this time is up, remove the bird from the oven. Next put a wooden spoon into the body cavity and, using a spatula to hold the breast end, tip the chicken and let all the buttery juices and slices of lemon pour out into the roasting tin, then transfer the bird on to a carving board, cover with foil and let it rest for 20 minutes.

Meanwhile, using a tablespoon, skim off the excess fat from the juices in the roasting tin, then place the tin over direct heat, add the wine and lemon juice and let the whole lot bubble and reduce to about half its original volume. Now add the remaining tarragon, then taste and check the seasoning. Carve the chicken on to warm plates and add any juices to the sauce. Spoon the sauce over the chicken and serve.

Crisp Roast Duck with Confit of Sour Cherries

This is it – the best method of roasting duck I've found to date, and of all the lovely sauces, this one – made with dried sour cherries – is the loveliest. It's important to remember, however, that the duck should be as dry as possible, so buy it 24 hours in advance, remove and discard the wrapping and giblets, dry it in a clean tea cloth and leave it uncovered on a plate in the fridge till needed.

Serves 4
1 x 4 lb (1.8 kg) Gressingham duck
(weight with giblets)
fresh watercress, to garnish
sea salt and freshly milled black pepper

For the confit of sour cherries:
3 oz (75 g) dried sour cherries
7 fl oz (200 ml) dry red wine (cabernet sauvignon, for example)
1 oz (25 g) golden granulated sugar
1 tablespoon good-quality red wine vinegar

You will also need a roasting rack or some kitchen foil, and a roasting tin measuring 9 x 11 inches (23 x 28 cm), 2 inches (5 cm) deep.

Pre-heat the oven to gas mark 8, 450°F (230°C).

You need to start this recipe the day before you want to serve it by first soaking the cherries for the confit in the red wine overnight.

The next day, prepare the duck by wiping it again. Now, using a small skewer, prick the fatty bits of the duck's skin, particularly between the legs and the breast. Now either place the duck on the roasting rack in the tin or make a rack yourself by crumpling the kitchen foil and placing it in the bottom of the roasting tin. Season with coarse sea salt and freshly milled black pepper, using quite a lot of salt, as this encourages crunchiness. Now place the tin on the centre shelf of the pre-heated oven and roast the duck for 1 hour and 50 minutes. During the cooking time, using an oven glove to protect your hands, remove the tin from the oven and drain the fat from the corner of the tin – do this about 3 times (the fat is brilliant for roast potatoes, so don't throw it away).

Meanwhile, to make the confit, place the soaked cherries and wine in a saucepan, along with the sugar and wine vinegar. Bring the mixture up to a gentle simmer, give it all a good stir and let it barely simmer, without a lid, for 50 minutes to 1 hour, stirring from time to time. What will happen is that the wine will slowly reduce so there's only about 3 tablespoons of free liquid left.

When the cooking time is up, allow the duck to rest for 20 minutes or so, then carve (see the photographs on page 101) and serve garnished with the fresh watercress, with the sour-cherry confit poured over each portion and the rest handed round separately in a jug.

Paella

I've had lots of hits and misses with this Spanish classic, adding ridiculous, overwhelming amounts of saffron to try getting it as yellow as it is in Spain. Then I found out the Spanish sometimes use colouring! So here at last is the Delia paella – easy, no fuss, and the good thing is it serves six people as a complete meal needing no accompaniment.

Serves 6

12 oz (350 g) Calasparra paella rice
2 tablespoons olive oil
1 x 3 lb (1.35 kg) Traditional Free Range chicken, jointed into 8 pieces (see page 98)
1 large onion, peeled and roughly chopped
1 red pepper, deseeded and roughly chopped into chunks
4 oz (110 g) Spanish chorizo sausage in a piece, skin removed and cut into ½ inch (1 cm) dice
2 cloves garlic, peeled and crushed
1 heaped teaspoon paprika
¼ teaspoon cayenne pepper
½ teaspoon saffron strands (½ x 0.4 g sachet)
8 oz (225 g) ripe red tomatoes, skinned and roughly diced
2 pints (1.2 litres) boiling water
12 raw tiger prawns, shell-on, defrosted if frozen, 4 with heads, 8 without
2 oz (50 g) fresh or frozen shelled peas
1 lemon, cut into wedges, to garnish
salt and freshly milled black pepper

You will also need a shallow paella pan with a base diameter of 10 inches (25.5 cm), a top diameter of 13 inches (32.5 cm) and a capacity of 7 pints (4 litres).

Once you have peeled, chopped, prepared and assembled everything, heat the oil in the pan over a fairly high heat. Now season the chicken joints, adding 4 of them to the hot oil to sauté on all sides until golden brown, then remove them to a plate and do the same with the other 4 joints. Next add the onion, pepper and chorizo and fry these over a medium heat for 6-8 minutes, or until they're nicely tinged brown at the edges. Now add the garlic, paprika, cayenne and saffron and cook for another minute, then return the chicken to the pan, followed by the tomatoes, plenty of seasoning and the boiling water. Next bring everything up to a gentle simmer, turn the heat down and cook, uncovered, for 10 minutes.

After that, remove the chicken pieces and set them aside, then pour the rice into the centre of the pan. Bring everything back up to the boil, give a final stir and simmer, still uncovered, for about 10 minutes. During that time, shake the pan occasionally and move it around on the hob a little if the hob plate is not as big as the base of the pan. Next return the chicken, along with the prawns and peas, to the pan and continue to simmer for 15-20 minutes, or until the rice is cooked, adding a little more hot liquid if you think it's necessary. Now shake the pan again, making sure the rice is completely immersed. Turn the prawns over halfway through the cooking time – they will turn pink when cooked. The rice at the edges of the pan will take longest to cook, so to test that the paella is ready, take a little of the rice from the edges and check it's cooked through, then remove the pan from the heat and cover with a clean tea cloth for 5 minutes to absorb some of the steam. The paella is now ready – just garnish with the lemon wedges and don't forget to have hot plates ready to serve it on.

Stir-Fried Chicken with Lime and Coconut

It's hard to credit that a recipe as simple and as quick as this could taste so good, but I can assure you it's an absolute winner.

First of all chop the chicken into bite-sized pieces and place them in a bowl with the lime juice and zest. Stir well and leave them to marinate for an hour.

When you're ready to cook the chicken, heat the oil in the pan or wok over a high heat, add the chicken pieces and stir-fry for 3-4 minutes, until they're golden. Then add the chilli, stir-fry for 1 more minute, and add the coconut milk, fish sauce and half the coriander and spring onions. Cook for another 1-2 minutes, then serve with Thai fragrant rice and the remaining coriander and spring onions sprinkled over.

Serves 2
2 Traditional Free Range boneless, skinless chicken breasts
grated zest and juice 1 large lime
5 fl oz (150 ml) tinned coconut milk
1 dessertspoon olive oil
1 green chilli, deseeded and finely chopped
1 dessertspoon Thai fish sauce
4 heaped tablespoons fresh coriander leaves
4 spring onions, cut into 1 inch (2.5 cm) shreds, including the green parts

You will also need a frying pan with a diameter of 10 inches (25.5 cm), or a wok.

Traditional Roast Chicken with Apple, Sage and Onion Stuffing, Cranberry and Sage Sauce and Chicken-Giblet Gravy

This is what I described at the beginning of this chapter – a family roast chicken, moist and succulent for Sunday lunch, with lots of crispy bacon, real chicken-flavoured gravy, some very savoury stuffing and a sauce. All it needs is some vegetables with piles of crunchy roast potatoes, and some family and friends to share the feast.

Apple, sage and onion stuffing

If you have a food processor, making stuffing is a doddle: all you do is switch the motor on, add the pieces of bread and process to crumbs, then add the parsley, sage, apple and onion quarters and process till everything is finely chopped. Next trim any sinewy bits from the chicken livers, rinse under cold water, pat them dry, then add them, together with the sausage meat, mace and seasonings. Give a few pulses in the processor until it is all thoroughly blended, remove the stuffing from the processor with a spatula, then place in a polythene bag and store in the fridge until it is required. If you're doing this by hand, just finely chop all the ingredients, combine in a bowl and refrigerate as above.

Traditional roast chicken

Pre-heat the oven to gas mark 5, 375°F (190°C).

First of all the chicken needs to be stuffed, and to do this you begin at the neck end, where you'll find a flap of loose skin: gently loosen this away from the breast and you'll be able to make a triangular pocket. Pack about two-thirds of the stuffing inside, as far as you can go, and make a neat round shape on the outside, then tuck the neck flap under the bird's back and secure it with a small skewer or cocktail stick. Take the remaining stuffing and place it in the body cavity (the fat in the pork will melt and help to keep the bird moist inside). Now place the chicken in the roasting tin and smear the butter over the chicken using your hands and making sure you don't leave any part of the surface unbuttered.

Season the chicken all over with salt and black pepper, then arrange 7 slices of the bacon, slightly overlapping, in a row along the breast. Cut the last rasher in half and place one piece on each leg. I like to leave the rind on the bacon for extra flavour, but you can remove it if you prefer.

Place the chicken in the oven on the centre shelf and cook for 20 minutes per lb (450 g), plus 10-20 minutes extra – this will be 1 hour and 50 minutes to 2 hours for a 5 lb (2.25 kg) bird, or 2 hours 10 minutes to 2 hours 20 minutes for a 6 lb (2.7 kg) bird. The chicken is cooked if the juices run clear when the thickest part of the leg is pierced with a skewer. It is important to baste the chicken at least 3 times during the cooking – spooning over the juices mingling with the bacon fat and butter helps to keep the flesh succulent.

During the last basting (about half an hour before the chicken is cooked), remove the now-crisp bacon slices and keep them warm. If they

Serves 6-8
For the roast chicken:
1 x 5-6 lb (2.25-2.7 kg) Traditional Free Range chicken
2 oz (50 g) butter, at room temperature
8 rashers traditionally cured smoked streaky bacon
salt and freshly milled black pepper

For the apple, sage and onion stuffing:
1 dessert apple, cored and quartered
1 heaped tablespoon fresh sage leaves
1 small onion, peeled and quartered
4 oz (110 g) fresh white bread, crusts removed
1 tablespoon fresh parsley leaves
reserved chicken livers from the giblets
8 oz (225 g) minced pork or good-quality pork sausage meat (I often use skinned sausages)
¼ teaspoon powdered mace
salt and freshly milled black pepper

You will also need a flameproof roasting tin measuring 10 x 14 inches (25.5 x 35 cm), 2 inches (5 cm) deep.

are not crisp, just leave them around the chicken to finish off. For the final 15 minutes of cooking, hike the heat up to gas mark 7, 425°F (220°C), which will give the skin that final golden crispiness.

When the chicken is cooked it is important to leave it in the warm kitchen (near the oven), covered in foil, for 30 minutes, which will allow it to relax. This is because when the chicken is cooking all the juices bubble up to the surface (if you look inside the oven you will actually see this happening just under the skin), and what relaxing does is allow time for all these precious juices to seep back into the flesh. It also makes it much easier to carve. When you serve the chicken, make sure everyone gets some crispy bacon and stuffing. Serve with the Chicken-Giblet Gravy and Cranberry and Sage Sauce.

For the chicken-giblet gravy

Simply place the giblets, water, carrot, onion, herbs, peppercorns and salt in a medium-sized saucepan and simmer very gently with the lid almost on for 2 hours. Then strain the stock into a jug and cool and chill in the fridge. Any fat on the surface is easily removed when cold. To make the gravy, after removing the chicken from the roasting tin, tilt the tin and remove most of the fat, which you will see separates quite clearly from the juices – you need to leave about 2 tablespoons of fat behind. Now place the roasting tin over direct heat turned to fairly low, and when the juices begin to sizzle, sprinkle in the plain flour, stirring vigorously till you get a smooth paste, then add the giblet stock, little by little, exchanging the wooden spoon for a whisk. Whisk thoroughly until all the stock is incorporated, bring the whole lot up to simmering point, then taste and season with salt and freshly milled black pepper.

For the cranberry and sage sauce

All you do here is combine everything in a small saucepan and whisk over a gentle heat until the cranberry jelly has melted. Then pour the sauce into a serving jug and leave till needed (it doesn't need re-heating – it's served at room temperature). Although I love to serve this sauce in summer, in winter my favourite accompaniment is Traditional Bread Sauce from my Christmas book.

For the chicken-giblet gravy:
8 oz (225 g) frozen chicken giblets (reserving the livers for the stuffing), thoroughly defrosted
1½ pints (850 ml) water
1 medium carrot, roughly chopped
½ onion
a few fresh parsley stalks
sprig fresh thyme
1 bay leaf
½ teaspoon black peppercorns
2 rounded tablespoons plain flour
salt and freshly milled black pepper

For the cranberry and sage sauce:
6 tablespoons cranberry jelly
2 dessertspoons chopped fresh sage
3 tablespoons balsamic vinegar
salt and freshly milled black pepper

Roast Quail Wrapped in Pancetta and Vine Leaves with Grape Confit

I am a self-confessed quail convert, having shunned them for years as being undersized and fiddly. I was wrong. They are plump and meaty and, because they are self-contained, they are one of the easiest birds to cook and serve. Vine leaves, which impart a lovely flavour, are available in some stores and specialised food shops, but if you can't find them, you can use foil loosely crumpled around each quail instead.

Serves 4
8 quail
3 oz (75 g) sliced pancetta, preferably smoked
16 fresh vine leaves or 1 x 227 g pack preserved vine leaves in brine
a little olive oil
salt and freshly milled black pepper

For the grape confit:
6 oz (175 g) red or black seedless grapes, halved
1 teaspoon golden granulated sugar
3 tablespoons red wine
1 tablespoon red wine vinegar

You will also need a baking tray measuring 10 x 14 inches (25.5 x 35 cm), and some string.

Pre-heat the oven to gas mark 7, 425°F (220°C).

First of all make the grape confit by dissolving the sugar in the wine and wine vinegar, then add the grapes and let them simmer very gently, without a lid, for 40 minutes, or until the liquid has reduced to a syrup.

If you are using fresh vine leaves, blanch them by dipping them in boiling water for a few seconds until they go limp, then pat them dry and remove the stalks. If you have preserved vine leaves, rinse them under the tap and pat them dry. Now wipe the quail with kitchen paper and remove any trussing string, then rub them with olive oil and season.

Next, cover the breasts with the pancetta, dividing it equally between them. Now sit each quail on a vine leaf, with the legs pointing towards the stalk end, and wrap the leaf up each side, then put another leaf over the breast and tuck it in underneath the quail. Now tie each quail with a piece of string to keep the leaves in place, then lay them on the baking tray and cook on a high shelf of the oven for 15 minutes. After that, take them out, untie the string and, holding the quail in a cloth, unpeel the top leaf (leaving the second leaf and pancetta intact). Now return the quail to the oven to brown and crisp, which will take another 15 minutes. When you've removed them from the oven, let them rest for about 10 minutes before serving with the grape confit.

Guinea Fowl Baked with Thirty Cloves of Garlic

Before you cry off this one, remember that garlic, simmered gently for 1¼ hours, mellows deliciously, losing much of its pungency. I have to admit it's probably not the thing to eat before a first date, but otherwise it's utterly sublime. In this recipe, an inedible huff paste is used to make a perfect seal for the lid of the casserole, ensuring that all the juices and fragrances remain intact. It's made in moments, but if you want to you could use foil instead – bearing in mind it will not be quite as effective.

First of all dry the guinea fowl as much as possible with kitchen paper and season it well. Next, melt the butter and oil in the casserole, then, keeping the heat fairly high, brown the guinea fowl carefully on all sides. This will seem a bit awkward, but all you do is protect your hands with a cloth and hold the guinea fowl by its legs, turning it into different positions until it is a good golden colour all over; this will take 10-15 minutes in all. After that, remove the guinea fowl from the casserole, add the cloves of garlic and rosemary sprigs, toss these around, then replace the guinea fowl and sprinkle the chopped rosemary all over. Next, pour the wine all around it and let it gently come up to simmering point.

Meanwhile, place the flour in a bowl and add the water – it should be enough to make a soft but not sticky dough – then divide the dough into 4 and roll each piece into a cylinder about 9 inches (23 cm) long on a lightly floured surface. Now position these all around the rim of the casserole – it doesn't matter what they look like. Place the casserole lid carefully on top, pressing down gently and making sure there are no gaps. Alternatively, simply place a double sheet of foil over the casserole before putting the lid on. Now place the casserole in the oven and cook for 1 hour exactly, then remove the lid and let the guinea fowl continue to cook for another 10 minutes, to re-crisp the skin. Next remove the guinea fowl from the casserole and allow it to rest for 10 minutes before carving.

Serve the carved guinea fowl with the garlic cloves alongside and the cooking juices poured around it. The idea is to squash the garlic cloves with a knife to release all the creamy pulp and, as you eat, dip the pieces of guinea fowl into it. Creamy mashed potatoes would be a wonderful accompaniment here.

Serves 4
1 x 4 lb (1.8 kg) guinea fowl
30 cloves garlic, unpeeled (3-4 heads)
½ oz (10 g) butter
1 dessertspoon olive oil
6 small sprigs fresh rosemary
1 heaped tablespoon rosemary leaves, bruised and chopped
10 fl oz (275 ml) white wine
salt and freshly milled black pepper

For the huff paste:
8 oz (225 g) plain flour, plus a little extra for dusting
5 fl oz (150 ml) cold water

You will also need a lidded flameproof casserole large enough to hold the guinea fowl comfortably – about 8 pints (4.5 litres).

Pre-heat the oven to gas mark 6, 400°F (200°C).

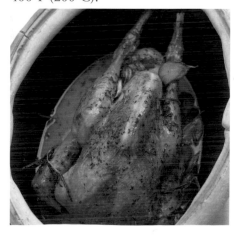

Grilled Lemon Chicken Kebabs with Gremolata

This is what we all need – something easy to prepare, really fast to cook that also tastes exceptionally good. Serve with rice or salad or both, or, instead of the rice, warm crusty bread to dip into the juices.

Serves 2

2 Traditional Free Range boneless chicken breasts, skin-on

juice 1 lemon, plus 1 teaspoon grated lemon zest

3 thick slices lemon, cut into quarters

2 fl oz (55 ml) olive oil

1 clove garlic, peeled and crushed

1 dessertspoon chopped fresh oregano

1 teaspoon white wine vinegar

2 bay leaves, torn in half

salt and freshly milled black pepper

For the gremolata:

1 clove garlic, peeled and finely chopped

1 heaped teaspoon grated lemon zest

1 tablespoon chopped fresh parsley

You will also need 2 wooden skewers, 10 inches (25.5 cm) long, soaked in water for at least 30 minutes before you start cooking.

Begin by chopping each piece of chicken into 5 chunky pieces, leaving the skin on, and place them in a bowl, along with the lemon juice and zest, oil, garlic, oregano, white wine vinegar and plenty of seasoning. Cover and leave to marinate overnight or for a few hours – or for as much time as you have.

To cook the chicken, pre-heat the grill to its highest setting at least 10 minutes ahead, then first thread half a bay leaf on to the first skewer, followed by a quarter-slice of lemon, then a piece of chicken. Carry on alternating the lemon and chicken until you have used 5 pieces of chicken, finishing off with a lemon quarter and another bay-leaf half at the end and making sure you pack everything together as tightly as possible. Repeat with the second skewer, then place them both on a grill rack, and underneath the rack place a heatproof dish to catch the juices. The kebabs should be 4 inches (10 cm) from the grill, and as they cook you need to baste them with the marinade juices. They will need 10 minutes on each side to cook through and become nice and dark and toasted at the edges.

While they're under the grill, mix the gremolata ingredients together and have it ready. When the chicken is done, transfer it to a serving plate and keep warm. Now put the rest of the marinade, plus the basting juices, in a saucepan and boil to reduce to a syrupy consistency, which will take about 2 minutes. Pour this over the chicken and sprinkle the gremolata all over as it goes to the table.

5

A vegetable calendar

I will always remember Victoria
Wood at the Albert Hall in
1996 doing one of her splendid
monologues in which she
described how an aunt of hers
always put the sprouts on for the
Christmas lunch in November!
It was the older people in the
audience who laughed the
loudest because, of course, we
all remembered the waterlogged,
rather grey, overcooked
vegetables of our schooldays.

Without going into the historical reasons for this poor culinary image British cooks are heir to, let's just say that things have thankfully changed. Though we are still very much a meat-loving nation, we have of late developed a much more healthy reverence and respect for vegetables, which have now become absolute stars in their own right and not some 'also-ran' to help the meat go down.

How to cook perfect vegetables

The answer to this question lies in just one word: carefully. Vegetables need care and attention if we're going to get the best out of them. 'Catch the moment' is a good phrase, because there is a moment when they are cooked to perfection and then, beyond that, they begin to deteriorate.

Whereas I suspect the problem of overcooking was related to a fear of the vegetables not being quite done enough, we now seem to be facing the absolute opposite problem – an equal fear of overcooking that results in almost raw, inedible vegetables that you'd be hard pushed to get your fork into. So whilst it can be argued that overcooked vegetables should be banned for ever, I would like to see the opposite extreme banned, too. I have nothing against good, honest, raw vegetables, but if they're meant to be cooked, they must be.

Catching the moment?

I am always being asked what my favourite piece of cooking equipment is, and the answer is unequivocal: a small, flat skewer – I keep a whole bunch of them hanging near where I cook. It's the only way I can tell if, say, a cauliflower floret, a potato or a Brussels sprout is cooked. As the skewer slides into the thickest part of the vegetable you can feel if it's tender by the amount of give. A very small, sharp paring knife will do the same job, but a skewer is better. If you practise the skewer test every time you cook vegetables you'll soon get the feel of 'catching the moment'.

Is water the enemy?

I would say yes, mostly, but not always. On the whole, the more water you have, the more it dilutes the flavour of the vegetable. If you're boiling, the water should barely cover the vegetables, because a brief encounter is what we're really looking for. Always use boiling water from the kettle so that you don't use too much – you can see instantly when it barely covers the vegetables and doesn't need more. So always be very sparing with water, except for boiling cabbage, where, after many years of experimenting, I have concluded that it needs plenty of boiling water to cover so that its brief encounter with the fast-boiling water cooks and tenderises it as quickly as possible. All vegetable cooking water contains nutrients, so use it as stock whenever possible. In the vegetable cooking methods that follow, I will indicate the amounts of water needed.

Is steaming better?

Sometimes quite definitely, other times not. As we have prepared *How To Cook*, my team and I have conducted side-by-side tests so that when steaming is better, it will be indicated. In some cases, steam rather than water helps to preserve more flavour, but in other cases, steaming does not tenderise sufficiently and because it takes longer it can affect flavour. I would urge you to invest in a fan steamer – a wonderful piece of equipment that can be slipped into any-sized saucepan, meaning you always have the choice of being able to steam.

Oven-roasting

When grilled vegetables became fashionable in other parts of the world, the vagaries of the British domestic grill were never going to be able to cope without a great deal of hassle. Since my first experience with high-temperature oven-roasting of vegetables in the *Summer Collection*, I am now thrilled and delighted to have discovered this method of cooking vegetables. I now almost never grill or sauté, which demands time, standing around watching, waiting and turning, whereas oven-roasting, besides leaving you in peace, has the huge advantage of requiring less fat. I do, however, sometimes use a ridged grill pan, which gives plenty of vision and no bending backaches from peering under a conventional grill.

Which is the best method?

There isn't one. All vegetables respond differently to different ways of cooking, so what I will do is indicate which method I think is best for each vegetable.

Eating vegetables in season

Once upon a time nature provided us with a perfectly varied diet, leaving us blissfully free of a large amount of decision-making. This in turn gave an added dimension to everyday eating in that we could enjoy anticipating what each month in each year would bring and really look forward to it.

Now modern technology and progress have provided something else. Fast jets. This means that at any given time in the calendar, produce from around the world can be dispatched within hours and absolutely everything is always available all year round. What this means is that, along with the good fortune of being able to eat almost anything we feel like when we like, we have also lost something, and that is an appreciation of what individual items taste like when they are harvested in their natural environment, in their best season. Thus we have pallid sprouts in July and woolly strawberries at Christmas. There's also the added problem of travel time and distribution, which often means fruits and vegetables are picked immature and unripened, with a resulting loss of flavour and quality.

I am not against progress and I do appreciate fresh shelled peas from Kenya – they don't have the tender melt-in-the-mouth flavour of home-grown in June, but they're better than frozen. I also love having fresh Israeli basil in the winter months when mine has died off. However, if we want to know how to cook we first need to know how to buy home-grown vegetables in season that have the finest quality and flavour: tight little button sprouts after the first November frost has sharpened their flavour; the finest young green stalks of asparagus in early May; the very red, sweet, sun-ripened tomatoes of early autumn; and the quite unmatched flavour and melting texture of British runner beans. For this reason I will indicate the best season for each vegetable and hopefully encourage you to reintroduce this natural rhythm of nature into your day-to-day eating.

Asparagus

Mid-April to the end of June, depending on the weather
I have now almost completely given up making things with asparagus, because apart from the very thin sprue, which I like to chop and put in Eggs en Cocotte (Book One), I think asparagus is best eaten as it is, hot with foaming melted butter or hollandaise sauce poured over, or warm or cold with a good vinaigrette (see page 153).

To cook asparagus, take each stalk in both hands and bend and snap off the woody end, then trim the ends with a knife to make them neater. Lay the asparagus stalks on an opened fan steamer (or an ordinary steamer will do) – they can be piled one on top of the other – then place them in a frying pan or saucepan, pour in about 1 inch (2.5 cm) of boiling water from the kettle, then season with salt, put a lid on and steam for 5-6 minutes, or until they feel tender when tested with a skewer.

Serve the asparagus on hot plates with some sauce poured over the tips. Pick them up with your hands and eat down to the tough ends, dipping in the sauce after each bite. Also, don't forget to have finger bowls and napkins at the ready. 1 lb 4 oz (570 g) of asparagus will serve 4 as a starter.

Aubergines

At their best July to September
Chefs and cooks seems to have an endless debate about aubergines – to salt and drain or not to salt and drain. I'm for the former. I do take the point that the modern aubergine has evolved to a state where it does not contain bitter juices, but the juices are there nonetheless and I find salting and draining gets rid of excess moisture and concentrates the flavour – there's nothing worse than a watery aubergine.

Aubergines also have a capacity to absorb other flavours, so are great mixed with tomatoes and spices, cheese or pulses. They also absorb oil at an incredible rate, so frying is not recommended. I find the best way to cook them is either by oven-roasting (page 136) or char-grilling (page 158).

Beetroot

Available all year round

A truly magnificent vegetable, but sadly its reputation in this country has been ruined by one thing alone – malt vinegar, a lethal culinary weapon that kills off the flavour of anything it comes into contact with (apart from its affinity with pickled onions and its ability to counteract the fattiness of fish and chips). So poor old beetroot is often despised as a consequence of formerly being confined to the pickle jar. Yet cooked as a vegetable or in a salad it has a superb earthy flavour and a wonderful rich, vibrant colour.

To cook beetroot: there are two methods here; one is long and slow in the oven, which is suitable for larger, older beetroot; and the other is for the first small bunches of fresh beetroot that appear in June.

To cook 1 lb (450 g) of winter-stored beetroot in the oven – try to use even-sized beetroot if you can – begin by pre-heating the oven to gas mark 3, 325°F (170°C). Now prepare the beetroot by leaving the trailing root intact but trimming the green stalk so only 1 inch (2.5 cm) is left. Wash well under cold running water, but leave the peel on. Now place the beetroot in a parcel of double foil, sealing well. Place the parcel on a baking sheet and bake on the middle shelf of the pre-heated oven for 3 hours. To test if it's cooked, you should be able to ease the skin away with your thumbs.

For boiled beetroot, take one bunch of small summer beetroot, prepare as above and place it in a medium saucepan, then add salt and enough boiling water to barely cover. Simmer, covered, for 20-30 minutes, until the skin eases away when pushed away with your thumbs.

Peel and serve hot as a vegetable or cold with vinaigrette in a salad.

Broad beans

Best late-June and July

In the *Cookery Course* I gave a recipe for very young broad beans in their pods; in fact the beans are hardly formed and the finger-thick pods are delicious. If you grow them or know someone who does, it's worth giving it a try. However, the beans themselves later on have much to offer. If they're young and tender just steam them for about 3 minutes; if they're a bit older, boiling is best as it softens and tenderises the skin – add salt, barely cover with boiling water and give them 3-4 minutes.

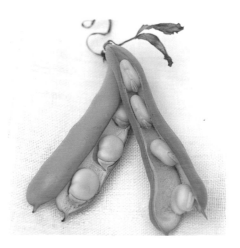

Older broad beans, when quite large, can be blanched in boiling water for 1 minute, then drained and, when cool enough, the skins slipped off. As you do this they will split in two, then you can finish cooking them in steam till tender – 2-3 minutes. Broad beans have a wonderful affinity with boiled ham and gammon steaks, and partnered with pancetta (Italian cured bacon) they make a brilliant salad (see page 155). 1 lb (450 g) of broad beans in the pod will serve 2.

Broccoli (calabrese)

English season, June to November

This is a vegetable that, because it's imported all year round, turns up far too often on restaurant menus. However, it's good to enjoy it in season. Prepare it by cutting it into even-sized florets measuring about 2 inches (5 cm) each, then steam them till tender – 4-5 minutes. Serve with a squeeze of lemon juice, a little butter or a sprinkle of grated cheese to just melt into the flower heads. You can also roast broccoli tossed in a little oil and seasoning – just place in a pre-heated oven at gas mark 6, 400°F (200°C) for 25 minutes.

Alternatively, to stir-fry for 2 people, separate 8 oz (225 g) of florets into 1 inch (2.5 cm) pieces and slice the stalk bits into tiny diagonal slices. Stir-fry in 1 dessertspoon of very hot oil for 1 minute, then add 1 teaspoon of grated ginger and a crushed clove of garlic, stir-fry for another minute, then add 1 tablespoon of soy sauce and 1 tablespoon of dry sherry. Cover with a lid and continue to cook until tender – about 2 more minutes.

Broccoli (sprouting)

February to March

After the lean winter months, the first fresh green vegetable to herald spring is sprouting broccoli, with its purple or white flowery heads. It has a lovely, sweet, very green kind of flavour and tender stalks. I like to eat the leaves, stalks and heads when it's very young. Steam them, sprinkled with salt, for 3-4 minutes. You will need 4 oz (110 g) per person.

Brussels sprouts

Best from November to February

Mini cabbages that grow on thick stalks is how I would describe Brussels. In Norfolk, on my way to football matches on Saturdays, I can buy them still attached to their two-foot-high stalks, which means I can 'pick' them fresh as I need them through the week.

People either love or hate Brussels sprouts, and I am devoted to them – with provisos. I never buy them till November, because I think that frost sharpens their flavour; sprouts at the end of summer are never as good. Also, they're difficult to cook if too large, so small, tight buttons about 1 inch (2.5 cm) in size are best. The larger, more opened, walnut-sized sprouts are more difficult to cook but can be used in purées or soups.

To cook Brussels sprouts, there's no need to make incisions in the stalks. All you need to do for 1 lb (450 g) of sprouts is take off the outer leaves if they look a bit weary (if not leave them on), sprinkle with salt and steam them for 5-8 minutes, depending on their size, but watch carefully and remember undercooking is just as bad as overcooking, so use a skewer to test when they're tender. Another way to serve them is to have a frying pan with ½ a teaspoon of butter and ½ a teaspoon of oil very hot, then, after giving them about one minute's less steaming, toss them around in the hot pan to finish cooking and to turn them fairly brown at the edges. This last method can be varied by adding a couple of rashers of chopped streaky bacon, cooked first till crisp, or at Christmas it's nice to add 4 oz (110 g) of chopped, peeled, cooked chestnuts and brown these, too. 1 lb (450 g) of Brussels sprouts will serve 2-3 people.

Cabbage

Varieties available all year

A cabbage is honest goodness with no pretensions. It is a supremely beautiful vegetable, an absolute work of art visually, and with its tight, audibly squeaky leaves bursting with goodness and vitality, why is it not acknowledged and revered? The overcooking of former years has made it a much-maligned vegetable in the western world. Chefs and restaurants continue to largely ignore seasons and prefer to offer endless dull green string beans and the ever in-season calabrese broccoli.

When were you last offered a bowl of fragrant, buttered green cabbage in a restaurant? Isn't it time for a rethink? Fresh cabbage lightly cooked is full of goodness, packed with vitamins, minerals and flavour and it's not expensive. So I hope I can encourage you to start eating more of it.

Types of cabbage

Spring greens or cabbage greens

Not really spring greens any more, as they are now available all year round, but they seem to have a luscious edge in spring that is lacking in the winter months. Look for small, tender leaves that look perky, sound squeaky and are not too floppy and tired.

Winter cabbages

These are the larger, fatter, rounded varieties. Savoy, *right*, has crinkly leaves and a superb flavour; January King has flowery leaves with a purple tinge; round cabbage has green outer leaves but gets whiter towards the centre and is good for coleslaw.

Pointed cabbage

This is a lovely variety – tight, green and leafy. Best in April, May and June, as it's home-grown, but still good imported from Spain at other times of the year.

Buying cabbage

Cabbage should always be eaten as fresh as possible – it loses nutrients if stored for too long. An unwrapped fresh cabbage should look bright and crisp, with its outer leaves intact (often if it's had its outer leaves removed, it was because they were limp, which is not a good sign). The heart should feel firm and the leaves should squeak as you pull them apart.

To prepare cabbage: with a leafy variety such as spring greens it's best to discard any tired, floppy outside leaves, then separate the other leaves down to the central bud and place them one by one on a flat board. Then, using a sharp paring knife, cut out the stalks, running the point of the knife down each side. When the stalks have been removed, pile the leaves on top of each other and, using a larger knife, shred the cabbage into strips, then do the same with the centre bud to shred that, too. For a more compact variety, such as Savoy, once the outer leaves have been discarded, halve and then quarter the cabbage lengthways, then cut out the hard core from each quarter and discard. Finally, slice thinly across each quarter to shred it.

To cook cabbage: I have tried every method under the sun and I am now convinced that boiled cabbage needs plenty of water. The secret is to shred it quite finely and cook it briefly in rapidly boiling water. What I do is pack it down quite tightly into a saucepan, sprinkle with salt, then place the pan over a high heat, pour boiling water from the kettle in, which re-boils instantly, and time it for 3-5 minutes.

The one way to tell if it's cooked is to bite a piece, as you would pasta. Then tip it into a colander and squeeze as much excess water out as you can, using a saucer to press the cabbage down. Then turn the saucer on its side and use chopping movements, which pushes any excess water out. Serve it straight away in a hot bowl, tossing it with a minute amount of butter, and season it with salt and pepper. One medium-sized cabbage will serve 4 people.

Carrots

June to November, or April and May from Spain
Summer bunched carrots (home-grown) are my favourites – sweet and delicate, great for simply munching raw or grated into salads. The first of these to appear in spring come from Spain and have a particularly good flavour.

To cook summer carrots, there's absolutely no need to peel here – just rinse them under a cold running tap and cut off the stalks only, just a fraction above the end. This leaves the inside of the carrot intact and, I feel, preserves the flavour. Place them in a steamer, sprinkle with a little salt and steam for about 7 minutes, or until tender when pierced with a skewer but still retaining some firmness and bite. Serve plain, or I like them tossed in butter mixed with some chopped fresh tarragon leaves.

To cook winter carrots: these are available from storage all year round. My favourite way to cook them plainly is to scrape off the skins and cut them into 2 inch (5 cm) chunks, then place them in a saucepan with salt and enough boiling water to barely cover them. Give them about 20 minutes, or until tender but with a little firm bite in the centre, then drain and place them in a food processor and, using the pulse movement, 'chop' the carrots quite small, but don't overdo it or you'll have a purée.

Quickly return them to the saucepan using a spatula to scrape them back in quickly, add a knob of butter and some freshly milled black pepper, then place them over a gentle heat and stir them around for a couple of minutes to get the heat back in. 1 lb (450 g) of carrots will serve 4.

Cauliflower and cape broccoli

December to March

Home-grown cauliflowers are available all year, but in the winter months we grow something called cape broccoli, which has dark-purple curds instead of the creamy-white. This has a more distinctive flavour and is good, I think, to ring the changes. They're both cooked in the same way, so remove the tough outer leaves, keeping the younger tender ones, which not only can be cooked and eaten, but their presence in the cooking imparts extra flavour.

To cook a cauliflower, first of all separate it into largish florets by turning the cauliflower upside down, then just insert a small sharp knife and cut through to separate the heads into about 3 inch (7.5 cm) florets. Then place them, along with the leaves, in a steamer, sitting them up vertically (ie stalk-side at the base, flower heads up). Now pop a bay leaf in, which has a fragrant affinity with cauliflower. I also add some salt, and I like to use another very English flavouring, nutmeg, which I grate lightly over the surface of the florets. Now pour in boiling water from the kettle and steam for 6-7 minutes, or until tender when tested with a skewer. Serve with a little butter or grated cheese, or in our modern variation of cauliflower cheese on page 135. One medium cauliflower will serve 4 people.

Celeriac

Best through the winter months

Celeriac, at first sight, is probably the ugliest, most uninteresting-looking vegetable there is, but there is a hidden agenda here, for underneath the spiney roots and ugly skin is a soft, velvety flesh that, when mashed, has the creaminess of potato with the added subtle flavour of celery. But that's not all: celeriac is excellent roasted in the oven and also raw in a salad, cut into tiny julienne matchstick strips and served with a creamy dressing.

To prepare celeriac, first of all have no fear in paring off the skin really thickly. What you need to do is peel off enough to leave behind only the creamy-white flesh, with no brown bits left behind. Because the root channels are interwoven into the base of the bulb you will need to cut all this away, so it's always useful to remember only three-quarters of what you buy can be used. Cut the rest into chunks and, as you do so, pop them in some cold salted water to prevent discolouring. Now you can either dry them well and roast (see page 134) or boil them and combine them with equal quantities of boiled potatoes and mash.

Celery

Available almost all year round

Celery is as English as the Stilton cheese it's often partnered and perhaps enjoyed best of all with: fresh, crunchy and crisp in the autumn with a good cheese board, some fresh-shelled walnuts and a glass of vintage port.

Originally, the older varieties of so-called 'dirty' celery from the flat black-earthed Fenlands of East Anglia had a short season – from October to January. If you're lucky enough to eat some there is much washing to do, but the flavour is exceptional, particularly after a light frost, when it's sweetest of all. However, a really severe frost can wipe the whole crop out, so growing it can be a hazardous occupation and in the past during hard winters there was sometimes none available. English Fenland growers have overcome this by not only developing new varieties that can be grown in summer, but have also overcome the severities of a British winter by growing English varieties in the warm climate of Spain. This means extremely good celery is available practically all year round, with a gap from about April to June. If you can get 'dirty' celery in November it is worth all the tedious washing, but it's also good to have English varieties available all year.

To prepare celery, first of all remove the tough, large outer stalks, and as these are usually distinctively stringy, take a sharp paring knife and pare off the strings, *above left*. Now trim off the outer skin around the root and cut the head vertically so that some of the sweet, edible root is still intact, then cut into 6-8 layered vertical strips, *left*.

Courgettes

Best home-grown from mid-June to October

Courgettes are baby marrows, and don't I know it! I used to grow them, but if I wasn't vigilant about picking them every day in season they seemed to turn into marrows overnight – and marrow for supper night after night is *not* a good idea! Now I would rather buy them small and tender. Courgettes are a delicate vegetable, with not a great deal of their own flavour, and like aubergines they have a high water content that can render them watery and dull. I like them chunkily cut and roasted in the oven, as in Oven-Roasted Ratatouille in the *Summer Collection*, or marinated in a vinaigrette with herbs (see page 139), which allows them to absorb some real flavour.

Fennel

Home-grown, May to September

Sometimes called Florence fennel, or its charming Italian name is *finocchio*. Fennel is like a fat, bulbous celery, with the same crunchy texture but with a marked aniseed flavour. Fennel can be thinly sliced and eaten raw in salads or shaved very finely with a mandolin and dressed with vinaigrette. It's also very good cooked and served as a vegetable.

To prepare fennel, first trim off the green shoot at the top; if the fronds aren't too droopy you can use them as a garnish. Then cut it diagonally into a pointed shape. Next slice off the root part at the other end and remove any outer toughened or brown layers. Slice the bulb in half and then again into quarters. Now you can take a little of the stalky core out, but not all, because you want the layers, including the inner green part, to stay intact.

To cook fennel, cut it into quarters, steam it for 10 minutes, or until tender, then have a frying pan with 1 teaspoon each of oil and butter really hot and sauté the fennel till it's golden brown at the edges. Finally, sprinkle with a tablespoon of freshly grated Parmesan whilst it's still in the pan and let it rest for a few seconds, then serve with a little more grated Parmesan sprinkled over and the chopped feathery fronds if there are any. Serves 2.

Leeks

Best home-grown from September to May

Leeks are a very fine vegetable indeed. Though they are related to onions, they have a far more subtle and somehow nobler taste, I think. Leeks lend themselves to other flavours superbly, too: great with potatoes, in a soup or with cheese (see Leek and Goats' Cheese Tart, Book One), in salads with vinaigrette, and they also respond beautifully to quick stir-frying. Watch the season, though, as home-grown leeks get a bit woolly and tired in the late spring and summer and the imported ones never seem quite as good. Remember, too, that the smaller and thinner the leeks are the sweeter their flavour is, so avoid the very fat, heavy ones.

To prepare leeks, buy a little more than you need, because there's going to be quite a bit of trimming. First take off the tough outer leaves and trim off most of the very green part. Now, using a sharp knife, place the leek on a flat surface and make an incision vertically about halfway down (because of the intricate layers, there can be dust and grit trapped in-between, usually in the upper part). Now turn on the cold tap and fan out the layers of leek to rinse them through and rid them of any hidden dirt, *right*.

This is my favourite way of cooking leeks – very gently, in their own juices and served as a vegetable, particularly at the end of winter when there's not an awful lot else available.

When the leeks are trimmed and washed, cut them all the way through vertically, then chop them into 1 inch (2.5 cm) pieces. Now place a small frying pan over a medium heat, add the butter and let it melt – it needs to lightly coat the surface of the pan. Now add the leeks and some seasoning, stir them around, then turn the heat down to low and let them cook gently for about 5 minutes without a lid, stirring them 2 or 3 times. There will be quite a lot of juice that collects in the pan, so use a draining spoon to serve.

Buttered Leeks

Serves 2

1 lb (450 g) leeks, trimmed – you need
12 oz (350 g) trimmed weight
½ teaspoon butter
salt and freshly milled black pepper

Mushrooms

Mushrooming is a word that's used to describe something that's grown overnight, and I have to say that's precisely the word I would use to describe the mushroom market. Whereas once we could buy only buttons or caps, we are now presented with an amazing variety of sizes, shapes and colours. Let's not be too dazzled by looks, though, because some of them appear more interesting than they actually taste.

Because season and availability fluctuate, here we need to concern ourselves mostly with how to get the best out of whatever is available. My own firm favourite cultivated mushrooms are the flat, open, dark-gilled variety and the smaller pink-gilled open caps. (I have never thought the pale, insipid button mushrooms were even worth bothering with.) There are now chestnut mushrooms and the large version called portabella, too. I also like shiitake (particularly in an omelette), a saffron-yellow variety called pied de mouton, and now we can buy the best-flavoured wild mushrooms of all, Italian dried porcini (known as ceps in France) and another French variety called morels. I now find getting the finest mushroom flavour in cooking is never a problem.

To prepare mushrooms, don't wash them is the first rule – they already have a lot of moisture and washing them means they absorb even more, which can make them soggy. Take a damp piece of kitchen paper and wipe each mushroom clean, or use a special mushroom brush, which brushes away any dirt. Don't peel them, either, because the peel has lots of flavour. I always use the mushroom stalks, except with shiitake, as they are a bit chewy in this case and so need to be trimmed down almost to the cup. If the mushrooms are small, leave them whole, if not, cut through the stalk, then into halves or quarters.

Sautéed Mushrooms

Serves 2
8 oz (225 g) mushrooms, prepared as described
1 teaspoon olive oil or butter
salt and freshly milled black pepper

First imagine a plump, round, fat, juicy mushroom, then think of a shrivelled dried mushroom – the difference is moisture, and because the dried one has masses more flavour, having lost the moisture, I feel that the thing to aim for when cooking mushrooms is to get as much of the moisture out as possible so as to concentrate the flavour. No need to use very much oil or butter, as mushrooms tend to soak this up at an alarming rate. Always remember, too, that as the moisture evaporates they lose half their original volume.

Heat the olive oil or butter in a frying pan and, when it's hot, throw in the mushrooms and toss them around by shaking the pan. Season with salt and pepper, then turn the heat down to very low and just let the mushrooms cook gently, uncovered, so that all the juice evaporates and the flavour of the mushrooms becomes more concentrated. Leave them like that for 30 minutes, stirring them around once or twice.

Once the mushrooms have lost much of their moisture content they can then be used in an omelette or simply as they are. You could also add a peeled and chopped clove of garlic 5 minutes before the end and finish off with a sprinkling of chopped fresh flat-leaf parsley.

Onions and shallots

Available all year

Where would cooks be without onions? One of the principal flavour-makers in the kitchen, stews, soups, casseroles, quick salads and sauces are all enhanced by this most humble but wonderful of vegetables, together with its tiny, milder cousin the shallot, which also plays an important role.

Over the years I've been given countless methods of how not to cry when preparing them. One enterprising person even sent me a battery-operated fan to fan away the fumes, but I can honestly say that nothing really works. For chopping, however, food processors have made things a lot easier, and now there aren't as many tears as there used to be.

How to prepare onions

Slicing: if you want to slice them, cut off the root end, then peel away the skin. Slice in whole round slices and separate into rings, or else cut the onion in half first and then slice into half-moon shapes.

Chopping: rough chopping is as above, making about 3 cuts vertically across each onion and then 3 horizontally.

Chopping small (without a processor): this time leave the root intact, then peel away the skin from the top end. Now cut the onion in half and place each half on a flat surface, round-side up. Next, make cuts vertically from the root end but leaving the root intact to hold it together, *top right*. Then make horizontal cuts across the vertical cuts whilst you hold on to the root end firmly, *right*. The last cut will be the little root bit, and this can be discarded.

Well, they're actually roasted, but you get the same effect without having to stand over them. They are particularly lovely served with sausages and mash or for steak and onions.

First of all you need to cut the onions into ¼ inch (5 mm) slices, then place them in a bowl, add the oil and sugar and toss the onions around to get the lightest coating. Then spread them out on a baking tray and place on a high shelf of the oven for 14-15 minutes – they need to be nicely blackened round the edges.

Oven-Fried Onions

Serves 2
8 oz (225 g) onions, peeled
1 teaspoon groundnut or other flavourless oil
1 teaspoon golden caster sugar

Pre-heat the oven to gas mark 7, 425°F (220°C).

Shallots

These are like little baby onions, sometimes bright purple-pink and sometimes creamy-white. Cooked slowly as a confit they make a lovely accompaniment to beef. In a medium pan, simmer 12 oz (350 g) of peeled whole shallots with 7 fl oz (200 ml) of red wine, 1 fl oz (25 ml) of red wine vinegar and seasoning. Keep the heat very low and cook, without a lid, for about 1 hour and 10 minutes, turning the shallots over halfway through. After this time, add half a teaspoon of sugar to give a lovely sticky glaze, and cook for another 5 minutes. Serves 4.

They are lovely pickled (see the Christmas book), or simmered whole in casseroles and braised dishes, and I love them chopped very finely in salads (see pages 155 and 161).

Parsnips

Best November to February
What an absolute star a parsnip is – full of soft, juicy flesh and fragrant, sweet flavour. They are lovely plain, steamed, mashed and roasted, and one of my favourite parsnip recipes is in the Christmas book, where they are baked in the oven with Parmesan.

I like them best after the frosts have arrived, which really does intensify their flavour. Because parsnips are stored, they tend to go a bit woody towards the end of the winter, so enjoy them at their best between November and February. If you can, buy small, young parsnips that don't need peeling and coring; the older, larger, late-winter parsnips need the peel taken off and the cores cut out. Then cut them into even-sized pieces and steam for 10-15 minutes, and serve with plenty of salt and freshly milled black pepper and a little butter. For roasting, prepare them in the same way, toss in a little oil and season. Place on a pre-heated roasting tray and roast in the oven pre-heated to gas mark 7, 425°F (220°C) for 30-40 minutes, depending on the size of the parsnips. 1 lb (450 g) of parsnips will serve 4 people.

Peas

Home-grown, best in June and July
One very sad but thought-provoking incident happened to me a few years ago. I was buying fresh peas in the pod in a supermarket, and the sixth-former doing a Saturday job on the checkout asked me if I could tell her what they were. Perhaps the positive side of that comment was a kind of affirmation that I really needed to do *How To Cook*.

Fresh-shelled peas are one of the most delightful vegetables of all – young and tender, they melt in the mouth when cooked and taste wonderful raw. Sure, it takes a bit of time to shell them, but sitting by an open window or in the garden on a bright summer's day shelling peas can be wonderful therapy. When they first arrive they're incredibly sweet and tender, but later on they get bigger and have quite a different character and flavour. I like both equally. Imported Kenyan peas are not quite as good as the summer home-grown peas, but I think we are very fortunate to have them available all year round, and ready-shelled, too.

To cook young, fresh shelled peas, first remember to buy 8 oz (225 g) in the pod per person. After shelling, pop them in a steamer with some salt and give them 1 minute before you bite one; they shouldn't take any longer than 2 minutes in all. If they are a bit older, they may need 3-4 minutes.

This is a good recipe for slightly older peas, which, in my opinion, sometimes have more texture and flavour than the younger ones. However, if the peas you are using are very young, give them far less cooking time – 8 minutes at the most.

First trim the spring onions: you need only the white bulbs (the rest can be chopped and saved for something such as a stir-fry). Pull off any thick, stalky bits from the rocket and tear the larger leaves in half. Now all you do is put all the ingredients in a large saucepan, cover with a lid, bring them up to simmering point and simmer gently for 8-15 minutes, depending on the age of the peas.

Peppers

Best season, summer and autumn

Once an exotic import from the Mediterranean, now an everyday, ever-available staple but best home-grown in the summer and autumn. Peppers actually come in all kinds of colours, but red, green and yellow are the most widely available. When peppers are grown they begin green, and then, if left on the stalks to mature, this mellowing results in red peppers, with a sweeter flesh (which is better if they are to be eaten raw or only lightly cooked). But the green ones do have a special character of their own – a sharper, more robust flavour, which stands up to long, slow cooking. For this reason I am very much against any snobbish dismissal of green peppers as being somehow inferior. In fact certain cuisines, such as Cajun and Creole, seem to only ever include green peppers in their recipes. Yellow peppers are more like red in flavour, and their golden-yellow colour can look very pretty in certain dishes.

To prepare peppers, firstly slice the top off the pepper, including the stalk, then, with the tip of a small knife, scrape out the seeds and core. Now slice the pepper into quarters, and again, using the tip of the knife, slice away any very white, pithy bits. Then slice or chop according to

Braised Peas, Rocket and Spring Onions

Serves 6
3 lb (1.35 kg) peas (unshelled weight), freshly shelled
2½ oz (60 g) fresh rocket
12 bulbous spring onions
1½ oz (40g) butter
3 tablespoons water
pinch golden caster sugar
1 rounded teaspoon Maldon sea salt

the recipe. If the recipe calls for finely chopped pepper, you can use the round lid bit around the stalk and chop that, too.

To cook peppers: to peel or not to peel is the vexed question. I say don't bother. After discovering the recipe for Piedmont-Roasted Peppers – which are lovely in the autumn when the peppers are in season and the tomatoes are ripe and red – and publishing it in the *Summer Collection*, I decided they were the very best cooked peppers I'd ever tasted, so I stopped going to the bother of peeling them. So all the recipes I have done since then use the peppers as they are, skins and all. They can be sautéed, stir-fried in strips till blackened at the edges and tender, or oven-roasted, sprinkled firstly with olive oil and seasoning, then placed in the oven at gas mark 8, 450°F (230°C) for 30-40 minutes.

Chilli peppers
Available all year

Forgive the pun, but the whole subject of chillies is a hotbed of confusion: there are so many varieties, and availability fluctuates from one variety to another. The only real guide is individual taste. I would avoid the fat, round, scorching Scotch bonnet pepper unless you are a real hot-chilli lover. What I tend to do is buy the larger, fatter kind, which are usually not so fiercely hot, and if I want really hot then the tiny Bird Eye chillies used in Asian cooking are the ones to go for, because they are always reliably hot. The other point to remember is that green is usually marginally hotter than red. There is a safety net, though: if you find you're using fresh chillies and they haven't given you quite enough heat, all you do is add a few drops of Tabasco (see page 16) to top up the fire.

How to prepare chillies: very carefully. Why? Because the membrane and the seeds inside are the hottest part and can burn delicate skin. American cookbooks often advise using rubber gloves, but washing your hands with soap and water after handling should be OK. What happens is if your hands touch the delicate skin on your face or, worse, eyes, it can burn the skin. So slice the tops off, cut them in half lengthways, hold down the tip of each chilli half with your finger and, using a sharp knife, scrape away all the membrane and seeds and discard them. After that, either slice the chilli or chop it finely, then carefully wash your hands.

Winter pumpkin and squash
Winter pumpkin: home-grown, October to November; imported, September to November. Squash: all year

The bright-orange lantern pumpkins available around Halloween do not have a great deal of flavour, so in my opinion are not worth serving as a vegetable. However, the smooth, silky texture makes wonderful soup, and gives the best texture in Pumpkin Pie (see Book One) or in pumpkin and sweetcorn soup (page 143).

Butternut squash is available all year, because when our season finishes we import it from Africa, and its buttery, nutty texture is one of my own favourites. It is shaped like a bottle and has both a nutty flavour and a good firm texture excellent for roasting and braising (see the recipes on pages 134 and 82 respectively).

To prepare pumpkin or squash, you need a good, sharp, heavy knife, and first you cut the vegetable in half and then into quarters. After that scoop out the fibrous bits and all the seeds with a spoon or knife, then, this time using a small but very sharp knife, peel away the tough skin. Finally, cut the pumpkin flesh into cubes or slices.

Runner beans

August to mid-September

This vegetable is, for me, the crown prince of all British vegetables. Although runner beans are imported all year round, they're never quite the same as our own end-of-summer crop, which provides a feast for almost two months. If you're growing your own the beans must be harvested young because the whole lot is eaten, pod and all. Runner beans have in the recent past been a misunderstood vegetable, rarely seen in restaurants, even in peak season. The problem is that people, chefs included, rarely know how to prepare and cook them. If they're simply chopped into little diamond shapes, the skins take longer to cook than the insides and they end up being either grey and overcooked or undercooked and tough.

Old-fashioned cooks like me use something called a bean slicer, *right*. The runner beans are simply fed through a channel, and a wheel with blades is turned by hand so that the runner beans are sliced very finely. This means only the briefest cooking time is needed and the beans taste deliciously fresh and green. So good are they that you don't ever need a specific recipe, maybe just a smidgen of butter and some salt and black pepper. In fact I could happily eat a whole plateful and nothing else.

To prepare and cook runner beans, first take a sharp paring knife and strip away the stringy bit on the join at either side of each bean. Then feed them through a bean slicer, which should be fixed to the edge of a table, and have a plate underneath it to catch the slices. If you don't have a bean slicer, slice the beans in exactly the same way using a paring knife. 1 lb 8 oz (700 g) of runner beans will serve 4 people.

Spinach

Home-grown, best from May to October

Very green and very good for you, spinach is packed with vitamin C. What you need to be most aware of is that spinach contains a great deal of water, so what looks like a huge amount won't be when it's cooked.

To prepare spinach: fresh spinach can be rather dusty or muddy. The best way to deal with this is to pick out and discard any damaged or brown leaves and remove any tough stalks, fill the sink with cold water, then plunge the spinach in the water and swirl the leaves around. Do this in two or three changes of water, then let it all drain in a colander, shaking it well over the sink. Young spinach leaves can be wiped and used raw in a delicious salad.

To cook spinach: absolutely no water ever. For 1 lb (450 g) of spinach leaves, melt ½ oz (10 g) of butter in a large, thick-based saucepan, then, keeping the heat at medium, pack the spinach leaves in. Add some salt, put on a tight-fitting lid and let it cook for about 30 seconds, then take the lid off and you'll find the spinach has collapsed down into the butter. Give it a stir so that the top leaves get pushed down to the base of the pan, replace the lid and give it another 30 seconds or so, shaking the pan a couple of times – I find the whole operation takes less than 2 minutes. Next drain the spinach in a colander, pressing it well with a saucer to get rid of any excess water. You can now return it to the pan and add seasoning: spinach is enhanced beautifully with a little cream or crème fraîche. It also, like cauliflower, has an affinity with nutmeg, so season with salt and freshly milled black pepper and a few gratings of whole nutmeg. Spinach as a vegetable goes beautifully with smoked haddock (see the recipe on page 174). If you're serving spinach as a vegetable you will need 8 oz (225 g) per person.

Swede

Home-grown, best in winter

I love the unique flavour of swedes, which seems to epitomise all the goodness of home cooking. They have long been of service to cooks because their presence in stews and casseroles not only ekes out the meat to make it go further, but also adds a presence that offers something of its own flavour, whilst at the same time absorbing some of the meat flavours as well. Swede is also good served solo as a vegetable.

To prepare swede, all you need here is use a potato peeler to peel it in precisely the same way as a potato, slicing off the root end first with a knife. Then just cut the swede into suitably sized chunks.

To cook swede, cut it into 1 inch (2.5 cm) dice and steam for about 10 minutes, or until tender, then whiz to a purée in a food processor or mash with a fork, adding a knob of butter, salt and lots of freshly milled black pepper. This method also works very well using half swede and half carrot, but in this case I like it chopped small rather than puréed.

For roast swede cut the chunks larger – 1½ inches (4 cm) – place the cubes in a bowl, adding (for 1 lb/450 g) 1 dessertspoon of olive oil and some seasoning. Toss the swede around to get all the pieces coated in the oil, then place them on a baking tray and roast in a pre-heated oven set to gas mark 7, 425°F (220°C) for 30-35 minutes, until the swede is nicely toasted brown at the edges. This amount will serve 4 people.

Sweetcorn

Home-grown from July to October

Aesthetically one of the most beautiful vegetables, I think – such a visual work of art. Outside, the pale-green casings cover firm, silky-white threads, and all this to protect the plump, pale-golden kernels, full of juicy sweetness.

To prepare sweetcorn you'll need to remove the kernels, so first of all remove the green part and all the silky threads. Then stand the cob upright on a flat board and, using a very sharp paring knife, carefully scrape off all the kernels, keeping the knife deep in the husk so you get the whole kernel.

To cook sweetcorn: for corn on the cob, one way is to steam the cobs for about 15 minutes, or until the kernels feel tender when tested with a small skewer. Then dress with a little melted butter, season well with plenty of salt and freshly milled black pepper and eat straight from the cob. If you stick a small fork into each end, you can pick the whole thing up, or you can chop the cob into smaller sections that can be lifted with your hands. Don't forget the napkins and finger bowls.

By far the best and most delicious way to cook and eat corn on the cob is to strip the casing and silky threads off as described above, toss the cobs in a little olive oil, season well with salt and black pepper and roast on an open barbecue. Watch them carefully, turning them all the time, until they're toasted golden brown – 5-10 minutes. You will need one medium head of corn per person.

Warning: never try to cut corn husks before cooking, as it's virtually impossible. After cooking, a very sharp knife will cut them into chunks you can bite straight into. Finally, sweetcorn kernels stripped from the cob and oven-roasted can be served as a vegetable or used to make the Pumpkin Soup with Toasted Sweetcorn on page 143.

Turnips

Baby turnips, best in June and July; winter turnips, all year

In early June I love seeing the first young bunches of carrots, and the same goes for turnips – so pretty, about the size of golf balls, with deep-purple tinges to their creamy-white flesh and topped with frilly leaves. In winter they're less tender and can be steamed and mashed to a purée with an equal amount of steamed potatoes, with the addition of a little cream and butter. I love them sliced wafer-thin in Cornish pasties and roasted as a vegetable (they can be used in the recipe on the following page). Turnips are prepared in exactly the same way as swede (see left).

To cook baby turnips, dice 1 lb (450 g) of peeled turnips into ¾ inch (2 cm) cubes. Steam them for 3 minutes, sprinkled with a little salt, then sauté in melted butter, tossing them around for about 10 minutes, until tender. This quantity of turnips will serve 4 people.

Oven-Roasted Winter Vegetables

This is always going to be an easy option if you're entertaining, as all the vegetables get cooked without any attention. One thing I have found invaluable, too, is being able to prepare them well ahead, which gives you that organised feeling. This is a particularly lovely combination of vegetables, but you can vary it with whatever is available.

Serves 6
Vegetable quantities are prepared weights
12 shallots, peeled
12 oz (350 g) peeled and deseeded butternut squash
12 oz (350 g) peeled sweet potato
12 oz (350 g) peeled swede
12 oz (350 g) peeled celeriac
1 tablespoon freshly chopped mixed herbs (rosemary and thyme, for example)
2 large cloves garlic, peeled and crushed
3 tablespoons olive oil
salt and freshly milled black pepper

You will also need a baking tray measuring 11 x 16 inches (28 x 40 cm).

Pre-heat the oven to gas mark 7, 425°F (220°C).

All you do is cut the vegetables into large, chunky pieces (no smaller than 1½ inches/4 cm) – leaving the celeriac until last, as it may discolour if left for too long – place in a large bowl, then add the herbs, garlic, olive oil and lots of seasoning and just use your hands to mix them. The prepared vegetables can now be kept in a sealed plastic bag in the fridge for 2-3 days.

When you're ready to cook the vegetables, spread them out on the baking tray and cook in the pre-heated oven on a high shelf for 30-40 minutes, until they're tender and turning brown at the edges.

Cauliflower with Two Cheeses and Crème Fraîche

No need to make a white sauce for this one – the beauty of half-fat crème fraîche is that you can simmer it into a creamy sauce in moments. This could be an accompanying vegetable for four, it could make a main course for two served with rice, or I like it with penne pasta – England meets Italy, sort of thing!

First of all place the cauliflower florets and a few of the inner leaves in a steamer with the pieces of bay leaf tucked amongst it. Pour in some boiling water from the kettle, add some freshly grated nutmeg and salt, then cover and steam the cauliflower till tender – about 12 minutes. After this time, test the thickest parts with a skewer to see if they are tender, then remove it to the baking dish and cover with a cloth to keep warm.

Now pour 3 fl oz (75 ml) of the steaming water into a saucepan, add the crème fraîche and simmer, whisking well, until it has thickened very slightly, then add the cheeses. Heat this gently for about 1 minute, whisking, until the cheeses have melted, then season the sauce to taste. Now pour the sauce over the cauliflower and scatter the spring onions and remaining Parmesan over, then sprinkle with the cayenne. Finally, place the dish under the hot grill until the cauliflower has browned and the sauce is bubbling.

Serves 4 as a vegetable or 2 for supper
1 medium cauliflower, separated into florets
1½ oz (40 g) Parmesan (Parmigiano Reggiano), finely grated, plus 1 heaped tablespoon extra to finish
1½ oz (40 g) Gruyère, finely grated
2 heaped tablespoons half-fat crème fraîche
2 bay leaves, torn in half
a little freshly grated nutmeg
2 spring onions, very finely chopped, including the green parts
pinch cayenne pepper
salt and freshly milled black pepper

You will also need an ovenproof baking dish measuring 7½ inches (19 cm) square and 2 inches (5 cm) deep.

Pre-heat the grill to its highest setting.

Tunisian Aubergine Salad with Coriander and Yoghurt

This is my adaptation of an Elizabeth David recipe. I never actually made it from her book, but one of my favourite restaurants, Chez Bruce, in Wandsworth, London, regularly serves it as a first course. It's so wonderful I never have anything else if it's on the menu.

Serves 4 as a starter

1 lb 8 oz (700 g) aubergine, chopped into ½ inch (1 cm) cubes
2 rounded tablespoons chopped fresh coriander
1 lb 8 oz (700 g) ripe red tomatoes
about 3 tablespoons olive oil
1 heaped teaspoon cumin seeds
1 teaspoon allspice berries
1 large onion, weighing about 10 oz (275 g), peeled and finely chopped
1 large red chilli, deseeded and finely chopped
4 cloves garlic, peeled and finely chopped
2 rounded tablespoons chopped fresh mint
salt and freshly milled black pepper

To serve:

1 tablespoon olive oil
8 pitta breads, warmed
4 tablespoons Greek yoghurt
1 rounded tablespoon chopped fresh coriander
1 rounded tablespoon chopped fresh mint

You will also need 2 baking trays, one measuring 11 x 16 inches (28 x 40 cm), the other measuring 10 x 14 inches (25.5 x 35 cm).

You'll need to start this recipe the day before you want to serve it. First salt and drain the aubergines: place them in a large colander and, as you add them, sprinkle with 1 tablespoon of salt, then cover with a plate and weigh it down with a few scale weights or a similar heavy object. Now place the colander on a plate and leave the aubergine to drain for 1 hour. When it has been draining for 30 minutes, pre-heat the oven to gas mark 8, 450°F (230°C).

Meanwhile, skin the tomatoes. To do this, pour boiling water over them and leave for exactly 1 minute before draining them and slipping off their skins, protecting your hands with a cloth if they are too hot. Cut them in half and place them cut-side up on the smaller baking tray, which should be lightly oiled, and brush the tomatoes with a little olive oil as well. Set to one side.

Now you need to dry-roast the cumin seeds and allspice berries, and to do this place them in a small frying pan or saucepan over a medium heat and stir and toss them around for 1-2 minutes, or until they begin to look toasted and start to jump in the pan. Now transfer them to a pestle and mortar and crush them to a powder.

When the aubergines are ready, squeeze them to get rid of any excess juices, dry them in a clean tea cloth, then place them in a bowl, add 1 tablespoon of the oil and toss them around so they get a good coating. After that, spread them out on the larger baking tray and place both baking trays in the oven, with the aubergines on the top shelf and the tomatoes on the next one down. Give them about 25 minutes, by which time the aubergines should be tinged golden brown at the edges and the tomatoes soft. Remove the vegetables from the oven and, when the tomatoes are cool enough, chop them into quite small pieces.

Meanwhile, heat 2 more tablespoons of the oil in a large frying pan over a medium to high heat and fry the onions until soft and pale gold – about 5 minutes – then add the chilli and garlic and fry for 1 more minute. Next add the chopped tomatoes, aubergines and crushed spices, stir well, add the herbs and season with salt and freshly milled black pepper. Bring everything up to a gentle simmer, then remove the pan from the heat and pile everything into a serving dish. Leave for 24 hours, or longer if possible, covered in the fridge. Serve the salad at room temperature, drizzled with the olive oil. Serve with the warm pitta breads, about a tablespoon of Greek yoghurt with each serving and the fresh herbs scattered over.

Quick-Braised Celery

Serves 4-6
1 head celery, trimmed, de-stringed and cut into 3 inch (7.5 cm) pieces
1 oz (25 g) butter
1 medium onion, peeled and thinly sliced
3 oz (75 g) carrot, peeled and thinly sliced
8 fl oz (225 ml) made up Marigold Swiss Bouillon stock
1 tablespoon chopped fresh parsley
salt and freshly milled black pepper

You will also need a frying pan with a diameter of 10 inches (25.5 cm).

Celery has such a lot going for it as a raw ingredient in salads, and because of that we rather forget how good it is cooked and served as a vegetable. This method is delightfully quick and easy, and tastes just wonderful.

First of all melt the butter in the frying pan and begin to cook the onions for 3-4 minutes over a medium to high heat, until lightly golden, then add the carrots and cook for a further 2 minutes. Now add the celery and continue to fry for 5 minutes more, or until everything is slightly browned at the edges. Season with salt and black pepper, then pour in the hot stock and place a lid on the pan. Turn the heat down and simmer gently for 20 minutes, until the vegetables are almost tender, then take the lid off and increase the heat to medium and continue to simmer till the liquid has reduced and become slightly syrupy – about 5 minutes. Serve the celery with the juices poured over and sprinkled with the parsley.

Oven-Roasted Carrots with Garlic and Coriander

This is a recipe for the large, chunky carrots of winter, which lack the sweet, delicate flavour of new carrots in summer. In the oven they turn slightly blackened and caramelised at the edges, which, together with the coriander seeds, gives an added flavour dimension.

Serves 4
1 lb (450 g) winter carrots, wiped if dusty
2 cloves garlic, peeled and crushed
1 dessertspoon coriander seeds
½ teaspoon black peppercorns
½ teaspoon Maldon sea salt
1 dessertspoon olive oil

You will also need a baking tray measuring 10 x 14 inches (25.5 x 35 cm).

Pre-heat the oven to gas mark 8, 450°F (230°C).

Begin by cutting the carrots into 1½ inch (4 cm) chunks, but no smaller. Next, dry-roast the coriander seeds and peppercorns in a small frying pan or saucepan over a medium heat, stirring and tossing them around for 1-2 minutes, or until they begin to look toasted and start to jump in the pan. Now empty them into a pestle and mortar and crush them coarsely, then put the carrot chunks and crushed spices in a bowl.

Next, put the garlic cloves and salt in the mortar, crush to a purée, then whisk in the oil. Now toss this mixture around with the carrots and spices, then spread it out on the baking tray. Pop it into the oven on a high shelf and roast until the carrots are tender when tested with a skewer – 30-40 minutes.
Note: the carrots can be prepared well in advance and kept in a polythene bag in the fridge.

Marinated Courgettes with a Herb Vinaigrette

If you grow courgettes then this recipe is superb for serving the ones that – if you don't keep a sharp eye on them – become baby marrows overnight. If you don't, then this is still a superb way to serve courgettes as a salad with cold cuts.

To prepare the courgettes, trim off the stalky ends and, if they are small, simply slice them in half lengthways; if they are larger, cut them in 4 lengthways. Then place them in the steamer, pour in some boiling water, sprinkle the courgettes with a little salt and let them cook, covered, for 10-14 minutes, depending on their size – they need to be firm but tender.

Meanwhile, prepare the dressing by pounding the garlic with the salt in a pestle and mortar until it becomes a creamy paste. Now work in the mustard, then the vinegar and a generous amount of black pepper. Next add the oil and give everything a good whisk, then add the herbs. When the courgettes are ready, remove them to a shallow serving dish, then pour the dressing over them. Allow them to get cold, then cover with clingfilm and leave in a cool place or the fridge for several hours, turning them over in the marinade once or twice. These still taste good after 3 days, so you can make them in advance if you prefer.

Serves 4
1 lb (450 g) courgettes
Maldon sea salt

For the herb vinaigrette:
1 teaspoon snipped fresh chives
1 teaspoon finely chopped fresh tarragon
1 teaspoon finely chopped fresh parsley
1 teaspoon fresh rosemary leaves, bruised and finely chopped
1 clove garlic, peeled
1 teaspoon Maldon sea salt
1 rounded teaspoon wholegrain mustard
2 tablespoons white wine vinegar
4 tablespoons olive oil
freshly milled black pepper

You will also need a steamer.

Below, left to right: Quick-Braised Celery, Oven-Roasted Carrots with Garlic and Coriander, Marinated Courgettes with a Herb Vinaigrette

Cabbage with Bacon, Apples and Cider

The flavours of this recipe combine beautifully, and I think it's an exceptionally good accompaniment to sausages and mash.

Serves 4-6
1 lb (450 g) green cabbage, cut into 4 sections and core and stalk removed
4½ oz (125 g) cubetti (cubed) pancetta or chopped bacon
1 Granny Smith apple, cored and chopped small
2 tablespoons strong dry cider
2 tablespoons cider vinegar
1 dessertspoon olive oil
1 small onion, peeled and finely chopped
2 cloves garlic, peeled and crushed
1 bay leaf
1 sprig fresh thyme
salt and freshly milled black pepper

You will also need a frying pan with a diameter of 10 inches (25.5 cm).

First of all shred the cabbage into ¼ inch (5 mm) pieces, then place the frying pan over direct heat and dry-fry the pancetta or bacon until crispy and golden – about 5 minutes – and remove it to a plate. Now add the oil to the pan and, when it's hot, fry the onions over a medium heat for 5 minutes: they also need to be turning golden brown at the edges. Now turn the heat up to its highest setting and add the cabbage, stirring continuously for about 3 minutes, keeping it on the move and tossing it around. Return the pancetta or bacon to the pan and add the apple, garlic, bay leaf and thyme, seasoning well with salt and black pepper. Toss the mixture around for a few seconds, then add the cider and cider vinegar and continue to cook, with the heat still high, for 1-2 minutes. Finally, remove the bay leaf and thyme, taste and season and serve as soon as possible.

Slow-Cooked Root Vegetable Soup

Something happens to vegetables when they're cooked very slowly for a long time: their flavour becomes mellow but at the same time more intense, and your kitchen is filled with aromas of goodness. This soup is also completely fat-free.

There's not much to do here once everything is peeled and chopped. All you do is place everything in the casserole and bring it up to a gentle simmer, then put the lid on, place it in the lowest part of the oven and leave it there for 3 hours, by which time the vegetables will be meltingly tender. Next remove the bay leaves and process or liquidise the soup in several batches to a purée, then gently re-heat, and serve the soup in bowls with a teaspoon of Greek yoghurt swirled into each and garnished with the fresh chives.

Serves 6
Vegetable quantities are prepared weights
8 oz (225 g) peeled carrots, cut into 2 inch (5 cm) lengths
8 oz (225 g) peeled celeriac, cut into 2 inch (5 cm) pieces
8 oz (225 g) trimmed and washed leeks, halved and cut into 2 inch (5 cm) lengths
8 oz (225 g) peeled swede, cut into 2 inch (5 cm) pieces
1 small onion, peeled and roughly chopped
2½ pints (1.5 litres) made up Marigold Swiss Bouillon stock
3 bay leaves
salt and freshly milled black pepper

To serve:
6 teaspoons fat-free Greek yoghurt
a few fresh chives, snipped

You will also need a lidded flameproof casserole with a capacity of 6 pints (3.5 litres).

Pre-heat the oven to gas mark 1, 275°F (140°C).

Bubble and Squeak Rösti

Bubble and squeak is a classic leftover recipe for greens, but making it rösti-style and adding some mature Cheddar adds a new dimension. These little individual rösti are brilliant served with sausages or leftover cold turkey and ham and a selection of pickles.

Serves 4 (makes 8 rösti)
1 lb (450 g) Desirée or Romano potatoes (this should be 3 evenly sized potatoes weighing about 5 oz/150 g each)
3 oz (75 g) spring greens or green cabbage (trimmed weight)
2 oz (50 g) mature Cheddar, coarsely grated
1 tablespoon plain flour
1 oz (25 g) butter
1 dessertspoon olive oil
salt and freshly milled black pepper

You will also need a baking tray measuring 10 x 14 inches (25.5 x 35 cm).

First scrub the potatoes, then place them in a medium saucepan with a little salt. Pour boiling water over to just cover them, then simmer gently with a lid on for 8 minutes. Drain the potatoes, then, while they are cooling, remove any stalks from the spring greens or cabbage and finely shred the leaves into ¼ inch (5 mm) slices. This is easy if you form them into a roll and then slice them. Drop the spring greens or cabbage into boiling water for 2 minutes only, then drain and dry well.

When the potatoes have cooled, peel them, then, using the coarse side of a grater, grate them into a bowl. Season with salt and freshly milled black pepper, then add the grated cheese and greens or cabbage and, using 2 forks, lightly toss together.

To assemble the rösti, shape the mixture into rounds 3 inches (7.5 cm) wide and ½ inch (1 cm) thick. Press them firmly together to form little cakes and dust lightly with the flour. If you want to make them ahead, place them on a plate and cover with clingfilm – they will happily sit in the fridge for up to 6 hours.

To cook the rösti, pre-heat the oven to gas mark 7, 425°F (220°C), placing the baking tray on the top shelf of the oven. Melt the butter and add the oil, then brush the rösti on both sides with the mixture. When the oven is up to heat, place the rösti on the baking tray and return it to the top shelf of the oven for 15 minutes, then turn the rösti over and cook them for a further 10 minutes. Once cooked, it's alright to keep them warm for up to 30 minutes.

Pumpkin Soup with Toasted Sweetcorn

This is a very fine combination: the soft, velvety texture of the pumpkin makes the soup deliciously creamy and the toasted sweetcorn provides contrasting flavour and some crunch.

Begin by melting the butter in the saucepan, then add the onion and soften it for about 8 minutes. After that add the chopped pumpkin (or butternut squash), along with half the sweetcorn, then give everything a good stir and season with salt and pepper. Put the lid on and, keeping the heat low, allow the vegetables to sweat gently and release their juices – this should take about 10 minutes. Next, pour in the milk and stock and simmer gently for about 20 minutes. Put the lid on for this but leave a little gap (so it's not quite on) because, with the presence of the milk, it could boil over. Keep a close eye on it anyway.

While that's happening, pre-heat the grill to its highest setting for 10 minutes. Mix the rest of the sweetcorn with the melted butter, spread it out on a baking tray, season with salt and pepper and pop it under the hot grill about 3 inches (7.5 cm) from the heat – it will take about 8 minutes to become nicely toasted and golden, but remember to move the sweetcorn around on the baking tray halfway through.

When the soup is ready, pour it into a food processor or blender and blend it to a purée, leaving a little bit of texture – it doesn't need to be absolutely smooth. You will probably need to do this in 2 batches. Serve the soup in warm bowls with the toasted sweetcorn sprinkled over.

Serves 6

1 lb 8 oz (700 g) pumpkin or butternut squash, peeled, deseeded and chopped into 1 inch (2.5 cm) dice
1 lb 4 oz (570 g) sweetcorn (off the cob weight, from 5-6 cobs)
1 oz (25 g) butter
1 medium onion, peeled and finely chopped
10 fl oz (275 ml) whole milk
1¼ pints (725 ml) made up Marigold Swiss Bouillon stock
1 teaspoon melted butter, for the sweetcorn
salt and freshly milled black pepper

You will also need a lidded saucepan with a capacity of 3 pints (1.75 litres).

6

Salads and dressings for beginners

The title of this chapter is meant, hopefully, to reassure those who find themselves rather confused about precisely what a well-dressed salad should actually be, something that has somehow eclipsed the simple joy of dressing and eating a salad.

Thirty years ago olive oil was, in this country, medicinal and came from chemists, and because we are a beer-brewing country rather than a winemaking one, our vinegar was distilled from malt. Boots' olive oil and malt vinegar were, as you can imagine, not the desired components of a good salad dressing, and in the lean post-war years salads in ordinary households were served with a dressing of bottled salad cream, a modern commercial version of an 18th-century recipe for English salad sauce made with cream and egg yolks.

We have now, thankfully, moved on from there, but, in my opinion, we have perhaps gone too far. Yes, it's wonderful to have a choice of olive oils and a selection of wine vinegars, but supermarkets now have wall-to-wall oils and sometimes half as many vinegars. It seems that every country in the world can produce oils and vinegars, and not just from the humble olive or the grape but from everything under the sun – witness pumpkin seed oil, grapefruit oil, seaweed vinegar, rose petal vinegar! Even tourist and gift shops sell designer oils and vinegars, which are often made from some unlikely ingredients. They are utterly superfluous to most people's everyday needs and end up lurking unused and abandoned in the back of a cupboard. Even worse, I get letters asking me what to do with them!

Because I feel that, were I a beginner today, I wouldn't actually know where to start learning, I thought it might be helpful to concentrate on basic everyday salads and dressings. Oils do not have a very long shelf life, so if we want to enjoy them at their best, having half a dozen varieties on the go is not helpful unless you are doing an awful lot of cooking on a daily basis. So let's start with what, in my opinion, is the best type of olive oil for a salad dressing, and tackle the most pertinent question first.

What is extra virgin olive oil?

Before we can understand 'extra virgin' we first have to clarify the word 'virgin'. What it describes, quite simply, is oil pressed from the fruit of the olive tree under conditions that cause no deterioration of the finished oil – the olives are not damaged, bruised or subjected to adverse temperatures or too much air, and they must not have undergone any additional treatment such as heat or blending (other than with other virgin olive oil). The supreme quality is measured by acidity or, more precisely, the lack of it – too much acidity gives a harsher flavour, which can, with skill, be refined out. What is simply termed olive oil is often a blend of lesser-quality refined oils with some virgin added to give the right balance of flavour.

Extra virgin olive oil could, in fact, have another name – perfect virgin olive oil, because this is precisely what it is: virgin olive oil with no flaws whatsoever. By law the acidity of extra virgin olive oil is never more than 1 per cent, and what does this mean? Flavour. First there is an aromatic fragrance, then a sweetness not marred by acidity, and then an abundant taste of fruit, verdant and luscious, not tasting like olives exactly but like some other mysterious, unique fruit. Like very fine wine, extra virgin olive oil is both rich and flavoursome.

Which country produces the best olive oil?

Difficult to answer, this. The olives of each country have their own character and flavour, which will even vary from region to region: a Tuscan olive oil, for instance, is different to a Ligurian olive oil. If I were being a purist I would suggest that Provençal dishes should be made with oils made in Provence, and Italian, Greek or Spanish dishes made with the oil produced in that country. But unless you do masses of cooking it's best to find an olive oil you're happy with, and my recommendation is to have an extra virgin oil for special occasions, along with an everyday blended oil.

What about other oils?

What you need to be careful of is having endless bottles of oils that you hardly use, because, as I've said, the shelf life of any oil is never very long. However, I would include the following in my store cupboard – along with olive oil – as a good selection for both cooking and making dressings.

Groundnut oil

An excellent all-rounder with the advantage of having no marked flavour yet at the same time being quite luscious. It is perfect for making mayonnaise, with just a little olive oil added for flavour, and it's an extremely useful oil for cooking – oriental dishes in particular, because with these the flavour of olive oil is alien and too strong. Warning: because groundnut oil is made from peanuts, people who suffer from any nut allergy should avoid it (and warn anyone cooking for them as well).

Grapeseed oil

This is an alternative mildly flavoured oil. It's more expensive than groundnut oil, but if you are at all worried about the nut-allergy problem, grapeseed oil will do the same work both in dressings and in cooking.

Sesame oil

An excellent oil, and rich in nutty sesame flavour. It's great in oriental dishes and dressings, but needs to be used very sparingly, as the flavour can be overwhelming.

Walnut oil

This is a great addition to the repertoire of oils. It has all the flavour of crushed walnuts and is therefore particularly good in salads that contain walnuts. However, it does become rancid quite quickly, so monitor its shelf life once it's opened.

Flavoured oils

These are definitely not for me. Apart from the fact that they take up valuable storage space, it seems logical that if you want to incorporate other flavours in your oils, they are best added fresh. So add your own garlic, chilli, lemon or herbs and so on as and when you want to.

How to store oils

This has to be in the coolest-possible place, though not in the fridge, as oil solidifies when it gets too cold. Light is not good for oils, either, so a cool, dark corner would be the best place to store them. Most oils have date stamps, so watch these, and although it is more expensive to buy in smaller quantities, it is still cheaper than throwing out stale oil that never got used.

Vinegars for salads

Personally I would want to have about half a dozen vinegars available. They keep better and for longer than oils, so it's good to have a varied selection suitable for different kinds of salads, confits and sometimes cooked dishes. You will find dozens of designer varieties available but, as always, I say keep it simple and buy the best quality you can afford – some cheaper vinegars are too acidic and lacking in flavour.

Wine vinegar

Originally the French word *vinaigre*, from which we get our word vinegar, meant sour wine, but now it embraces all similar liquids where alcohol is turned into acetic acid. As you might expect, wine vinegar comes either red or white, and the best quality is that made by the Orléans method, which, because of its long, slow fermentation in oak casks, has depth of flavour without the overpowering acidity.

Balsamic vinegar

After struggling in the past to find good-quality wine vinegar, when *aceto balsamico* (as it's called in Italy) appeared, it was like discovering heaven. It is not a wine vinegar but a grape vinegar, made from fresh-pressed grape juice, aged in barrels of oak, ash, cherry wood, mulberry and juniper – all contributing to its unique flavour. Each year new grape juice is added and skilfully blended over a period of 8 to 12 years to produce the dark, sweet-sour amber liquid that makes one of the best salad dressings of all.

Sherry vinegar

A very special vinegar made, if I may say, from a very special drink. I love Spanish sherry, both to drink and to cook with, and the vinegar from the sherry grape must has its own delightfully rich, sweet, nutty flavour. Though quite different from *balsamico*, it is equally good sprinkled over salads and cooked vegetables just by itself.

Cider vinegar

As you'd expect, a vinegar distilled from cider, milder and less acidic than wine vinegar. It has a lovely fragrant apple flavour and is good for salad dressings, particularly if the salad contains fruit.

Rice vinegar

It's marvellous how vinegar turns up around the world distilled from whatever grows locally, so it's not surprising that in the Far East vinegar is made from rice. The Japanese have the best quality, and I always have some handy for making oriental salads and dipping sauces.

There are times when vinegar can be dispensed with and the acidic content of a salad dressing can be provided by lemon or lime juice. In fact I would say that if you want to cut the fat in your diet for any reason, lemon and lime juice alone squeezed over salad ingredients give a lovely zest and piquancy of their own. Lime is especially good for oriental dressings, while the combination of lemons and olive oil gives the classic flavours of the Mediterranean to a bowl of very simple salad leaves.

Other ingredients

Mustard, both plain and wholegrain, have an emulsifying effect that thickens the dressing. Garlic, if you like it, adds flavour, and Maldon sea salt and freshly milled black pepper are two absolute essentials.

What makes the perfect dressing?

For once there are no rules. Food snobs sometimes like to make them, but the truth is it's about personal taste: some like more vinegar, some less, some like to add sugar, others (me) never do. So when you begin to make salad dressings, it's you who should taste and you who should decide just how much of this or that you want.

Equipment

Do invest in a pestle and mortar, a simple time-honoured item that will serve you for a lifetime. With a pestle and mortar you can pound and crush the ingredients needed for making most salad dressings. Blenders will do the job and are occasionally preferable for large quantities, but you don't always want to be bothered with them for small amounts. Once you have blended your dressing, a small loop whisk, *right*, will combine it quickly and efficiently; alternatively you can keep a small screw-top jar handy and use it to shake and amalgamate the ingredients together.

Salad ingredients

Herein lies the subject for a book by itself, because most ingredients can be made into salads – meat, fish, vegetables, rice and so on. Here I will confine myself to specific salad vegetables, starting with a very pertinent point.

Lettuce or leaves?

For me it would be lettuce all the way; a salad needs bite, crunchiness and some substance. Yes, there are leaves that make good salads, but there are now too many kinds of designer leaves grown, bought and used merely for their looks. That's OK up to a point – we can all appreciate a pretty garnish of colourful leaves – but delicate leaves that get soggy when they're washed, before being packed in plastic bags, and just disintegrate once they meet with a dressing are, in my opinion, to be avoided (except for garnishing).

What kind of lettuce?

Again, it's what you personally like, but my own recommendations would be as follows.

Round lettuce

Sometimes called Butterhead, it may not look very promising, but usually has a cluster of crisp, sweet leaves nestling in the centre that partner most dressings very well.

Cos lettuce

If fresh, this is reliably crisp and crunchy, with a good flavour, and can take strong, thick, creamy dressings such as Caesar.

Crispheart lettuce

As good as its name, this is a lettuce with good flavour and lots of crunch.

Escarole lettuce and Quattro Stagioni (Four Seasons)

A colourful pair, the former has pale-green leaves and the latter pinkish-red edges. They are not crisp, but their flavour is good as long as you give them lighter dressings.

Frisée

This comes with very crunchy, curly leaves, but because it is related to the chicory family, it has a slightly bitter taste, which is fine if matched with highly flavoured dressings.

Rocket

I make no secret of the fact that this is one of my favourite salad leaves. Why? It's traditionally English and has been used in salads since Elizabethan times. It has a lovely concentrated buttery flavour and goes with any dressing. Not, I think, good as a salad leaf just on its own, because it's not crisp, and a lot of it seems somehow to be too concentrated and 'in your face'. However, added fifty-fifty to crisp lettuce, it makes, I think, one of the nicest green salads of all.

Lamb's lettuce

This leaf comes in delicate little sprigs with clusters of leaves, and is good both for garnishing and mixing with other lettuce types. Because it does not keep well, it needs to be used fairly quickly.

Watercress

Popular with everyone, watercress is a bit like rocket, with its own distinctive, fresh, peppery flavour. I think it's too strong to be used on its own, but it's wonderful combined with lettuce, used as a garnish and for giving its own unmatched flavour to soups and sauces.

Not recommended

Given that everything is largely a matter of personal taste, I would nevertheless explain why I would not recommend certain lettuces and leaves. Iceberg is crunchy but that's all: it tastes of absolutely nothing. As for Little Gem, I have a feeling this was originally grown for its long shelf life. For housebound people, a Little Gem is better than no lettuce at all, but for those who have a choice I would give it a miss; it's rather tough and stalky, with an earthy flavour. Lollo Rosso, Lollo Biondo, Oak Leaf and others are good to look at but pretty dull to eat.

How to prepare salad leaves

All lettuces and salad leaves should be eaten as fresh as possible, but first of all I've found the best way to store lettuces is to remove the root, but otherwise leave them whole and enclose them in a polythene bag in the lowest part of the fridge. I believe washing should be avoided if possible, as once the leaves are wet it's difficult to dry them again and you simply can't get dressing on to wet salad leaves. What I prefer to do is take a damp piece of kitchen paper and wipe each leaf – this way the lettuce leaves remain dry and can more easily be coated with dressing. Now, I realise many people will not agree with me here and will want to wash the leaves: in that case plunge the separated leaves briefly into cold water and place them in a salad basket, then either hang them up after a good shaking or else swing the basket round and round out-of-doors. Finish off by drying the leaves carefully with kitchen paper.

Never use a knife when you prepare lettuce, because cutting tends to brown the edges of the leaves. Breaking up the leaves too soon can cause them to go limp quickly, so always leave them whole, if possible, until you're ready to serve the salad (and even then use your hands to tear them rather than a knife).

Other salad ingredients

Avocados

A ripe, buttery-textured avocado, served with a really good vinaigrette, is simplicity itself. The way to tell if an avocado is ripe is to hold it in the palm of your hand and give it some gentle pressure; if ripe, you'll feel it 'give' slightly.

Salad or spring onions

Indispensable in the kitchen, and especially in salads. You won't find the best kind in the supermarket, but if you are near a farm shop, tiny, thin, very young spring onions are delicious served whole with just the root trimmed.

Cucumber

A home-grown cucumber in the late-English summer is a luxury for its fragrant, cool, pronounced cucumber flavour – if you can get hold of one. In any case, English home-grown cucumbers do have the best flavour and it's difficult to find a well-flavoured imported cucumber in the winter. For the best results, and if you have time, salting, as you would an aubergine, does draw out some of the excess water content and helps concentrate the flavour.

What about the seeds? No problem. These are part and parcel of the cucumber, so I never bother to remove them. Then there's the question of whether to peel or not to peel. I say not, because I like the colour, texture and flavour of the peel, but if the cucumber has a very tough skin, use a potato peeler so only the outer skin is pared off. It's also possible to just pare off strips of skin, a kind of halfway house. The exception is small, ridged cucumbers, which sometimes have quite knobbly skins and are usually best peeled.

Chicory heads

Tight little buds of crunchy leaves, sometimes with pale-green edges, sometimes pink-edged. They have a slightly bitter taste that calls for a flavourful dressing.

Fennel

This is brilliant cooked, but sliced very thinly it's also lovely raw in a salad.

Beetroot

This can be added to salads cooked (see page 119), or else raw and thinly shredded into julienne strips.

How to make a vinaigrette dressing

It has to be said that this is always going to be a matter of personal taste according to how much acidity you like and what your preferences are as to flavourings and so on. I seem to suffer from some kind of mental handicap with dressings, which roughly means that other people's salad dressings always seem to taste better than my own – my husband's particularly. Here I have set out my favourite version of vinaigrette, but it's adaptable: you can use red or white wine vinegar, a different mustard or no mustard; if you like it sharper, use a higher ratio of vinegar, and if you want it less sharp use a higher ratio of oil. The following combination is my own personal favourite.

Begin by placing the salt in the mortar and crush it quite coarsely, then add the garlic and, as you begin to crush it and it comes into contact with the salt, it will quickly break down into a purée. Next add the mustard powder and really work it in, giving it about 20 seconds of circular movements to get it thoroughly blended. After that, add some freshly milled black pepper.

Now add the vinegars and work these in in the same way, then add the oil, switch to a small whisk (see the photograph on page 149) and give everything a really good, thorough whisking. Whisk again before dressing the salad.

Note: vinaigrette dressing is best made and used as fresh as possible, because once the oil is exposed to the air it loses some of its fragrance. If you want to prepare things ahead, proceed up to the vinegar stage and leave adding the oil till the last minute.

Serves 4-6; halve the ingredients for 2-3
1 rounded teaspoon Maldon sea salt
1 clove garlic, peeled
1 rounded teaspoon mustard powder
1 dessertspoon balsamic vinegar
1 dessertspoon sherry vinegar
5 tablespoons extra virgin olive oil
freshly milled black pepper

You will also need a pestle and mortar.

American Chef's Salad

A chef's salad is so named because it is supposed to be an innovative way of using whatever you happen to have handy to create a main-course salad. Ham, salami, chicken, turkey or any cold meat could be used for this one; similarly any kind of cheese or salad vegetable. This happens to be one of my favourite combinations, but once you get the gist of it I'm sure you'll have lots of other ideas.

Serves 6-8 as a main course
6 oz (175 g) lean streaky bacon
8 oz (225 g) French garlic sausage
in one piece
4 oz (110 g) small open-cup
mushrooms
3 oz (75 g) Roquefort or other cheese
2 ripe avocados
1 round lettuce, outer leaves removed
1 Cos lettuce, outer leaves removed
2 oz (50 g) watercress, stalks removed
2 oz (50 g) rocket, stalks removed
4 spring onions, finely chopped

For the dressing:
5 fl oz (150 ml) soured cream
1 small clove garlic, peeled and
crushed
2 tablespoons good-quality mayonnaise
1 heaped teaspoon wholegrain mustard
2 tablespoons extra virgin olive oil
1 tablespoon white wine vinegar
1 tablespoon lemon juice
salt and freshly milled black pepper

Before you start, pre-heat the grill to its highest setting and let it heat up for at least 10 minutes. Meanwhile, combine all the dressing ingredients in a jug or bowl and whisk them together well, tasting to check the seasoning.

Now place the bacon on some foil on the grill pan, and grill until it's very crispy – about 7 minutes – then remove it to drain on some kitchen paper and crumble it into small pieces. Next slice the garlic sausage, first into ¼ inch (5 mm) slices, then cut the slices into ¼ inch (5 mm) strips. After that, wipe the mushrooms and slice them fairly thinly (but not paper-thin). Next crumble the cheese and peel and slice the avocados.

To serve the salad, tear up the lettuce leaves and place them in a large bowl with the watercress and rocket. Scatter in the bacon, sausage, mushrooms, cheese and avocado and mix well. Just before serving, add half the dressing and mix together. Add the remaining dressing and toss again so that everything gets a good coating. Finally, sprinkle over the spring onions and serve immediately. This needs lots of good rustic bread on the table.

Broad-Bean Salad with Pancetta and Sherry Vinegar

The fresh broad bean season seems to be so short, I always feel the need to feast as much as possible when I can, hence this salad. It's good as a first course or to serve alongside other salads in a cold buffet. Remember, when buying broad beans in the shell you'll need 1 lb (450 g) in weight to get 4 oz (110 g) once shelled.

Begin this by pre-heating the grill to its highest setting for 10 minutes or so, then place the pancetta (or bacon) on a piece of foil and grill it 3 inches (7.5 cm) from the heat for about 4 minutes; it's important to get it really crisp. Then, as soon as it's cool enough to handle, crumble it into tiny pieces. Now place the shelled beans in a medium saucepan, add a level teaspoon of salt and pour in enough boiling water to barely cover them. When they come back to the boil, put a lid on, turn the heat down and simmer them gently for about 5 minutes. It's very important not to overcook them, so a timer would be useful here.

While they're cooking, make the dressing by first crushing the garlic and salt with a pestle and mortar until it becomes a creamy paste, then work in the mustard powder and follow this with the vinegar and a generous amount of coarsely milled black pepper. Next add the oil and give everything a good whisk. When the beans are cooked, drain them in a colander, then place them in a serving bowl, toss them in the dressing and give it all a good stir. Now sprinkle in the pancetta, herbs and chopped shallots, taste to check the seasoning, give everything one more good mix, then cover the bowl with a cloth and leave aside for a couple of hours so the beans can absorb all the flavours.

Serves 4 generously
4 lb (1.8 kg) young broad beans, shelled
4 oz (110 g) sliced smoked pancetta or smoked streaky bacon
1 tablespoon chopped mixed fresh herbs (parsley, chives, basil and thyme, for example)
2 shallots, peeled and finely chopped
salt and freshly milled black pepper

For the dressing:
2 tablespoons sherry vinegar
1 large clove garlic, peeled
2 teaspoons Maldon sea salt
2 teaspoons mustard powder
5 tablespoons extra virgin olive oil
freshly milled black pepper

White Bean and Tuna Fish Salad with Lemon Pepper Dressing

This is my version of an old Italian favourite, and I think the addition of a sharp lemon dressing and some buttery rocket leaves gives a lovely edge.

*Serves 4 as a main course or
6 as a starter*
9 oz (250 g) cannellini beans
2 x 200 g tins tuna fish in oil
1 oz (25 g) rocket, stalks removed
2 oz (50 g) red onion, peeled and
sliced into thin rounds
salt and freshly milled black pepper

For the dressing:
grated zest 1 lemon
3 tablespoons lemon juice
1 rounded teaspoon black peppercorns
2 cloves garlic, peeled
1 tablespoon Maldon sea salt
1 heaped teaspoon mustard powder
3 tablespoons extra virgin olive oil
3 tablespoons tuna oil, reserved from
the tins of tuna

Begin this the night before you are going to make the salad by placing the beans in a bowl and covering them with cold water to soak. Next day, drain the beans, then put them in a large saucepan, cover with fresh water and bring them up to simmering point. Boil for 10 minutes, then cover and simmer gently for 1¼-1½ hours, or until tender.

Meanwhile, empty the tuna fish into a sieve fitted over a bowl and allow it to drain. Then, to make the dressing, first crush the garlic and salt using a pestle and mortar till the garlic is pulverised, then work the mustard powder into this. Now push the mixture to one side, add the peppercorns and crush these fairly coarsely. Next add the grated lemon zest, along with the lemon juice, olive oil and tuna oil (the rest of the tuna oil can be discarded). Whisk everything together very thoroughly, then, when the beans are cooked, drain them, rinse out the saucepan and return the beans to it. Now pour the dressing over while the beans are still warm, give everything a good stir and season generously.

To serve the salad, arrange three-quarters of the rocket leaves over the base of a serving dish, spoon the beans on top and add the tuna fish in chunks. Then add the rest of the rocket leaves, pushing some of the leaves and chunks of tuna right in amongst the beans. Finally, arrange the onion slices on top and serve straight away, allowing people to help themselves. Warm, crusty ciabatta bread would be an excellent accompaniment.
Note: if you forget to soak the beans overnight, you can rinse the beans with cold water and place them in a saucepan, cover with plenty of water, bring up the boil for 10 minutes, then turn off the heat and leave them to soak for 2 hours. Next, bring them up to the boil and boil gently for 1½-2 hours, or until the beans are tender.

Char-Grilled Aubergine and Roasted-Tomato Salad with Feta Cheese

I am indebted to Chris Payne, who very generously gave me this splendid recipe. If you don't possess a ridged grill pan, you could grill the aubergine slices till nicely browned and tender. Either way, this is a truly delicious combination of textures and flavours.

Serves 4

2 medium aubergines

8 small, ripe plum tomatoes

7 oz (200 g) Feta cheese, cut into thin slices

8 tablespoons extra virgin olive oil

1 heaped tablespoon torn fresh basil leaves

2 tablespoons balsamic vinegar

4 oz (110 g) assorted salad leaves

7 fl oz (200 ml) half-fat crème fraîche

a little paprika

salt and freshly milled black pepper

You will also need a baking tray measuring 10 x 14 inches (25.5 x 35 cm), and a ridged grill pan.

Pre-heat the oven to gas mark 6, 400°F (200°C).

First of all skin the tomatoes by covering them with boiling water for 1 minute, then drain them and slip off their skins. Cut them in half and place them on the baking tray, cut-side up, then season well, drizzle 1 tablespoon of the olive oil over and place them on the top shelf of the oven to roast for 50-60 minutes. After this time, leave them aside to cool.

While they're cooling, cut the aubergines across into ½ inch (1 cm) slices, lay the slices on a board and lightly sprinkle them with salt on both sides. Leave them for 20 minutes to draw out some of the excess moisture, then blot them dry with kitchen paper. Next, brush them on both sides using 1 tablespoon of the olive oil and season with freshly milled black pepper. Brush the grill pan lightly with olive oil and place it over a high heat, then, when it is very hot, cook the aubergines in batches for about 2½ minutes on each side (this should take about 20 minutes in all).

Now pour the remaining 6 tablespoons of olive oil into a large bowl, add the basil and balsamic vinegar, then toss the cooked aubergines in this marinade and leave them in a cool place until you are ready to serve.

Divide the salad leaves between 4 plates and arrange the tomatoes and aubergines alternately all around. Then place equal quantities of the Feta slices in the middle of each salad and drizzle with the remaining marinade. Finally, put 1 tablespoon of crème fraîche on top of each salad and sprinkle a little paprika over.

Spiced Carnaroli Rice Salad

This is a lovely spicy salad with Moroccan overtones – perfect for a buffet lunch, party or serving with cold cuts and spicy chutneys.

Serves 4
10 fl oz (275 ml) carnaroli rice
¾ teaspoon cumin seeds
½ teaspoon coriander seeds
2 cardamom pods
1 dessertspoon groundnut or other flavourless oil, plus 1 teaspoon
1 oz (25 g) pine nuts
1½ oz (40 g) currants
1½ oz (40 g) ready-to-eat dried apricots, chopped into ¼ inch (5 mm) pieces
1 inch (2.5 cm) piece cinnamon stick
1 bay leaf
1 pint (570 ml) boiling water
1 large red onion
3 spring onions, trimmed and finely chopped
Maldon sea salt

For the dressing:
2 tablespoons groundnut or other flavourless oil
4 tablespoons lemon juice

You will also need a lidded frying pan with a diameter of 8 inches (20 cm).

First roast and crush the spices. To do this you need to place the cumin and coriander seeds and cardamom pods in the frying pan over a medium heat and stir and toss them around for 1-2 minutes, or until they begin to look toasted and start to jump in the pan. Now transfer them to a pestle and mortar and crush them to a powder.

After that, add the dessertspoon of oil to the frying pan set over a medium heat. When the oil is hot, sauté the nuts, currants and apricots until the nuts are golden brown. Next stir in the rice and roasted spices, cinnamon stick and bay leaf and turn the grains over in the pan till they're nicely coated and glistening with oil. Now pour in the boiling water, add some salt, stir once only, then put the lid on, turn the heat down to its lowest setting and let the rice cook for exactly 15 minutes. Don't remove the lid, and remember what was said in Book One – absolutely no stirring.

While the rice is cooking, pre-heat the grill to its highest setting. Peel and slice the red onion into ¼ inch (5 mm) rounds, then brush one side with half the teaspoon of oil, place them on a grilling rack directly under the grill and cook till the edges have blackened – 4-5 minutes – then turn them over. Brush the other side with the rest of the oil and grill them as before. After that, remove them and let them cool.

When the rice is cooked, take the pan off the heat, remove the lid and cover with a clean tea cloth for 5 minutes to absorb the steam. Now empty the rice into a warm serving dish and add about two-thirds of the spring onions. Whisk the oil and lemon juice together and pour this over the rice before fluffing it up with a fork, then garnish the salad with the grilled onions and remaining spring onions before serving.

Salade Niçoise

Nothing has changed much here over the long years I've been cooking and writing recipes – this is still one of the best combinations of salad ingredients ever invented. Slick restaurants often attempt to do trendy versions with salmon, char-grilled tuna and the like, but the original reigns supreme. In Provence lettuce was sometimes used, sometimes not, but I now like to abandon the lettuce in favour of a few rocket leaves.

To make the vinaigrette dressing, start off with a pestle and mortar. First of all crush the flakes of sea salt to a powder, then add the peeled clove of garlic and pound them together, which will immediately bring out the garlic's juices and turn it into a smooth paste. Next add the mustard powder, work that in, then add the vinegar and some freshly milled black pepper and mix thoroughly until the salt dissolves. Finally, add the olive oil. Now stir the herbs into the vinaigrette – it will look rather thick but will spread itself out beautifully once you toss it into the salad. Just before you dress the salad, pour everything into a screw-top jar and shake vigorously so it's thoroughly blended.

For the salad, begin by preparing the tomatoes. Place them in a bowl, pour boiling water over them, then, after 1 minute, drain and slip off their skins, protecting your hands with a cloth if you need to. Now cut each tomato in half and hold each half in the palm of your hand (cut-side up), then turn your hand over and squeeze gently until the seeds come out; it's best to do this over a plate or bowl to catch the seeds. Now cut each tomato into quarters. Then, in a large salad bowl, arrange the tomatoes, rocket leaves, cucumber, potatoes, beans and chopped shallots in layers, sprinkling a little of the dressing in as you go. Next arrange chunks of tuna and egg quarters on top, then arrange the anchovies in a criss-cross pattern, followed by a scattering of olives, the chopped parsley and a final sprinkling of dressing. Now you need to serve the salad fairly promptly, and needless to say it needs lots of warm, crusty baguette with Normandy butter to go with it.

Serves 4-6 as a light lunch
12 oz (350 g) red ripe tomatoes
4 oz (110 g) rocket, stalks removed
½ small young cucumber, cut into smallish chunks
1 lb (450 g) new potatoes, cooked and sliced
4 oz (110 g) French beans, cooked
4 shallots, peeled and finely chopped
2 x 200 g tins tuna fish in oil, well drained
2 large hard-boiled eggs, peeled and quartered
2 oz (50 g) anchovy fillets
2 oz (50 g) black olives
1 tablespoon chopped fresh parsley

For the vinaigrette dressing:
1 teaspoon Maldon sea salt
1 clove garlic, peeled
1 rounded teaspoon mustard powder
1 tablespoon wine or balsamic vinegar
6 tablespoons extra virgin olive oil
2 tablespoons finely chopped fresh herbs (chives, tarragon, parsley, basil, chervil or mint, for example); if using fresh oregano and thyme, use just ½ teaspoon each in the mix
freshly milled black pepper

Thai Grilled-Beef Salad With Grapes

This recipe was given to me by chef Norbert Kostner at the Mandarin Oriental Hotel in Bangkok when I visited the cookery school there. It's lovely served as a first course or included in a cold-buffet menu.

Serves 4

1 lb (450 g) rump steak in 1 piece,
1 inch (2.5 cm) thick
6 oz (175 g) red or black seedless
grapes, halved
2-3 medium red chillies, halved
and deseeded, or 3-4 Bird Eye
chillies, whole
2 cloves garlic, peeled
1 inch (2.5 cm) piece fresh root
ginger, peeled
6 sprigs fresh coriander, plus 3
tablespoons chopped fresh coriander
1 sprig fresh mint, plus 3 tablespoons
chopped fresh mint
3 tablespoons Thai fish sauce
grated zest 1 lime, plus 3 tablespoons
lime juice (juice of about 2 limes)
2 teaspoons palm sugar or light
brown soft sugar
3-4 stems lemon grass, very finely sliced
6 kaffir lime leaves, rolled into a
cigar shape and very finely shredded
(optional)
4 oz (110 g) rocket, stalks removed

To garnish:

1 teaspoon toasted sesame seeds
1 teaspoon chopped fresh chives

Pre-heat the grill to its highest setting.

First you need to grill the beef in advance, and for medium-rare give it 2-3 minutes on each side. Be careful not to overcook the steak: it needs to be quite pink, as the lime juice in the dressing 'cooks' the beef a bit further. If you'd prefer to use a ridged grill pan, pre-heat it for 10 minutes, then cook the steak for 1½-2 minutes on each side. Once the beef is grilled, allow it to rest for 10 minutes before slicing it into thin strips.

Meanwhile, to make the dressing, blend the chillies, garlic, ginger and sprigs of coriander and mint in a processor until finely chopped, then add the fish sauce, lime juice and sugar and whiz again to blend everything. Pour the dressing over the beef strips, then sprinkle the lemon grass, lime leaves (if using), lime zest and remaining herbs over. Add the rocket and grapes and toss everything together, then scatter the garnish over.

American Blue-Cheese Dressing

I love American salad dressings, and especially this one. The blue cheese can be Roquefort, if you want to splash out, or Gorgonzola, which crumbles particularly well. The only stipulation is that the cheese has to be gutsy; a subtle, faint-hearted one will get lost amongst all the other strong flavours.

Start off by crushing the garlic clove (or cloves), together with the salt, to a creamy mass in a pestle and mortar, then add the mustard and work that in. Next add the lemon juice, vinegar and, after that, the oil. Mix everything together thoroughly, then, in a bowl, combine the soured cream and mayonnaise and gradually whisk into the dressing ingredients. When all is thoroughly blended, add the chopped spring onions and the crumbled blue cheese and season with freshly milled pepper. The dressing is now ready to use, and I think a few crunchy croutons are a nice addition here.

To make these, toss ¼ inch (5 mm) cubes of bread – approximately 4 oz (110 g) in all – in a bowl with a dessertspoon of olive oil, spread them out on a baking sheet and bake in an oven pre-heated to gas mark 5, 375°F (190°C) for 10 minutes.

Serves 4-6

1½ oz (40 g) blue cheese, crumbled
1 large or 2 small cloves garlic, peeled
1 teaspoon Maldon sea salt
1 rounded teaspoon mustard powder
1 tablespoon lemon juice
1 tablespoon balsamic vinegar
2 tablespoons light olive oil
5 fl oz (150 ml) soured cream
2 tablespoons good-quality mayonnaise
2 spring onions, finely chopped
freshly milled black pepper

Marinated Kipper Fillets and Potato Salad with Coriander Seeds and Cracked Pepper

This is a salad that can mostly be made way, way ahead – up to a week, believe it or not. Then all you do is steam some potatoes to go with it, or alternatively you can serve the kipper fillets as they are, and instead of the potatoes have a pile of buttered wholemeal bread on the table.

Serves 4 as a main course or 8 as a starter
6 kipper fillets
2 teaspoons coriander seeds
2 teaspoons black peppercorns
6 shallots, peeled and cut into
thin rings
2 bay leaves, each snipped into
3-4 pieces
1 lemon, thinly sliced and cut in half
juice 2 lemons
1 dessertspoon dark brown soft sugar
2 rounded teaspoons wholegrain
mustard
5 fl oz (150 ml) extra virgin olive oil

To serve:
1 lb 8 oz (700 g) new potatoes,
scrubbed but skins left on
a few sprigs fresh flat-leaf parsley
Maldon sea salt

You will also need a shallow dish with
a capacity of 1½ pints (850 ml).

To get the best fragrance from the coriander seeds and peppercorns, pop them in a small frying pan and place them over a medium heat to dry-roast for 2-3 minutes. Move them around the pan until they start to jump, then put them in a pestle and mortar and crush them fairly coarsely.

Next, prepare the kipper fillets by turning them skin-side up on a flat surface, then, with a sharp knife, lift the skin away at the tail end. Now discard the knife and simply pull the skin from the flesh. If it clings at any point, just use the knife again and ease it away. Now snip each one in 4 lengthways, then cut them into 1½ inch (4 cm) pieces and lay the strips in the dish – this will probably have to be in 2 layers to fit them in – sprinkling the pepper and coriander mixture all over each layer. Next, scatter the shallot rings, bay leaves and lemon slices all over, tucking them in-between the kipper fillets here and there.

Now, in a bowl, whisk together the lemon juice, sugar, mustard and oil, and when they're very thoroughly mixed, pour the mixture over the kippers. Cover with clingfilm and put a plate on top with some kind of weight on it to keep the kippers submerged, then place in the fridge and let them marinate for a minimum of 24 hours or up to a week.

When you want to serve the salad it's important to remove the kippers from the fridge at least an hour beforehand. Now steam the potatoes, generously sprinkled with salt, for 20-30 minutes (depending on their size), and, when they're cooked, place a cloth over them to absorb the steam for 5 minutes. Chop them roughly, divide them between the plates, spoon some of the kipper marinade over, then arrange the kippers and everything else on top. Finish off with a few sprigs of flat-leaf parsley.

7

What's new in the dairy

'You may drive out Nature with a pitchfork, but she will ever hurry back to triumph in stealth over your foolish contempt.'

Never were these words, from Horace, *Epistles*, more true than in the dairy. In my long career of food writing, I have seen fashions, fads and so-called health scares arrive with the force of a destructive tidal wave one moment, then recede and disappear without trace the next, leaving everyone reeling in confusion.

My conclusion is that nutritionists a) often disagree with each other, and b) change their minds anyway as more and more facts come to light.

Meanwhile nature, thankfully, remains steadfast and does – if you wait long enough – still have the last word. Perhaps dairy foods more than any other have suffered being in the nutritional firing line in the past, but thankfully they have now been reinstated, as everyone's now discovered that the so-called-healthy hydrogenated-fat alternatives were not so healthy after all, and added to that, nature's very own dairy products have a unique and magical property called flavour that no man-made alternative has ever been able to match.

The fat problem

Yes, it's true that since we have evolved a more sedentary way of living we have had to cut the fat content in our diets. We now no longer serve our vegetables swimming with butter, perhaps we spread a little less of it on our bread and, of course, we now all love and applaud olive oil. But believe me, the home kitchen is not where our excess of eating fat has come from – we cannot blame dairy foods or the fat content of a good square meal. If we want to know why we consume more fat, we have to look, I'm afraid, at how our consumption of processed and snack foods and chocolate bars has grown. These have hidden amounts of fat that we don't take into account. What we eat per head in this country in chocolate bars alone adds up to 10 fl oz (275 ml) of double cream per person per week. Not that chocolate bars and other snacks foods are bad in themselves, but we desperately need to find the balance that so often gets overlooked in the heat of the health debate.

There is a crazy kind of imbalance, largely due to ignorance, that people seem hardly aware of – we eat fattening snacks and then have only skimmed milk because we are 'cutting down', or a Danish pastry with a high fat content accompanied by an artificial sweetener in our coffee. Someone who never eats snack foods but pours double cream on their apple pie at the weekend is, I'm quite positive, consuming far less fat. So, let's get dairy foods out of the firing line and enjoy them not in excess but in the perfect balance of a normal healthy diet.

A dairy explosion

When I first started writing about cooking, dairy foods were simply whole milk, single cream and double cream. Soured cream was not that widely available – perhaps just sometimes in specialised food shops; yoghurt was only available in health shops; and you only ever ate clotted cream if you went to the West Country. Now if you approach the dairy section in any large supermarket you can see a veritable explosion has taken place: miles and miles of yoghurts of every type and flavour, and an enormous range of different kinds of dairy products that, for me personally and for cooks everywhere, have been such a delight to discover and introduce into a whole range of cooking and recipes. But, with all this enormous choice available, it can be confusing, so here, before we move into the recipes, I want to give each dairy product an explanation.

Whole milk

The reason whole milk is so good for growing children is that it has many nutrients needed for good health. It has a natural fat content of 3.5 per cent, contains protein and carbohydrates, and is a good source of calcium, an important mineral for growing children's bones and teeth. In addition to all that, it's packed with vitamins and minerals. It's for these reasons that anyone living on a budget should choose milk first and foremost – in fact milk is the cheapest nourishment on offer.

In cooking, whole milk should be used to make white sauces and milk puddings, and substituting half the amount of stock needed with milk when making vegetable soups gives a lovely creamy texture and flavour.

Semi-skimmed milk

This has all the virtues of whole milk, except that some of the fat has been removed, leaving between 1.5 and 1.8 per cent. Because of this, it is actually better in tea and coffee, and, I think, works better in batters for pancakes or Yorkshire puddings. For anyone wishing to cut some of the fat content in their diet, semi-skimmed milk is an excellent choice, as it still retains some creaminess.

Skimmed milk

This is the one for people who are following a low-fat diet, as only a trace (0.3 per cent) remains. Even so, skimmed milk is still highly nutritious and is an excellent source of calcium, and contains everything whole and semi-skimmed milk has but without the fat. It can be used in all recipes requiring milk, but obviously won't give the same degree of creaminess.

Breakfast milk

This is also sometimes known as Channel Island milk, which comes from Guernsey and Jersey cows. It is the richest, creamiest milk of all and has the highest fat content at around 5 per cent. Really you could describe this as luxury milk and, as the name suggests, it's best of all for pouring on cereals or porridge. Needless to say, though, it is also wonderful for making creamy sauces and milk puddings.

Pasteurised milk

This is simply milk that has undergone heat treatment: a mere 5 seconds at 72°C purifies it but, at the same time, leaves all the important vitamins, minerals and proteins virtually unchanged.

Homogenised milk

When you leave pasteurised or other milk to stand, the small amount of cream present settles at the top. What homogenisation does, through a special treatment, is distribute the cream (milk-fat globules) evenly throughout the milk so this separation does not occur.

Buttermilk

This used to be a by-product of butter-making, hence its name, but now we have specially cultured buttermilk, which is made by adding a culture to skimmed milk. It has the same acidic flavour as the original and is perfect for making extra-light scones, soda bread and American-style pancakes.

Double cream

When cows' milk reaches the dairy, it contains a liquid substance called butterfat, and this, when it's skimmed off the surface of the milk, is cream, or what we know as double cream. It is extremely rich, with a minimum fat content of 48 per cent. Because of this it can stand being boiled in cooking without separating, and can be whipped to a fluffy, spreadable consistency.

When whipping double cream, though, you have to be extra careful, as overwhipping can give a grainy, slightly separated appearance (and if you really overwhip it, you'll end up with butter). One of the ways to prevent this happening is to add a couple of tablespoons of milk per pint (570 ml) of cream and, if you are using an electric hand whisk, make sure that you turn the speed right down when it looks thick enough. Double cream is also rich and luscious served just as it is, chilled as a thick pouring cream.

Whipping cream

This is a lighter version of double cream, with at least 35 per cent fat, and it whips beautifully without being quite so rich. Whipping cream is also good as a pouring cream, again, if you want something that's not too rich. If you're not Scottish (Scots don't approve), try pouring whipping cream over hot porridge, along with some unrefined brown sugar to melt and marble into little pools. I also think whipping cream is good for swirling on top of desserts, giving you that 'not-quite-so-high-in-calories' satisfaction.

Single cream

This is a much thinner cream, good for pouring and for cooking with when you need more creaminess than milk. Because it has only a minimum of 18 per cent fat, it's not suitable for boiling, as it will curdle.

Extra-thick double or single cream

These are as described for double or single cream, but have been treated to give them a consistency that is suitable for spooning on to pies and desserts without having to bother with whisking them first.

Soured cream

This is a lovely product, made with fresh single cream that is soured by adding a natural culture similar to that used in yoghurt. It is unique as a dairy product, and, in my opinion, is the very best topping for jacket potatoes (mixed with snipped fresh chives). If you are lucky enough to get some caviar, soured cream and chives make wonderful accompaniments.

Crème fraîche

For me, crème fraîche is the number one top of the pops cook's ingredient in the cream family. Because, by law, milk for cream has to be pasteurised, this has undoubtedly affected the flavour and made it blander than it was in former times. The French (more particularly the Normans, as Normandy is the world's richest dairy area), not content with this diminished flavour, created a special way of adding a culture to their cream and allowed it to mature and develop the faintly acidic flavour that was lost in pasteurisation.

The best crème fraîche comes from a strictly controlled area of Normandy and has all the rich, luscious flavour that the area is famous for. If you open a pot and closely look at it, you can see the wonderful creamy-yellow colour of the real thing, *right*. The reason it is specially loved by cooks is it has a longer shelf life than double cream, so you can take a spoonful here and there, replace the lid and use it again. Now we can also buy half-fat crème fraîche, which is less rich but still contains all the creamy flavour of the full-fat version. Finally, the other supreme virtue of crème fraîche is that when you use it in cooking, it never curdles and separates – you can bubble and boil it and never be afraid.

Clotted cream

Wait for it – this is the big one! Perhaps you'd rather not know, but it has at least 55 per cent butterfat. Clotted cream has a unique and special dairy colour, like pale buttercups, and is thick, rich and utterly irresistible. It is a speciality of the rich pastureland of the West Country, and is made by heating the cream to evaporate some of the liquids, so, in a sense, you could call it concentrated cream. It is heaven spread on scones with home-made preserves, and extra special on tart fruit pies. It's not for every day, but everyone should treat themselves to some just once in a while.

Yoghurt

The staple snack of the 1980s and 1990s has proved to be yoghurt, and producers never seem to tire of yet more variations and flavours. In the kitchen, yoghurt is a useful dairy ingredient and can be used in many ways. But what exactly is yoghurt? Very briefly, it's milk – whole, semi-skimmed, skimmed or dried – first pasteurised by heat treatment, then cooled to 41°C or 45°C and inoculated with a specially prepared culture. Then the whole thing is incubated at a warm temperature until the acidity reaches a certain level and setting takes place. The yoghurt is then cooled and chilled, ready to be eaten or stored. Apart from preserving the milk, the process adds acidity to the flavour, which is pleasant to eat as it is but is also incredibly good for adding character and flavour to all kinds of dishes. Wholemilk yoghurt contains 3.4 per cent fat; low-fat yoghurt contains 1-2 per cent fat; and diet, virtually fat-free yoghurt contains 0.2 per cent fat or less.

Organic wholemilk yoghurt

This is a yoghurt made with organic whole milk produced on dairy farms that meet Soil Association requirements, who control the animal feeds and pastureland. It is a completely natural product and contains only 3-4 per cent fat. This is suitable for vegetarians.

Genuine Greek yoghurt

This is another of my absolute favourite dairy ingredients. It's a special yoghurt made from cows' or sheep's milk, which is boiled in open vats so that its liquid content is reduced. The result is a much thicker consistency, giving a more concentrated yoghurt with a fat content of 8-10 per cent. I have a special fondness for it and I love serving it well chilled with lots of lovely Greek mountain honey poured over and pistachios sprinkled on top – in fact I think this is one of the simplest and nicest desserts. Greek yogurt is also a very useful ingredient in cooking, since it can replace some of the cream when you wish to lighten dairy desserts. Now you can buy low-fat Greek yoghurt, with 9 per cent fat, and an amazing 0 per cent, too. Don't buy Greek-*style* yoghurt, though, as it simply isn't the same. Look for the genuine Greek version, which is very widely available.

Cottage cheese

This is a very popular cheese because of its low fat content, and is a firm friend of the waistwatcher. It is made from skimmed milk that is first heat-treated, then a starter culture is added that forms the curds and whey. These are then washed several times in chilled water to remove the whey, and the curds are then drained and, finally, given a very light dressing of cultured cream. The result is a mild, faintly acidic cheese with just a hint of creaminess but not a great deal of character and flavour. Cottage cheese should always be eaten as fresh as possible, and is best served sprinkled with snipped fresh chives and seasoned with coarse salt and black pepper.

Cream cheese

This has a soft, smooth, buttery texture and varies enormously according to its fat content. Standard cream cheese has 45 per cent fat, but there are many variations, such as the light and extra-light versions, which can be used in recipes to replace full-fat cream and curd cheese if a lower fat content and fewer calories are required.

Curd cheese

This is similar to cream cheese but with a lower fat content and which, like cottage cheese, has had a lactic starter added. This gives it a light acidity and a light flavour, colour and texture. It is sometimes called medium-fat soft cheese. I like it best of all for cheesecakes because it gives them a lighter flavour and texture, as you will discover on page 232.

Quark

This is a soft white cheese made from skimmed milk, so it is very low in fat and ideal for slimmers. Use it instead of butter in scrambled eggs or mashed potatoes (Book One), or in place of full-fat curd cheese.

Ricotta

This, strictly speaking, is not really a cheese but a sort of by-product of cheesemaking. It is made from the drained whey and then cooked; in Italian, the word ricotta means re-cooked. It has a mild, fresh lactic flavour and contains only 14 per cent fat. It is actually delicious just by itself served with summer fruits, and I have eaten it freshly made in Apulia, Italy, sprinkled with coarse salt, pepper and olive oil, with really good bread.

Mascarpone

In my opinion, Mascarpone is the richest and most aristocratic of the new wave of dairy products. Thick, yellow and creamy, with a very high fat content (40 per cent) but a distinctive, rich dairy flavour, it forms the main part of the famous tiramisu. There again, it is lovely served alone with soft fruits or in a cheesecake. Because of its high fat content, it can be lightened by mixing it with an equal quantity of fromage frais and used as a filling for sponge cakes or as a topping for desserts. Add a small amount of sugar to sweeten the mixture and what you get is the flavour of Mascarpone given a lighter texture, and, if you are watching your waistline, far less guilt! I can also recommend Mascarpone spread on sweet biscuits (digestives or sweet oat biscuits) with fresh strawberry jam. Mascarpone is also brilliant for adding to sauces.

Fromage frais

Fromage frais is a fresh curd cheese introduced to this country from France and made from pasteurised cows' milk. Basically, it has very little fat, but cream is added to make 4 per cent (or 8 per cent) fromage frais. The 4 per cent is fine eaten on its own with honey or fruit purée, or used as a topping – especially for anyone on a low-fat diet. The 8 per cent is the best one for cooking. Either of these can be used in savoury sauces or as a topping for jacket potatoes with a few snipped chives. Alternatively, there is a diet virtually fat-free version (0.1 per cent), which is ideal in dips. For a cool, light, low-fat dessert, see the recipe on page 186.

Smoked Haddock with Crème Fraîche, Chive and Butter Sauce

This is a great recipe, a) because it's the most wonderful combination of flavours, and b) because it takes only 12 minutes from start to finish. Serve it with spinach cooked in its own juices with a little butter, then drain well and you'll have a sublime meal in no time at all.

Serves 2

12-14 oz (350-400 g) smoked haddock or smoked cod, skinned, or same weight golden haddock cutlets, skinned

2 rounded tablespoons crème fraîche

1 heaped tablespoon snipped fresh chives

½ oz (10 g) butter, diced

5 fl oz (150 ml) whole milk

freshly milled black pepper

You will also need a frying pan with a diameter of 10 inches (25.5 cm).

First place the fish in the frying pan and add a little freshly milled black pepper but no salt. Then pour in the milk (it won't cover the fish, but that doesn't matter), bring it up to simmering point and simmer gently, uncovered, for 8-12 minutes if you're using pieces of smoked haddock or cod, or 8 minutes for golden haddock cutlets. You will be able to see quite clearly when they are cooked, as the whole thing will become pale and opaque.

Now carefully remove the fish to a plate using a fish slice, increase the heat and add the crème fraîche to the pan. Continue to simmer, uncovered, for 2-3 minutes, until the sauce reduces and thickens slightly, then whisk in the butter and return the fish to the sauce briefly. Scatter in the chives, let it bubble for about 30 seconds and it's ready to serve.

Entrecôte Steak With Crème Fraîche And Cracked Pepper Sauce

This is a special supper dish for two people celebrating a birthday or anniversary or for those who just want a treat. It needs a good bottle of red wine, and jacket potatoes with a leafy salad would be good accompaniments. I usually make this with a tub of fresh beef stock from the supermarket.

First of all you need to reduce the stock to half its original volume, so put it in a small saucepan and boil rapidly for about 10 minutes, then taste and add some salt if it needs it. Now measure the Cognac into a jug.

When the steaks are at room temperature, season them well with salt, then place the frying pan over a high heat and, when it's really hot, add the butter and oil, which should start to foam immediately. Now drop the steaks into the hot pan and, keeping the heat high, give them 3 minutes on one side for medium or 2 minutes for rare. Use a timer and try to leave them alone – no prodding! Now turn them over and give them another 2 minutes on the other side for medium or 1 minute for rare. After that pour in the Cognac, let it splutter and reduce, and follow it first with the reduced stock and finally the crème fraîche and crushed pepper. Give it all a good stir, then let everything bubble, reduce and amalgamate for about 1 more minute, then serve the steaks on warmed plates with the sauce spooned over.

Serves 2

2 x 8 oz (225 g) entrecôte or sirloin steaks, at least 1 inch (2.5 cm) thick, removed from the fridge about 1 hour before you need them
2 rounded tablespoons crème fraîche
2 teaspoons black peppercorns, coarsely crushed
10 fl oz (275 ml) fresh beef stock
2 tablespoons Cognac
1 teaspoon butter
1 teaspoon oil
Maldon sea salt

You will also need a solid frying pan with a diameter of 10 inches (25.5 cm).

Gooseberry Yoghurt Fool

I now find that lusciously thick genuine Greek yoghurt makes the best fruit fool of all, as it allows the full flavour of the fruit to dominate. If you're serving this to someone who doesn't like yoghurt, don't worry – they won't know.

Serves 6
2 lb (900 g) gooseberries, topped and tailed with scissors
10 oz (275 g) Greek yoghurt
5 oz (150 g) golden caster sugar

You will also need a shallow 9 inch (23 cm) square or round ovenproof baking dish and 6 serving glasses, each with a capacity of 6 fl oz (175 ml).

Pre-heat the oven to gas mark 4, 350°F (180°C).

For the fullest flavour, I think gooseberries are best cooked in the oven. So first place them in the baking dish, sprinkle in the sugar and bake them on the centre shelf of the oven, uncovered, for 20-30 minutes, or until tender when tested with a skewer. After that tip them into a sieve set over a bowl to drain off the excess juice. Now reserve about a quarter of the cooked gooseberries for later, then place the rest in the bowl of a food processor, add 4 tablespoons of the reserved juice and whiz to a thick purée.

After that, leave the purée to get quite cold, then empty the yoghurt into a bowl, give it a stir, then fold in half the purée. Now spoon this mixture into the serving glasses, spoon the rest of the purée on top and, finally, add the reserved gooseberries. Cover the glasses with clingfilm and chill till you're ready to serve, then serve with some Pecan Shortbreads (see page 184) cut into smaller rounds.

Rhubarb Yoghurt Fool

For a delicious variation on the recipe above, trim and wash 1 lb 4 oz (570 g) of rhubarb and cut it into 1 inch (2.5 cm) chunks. Place in a baking dish, sprinkle with 3 oz (75 g) of golden caster sugar and add 1 teaspoon of chopped fresh root ginger, then cook in the oven, at the same temperature, for 30-40 minutes, until tender. Now drain the rhubarb as above, then purée all the rhubarb, along with 2 tablespoons of the reserved juice. When cool, fold half the purée into 7 fl oz (200 ml) of Greek yoghurt in a bowl, then divide it between 4 serving glasses and spoon the remaining purée on top. Finally, cut 2 pieces of stem ginger into matchstick lengths and use them to garnish the fool. Cover and refrigerate until needed. This amount will serve 4 people.

Toffee-Fudge Bananas with Toasted Nuts

The world record for making this recipe is not five minutes, but just three – it's quite simply the fastest dessert recipe I've ever come across. It's also amazingly good, and if it is conceivable that anybody on this earth does not love delectably thick Greek yoghurt, then you can make it just as well with whipped cream.

Right, on your marks, get ready… Pop the brazil nuts, spread out on some foil, under the grill about 4 inches (10 cm) from the heat and put a timer on for 3 minutes (if you don't have a timer keep an eye on them, because they will burn if you forget them), then keep them to one side for later.

Now peel and slice the bananas into thin rounds and place them in a large bowl, then add the yoghurt and mix well. Next divide the mixture between the serving glasses and simply sprinkle the sugar equally over the 4 portions of banana. Now cover with clingfilm and leave in the fridge for about 3 hours – after this time the sugar will have transformed itself into lovely pools of fudge sauce. Now all you need to do is chop the toasted nuts, sprinkle them on top, serve and wait for the compliments.

Serves 4
2 large, ripe bananas
2 oz (50 g) brazil nuts
1 lb 2 oz (500 g) Greek yoghurt
5 oz (150 g) molasses sugar

You will also need 4 individual serving glasses, each with a capacity of 7 fl oz (200 ml).

Pre-heat the grill to its highest setting.

Classic Crème Caramel

Over the years I've experimented with what should be the best crème caramel, using double cream, crème fraîche and half and half of these in the mixture. Now I prefer to use just single cream, which gives the whole thing a sort of wobbly lightness. So this, I now think, is the ultimate.

Serves 4-6
For the caramel:
6 oz (175 g) white caster sugar
2 tablespoons tap-hot water

For the custard:
5 fl oz (150 ml) whole milk
10 fl oz (275 ml) single cream
4 large eggs
1 teaspoon pure vanilla extract

To serve:
about 10 fl oz (275 ml) pouring cream

You will also need a soufflé dish with a capacity of 1½ pints (850 ml), 5 inches (13 cm) in diameter, 3 inches (7.5 cm) deep, and a deep roasting tin.

Pre-heat the oven to gas mark 2, 300°F (150°C).

Begin by making the caramel (see the pictures on page 247). To do this put the sugar in a saucepan and place it over a medium heat. Leave it like that, keeping an eye on it, until the sugar begins to melt and just turn liquid around the edges, which will take 4-6 minutes. Now give the pan a good shake and leave it again to melt until about a quarter of the sugar has melted. Now, using a wooden spoon, give it a gentle stir and continue to cook and stir until the sugar has transformed from crystals to liquid and is the colour of dark runny honey – the whole thing should take 10-15 minutes. Then take the pan off the heat and add the water, being a bit cautious here, as it sometimes splutters at this stage. Now you may need to return the pan to a low heat to re-melt the caramel, stirring until any lumps have dissolved again. Then quickly pour two-thirds of the caramel into the soufflé dish, tipping it round the base and sides to coat.

Now make the custard. To do this, pour the milk and cream into the saucepan containing the rest of the caramel, then place this over a gentle heat and this time use a whisk to thoroughly combine everything. Don't panic if you get a great clag of caramel clinging to your whisk or there's some stuck around the edges of the pan – remember that the saucepan is over the heat and the heat *will* melt it. Eventually is the word, so be patient. When it's all melted, remove the pan from the heat. Next break the eggs into a large bowl or jug and whisk them, then pour the hot milk that's now blended with the remaining caramel into this mixture, whisking it in as you pour. Next add the vanilla extract and, after that, pour the whole lot through a sieve into the caramel-lined dish. If you have any unmelted caramel left on the base of the pan, fill the pan with hot water and a drop of washing-up liquid and place it over the heat again to clean it off.

Now place the soufflé dish in the roasting tin and pour in enough tap-hot water to come two-thirds of the way up the dish. Place the whole thing on the centre shelf of the pre-heated oven and leave it there for 1¼ hours, until the custard is set in the centre, which means it should feel firm and springy to the touch. Then remove it from the roasting tin and, when it's completely cold, cover with clingfilm and chill thoroughly for several hours in the fridge before turning out.

When you're ready to serve, loosen it around the sides with a palette knife, put quite a deep serving plate on top and then turn it upside down and give it a hefty shake. What you will then have is a delicious, light, set caramel custard surrounded by a pool of golden caramel sauce. Serve it cut in slices with some pouring cream to mingle with the caramel.

Buttermilk Scones with West Country Clotted Cream and Raspberry Butter

These are the lightest little scones you'll ever come across, but what is raspberry butter, you're wondering. The answer is that, traditionally, country people used to use up surplus summer fruits by making fruit cheeses. Damsons, for instance, can be cooked long and slow until they are concentrated into a thick, cheese-like consistency. Fruit butters are similar, but not quite so thick. This version, made with raspberries, has all the concentrated flavour and aroma of the fruit, perfect for piling on to scones with generous amounts of clotted cream.

To make the raspberry butter, purée the raspberries in a food processor, then pass them through a fine nylon sieve, pressing with a wooden spoon so that as much juice as possible gets through – you should get about 15 fl oz (425 ml). Now place the purée in a medium saucepan with the sugar and heat very gently until the sugar has dissolved. Then turn up the heat so the mixture boils rapidly for 8-10 minutes, but keep stirring from time to time so it doesn't catch on the base. When it's ready, the mixture should have reduced by one third and a wooden spoon drawn across the base of the pan should leave a trail for 1-2 seconds only, but be careful not to overcook it, or you will get glue. Then pour it into a serving dish and leave to one side to cool and set for at least an hour.

For the scones, begin by sifting the flour and salt into a bowl, rub the butter lightly into the mixture until it looks like breadcrumbs, then add the sugar. Now, in a jug, beat the egg and 2 tablespoons of the buttermilk together and start to add this to the rest, mixing the dough with a palette knife. When it begins to come together, finish off with your hands – it should be soft but not sticky (if the dough seems too dry, add a little more buttermilk, a teaspoon at a time).

When you have formed the dough into a ball, tip it on to a lightly floured surface and roll it into a circle at least 1 inch (2.5 cm) thick – be very careful not to roll it any thinner; the secret of well-risen scones is to start off with a thickness of no less than an inch. Cut out the scones by placing the cutter on the dough and giving it a sharp tap – don't twist it, just lift it up and push the dough out. Carry on until you are left with the trimmings, then bring these back together to roll out again until you can cut out the last scone.

Place the scones on the baking tray, brush them lightly with the buttermilk and dust with a little flour. Now bake on the top shelf of the oven for 10-12 minutes, or until they are well risen and golden brown, then remove them to a wire rack to cool. Serve the scones thickly spread with raspberry butter and lots of clotted cream.
Note: don't forget that scones don't keep well, so in the unlikely event of there being any left, pop them in the freezer. The raspberry butter, however, can be kept in the refrigerator for a couple of weeks.

Makes about 10 scones
2-3 tablespoons buttermilk, plus a little extra for brushing
8 oz (225 g) self-raising flour, plus a little extra for dusting
pinch of salt
3 oz (75 g) butter, at room temperature
1½ oz (40 g) golden caster sugar
1 large egg, beaten

For the raspberry butter:
1 lb (450 g) raspberries
6 oz (175 g) golden granulated sugar

To serve:
clotted cream

You will also need a lightly greased baking tray dusted with flour, and a 2 inch (5 cm) pastry cutter.

Pre-heat the oven to gas mark 7, 425°F (220°C).

Eton Mess

This recipe, inspired by the strawberry and cream dessert traditionally served at Eton College on the 4th of June, is great for nervous meringue makers – because the meringues are broken up it simply doesn't matter if they weep, crack or collapse. So you can practise making them over and over with this dish until you get them perfect and, at the same time, enjoy this amazingly good summer dessert. Don't forget, though, to make the meringues the day before you want to serve the pudding.

Serves 6

6 oz (175 g) golden caster sugar
3 large egg whites
1 lb (450 g) fresh strawberries, hulled
1 rounded tablespoon unrefined icing sugar
1 pint (570 ml) double cream

You will also need a baking tray measuring 11 x 16 inches (28 x 40 cm), lined with non-stick silicone paper (parchment).

Pre-heat the oven to gas mark 2, 300°F (150°C).

First have the caster sugar measured out ready, then place the egg whites in a scrupulously clean bowl and whisk until they form soft peaks that slightly tip over when you lift the whisk. Next, add the sugar, about a tablespoon at a time, and continue to whisk until each tablespoon of sugar has been thoroughly whisked in. Now simply take rounded dessertspoonfuls of the mixture and place them in rows on the lined baking tray. Place the baking tray in the oven on the centre shelf, turn the heat down to gas mark 1, 275°F (140°C) and leave the meringues there for 1 hour. After that, turn the oven off and leave the meringues in the oven to dry out overnight, or until the oven is completely cold.

When you're ready to make the pudding, chop half the strawberries and place them in a blender together with the icing sugar. Whiz the whole lot to a purée, then pass it through a nylon sieve to remove the seeds. Now chop the rest of the strawberries and whip up the double cream to the floppy stage.

All the above can be done in advance, but when you are ready to serve, break up the meringues into roughly 1 inch (2.5 cm) pieces, place them in a large mixing bowl, add the chopped strawberries, then fold the cream in and around them. After that, gently fold in all but about 2 tablespoons of the purée to give a marbled effect. Finally, pile the whole lot into a serving dish, spoon the rest of the purée over the surface and serve as soon as possible.

Pecan Shortbreads with Raspberries and Raspberry Purée

If you like classic crème pâtissière (French pastry cream) but have no time to make it, a combination of ready-made custard and crème fraîche makes a lovely alternative. If you use it to sandwich together crisp, wafer-thin pecan shortbreads, raspberries and raspberry purée, you have a real winner for summer entertaining.

Serves 8

For the pecan shortbreads:
4 oz (110 g) pecans
5 oz (150 g) softened butter
2½ oz (60 g) unrefined golden icing sugar
5 oz (150 g) plain flour, sifted
2½ oz (60 g) rice flour or ground rice, sifted

For the raspberry purée:
8 oz (225 g) fresh raspberries
2 tablespoons golden caster sugar

For the raspberry filling:
1 lb (450 g) fresh raspberries, reserving 24 for the garnish
7 fl oz (200 ml) crème fraîche
5 fl oz (150 ml) fresh custard
2 drops vanilla extract

To garnish:
24 whole fresh raspberries, reserved from the filling
unrefined golden icing sugar, to dust

You will also need 2 baking trays measuring 11 x 16 inches (28 x 40 cm), lightly greased, and a 3½ inch (9 cm) round pastry cutter.

Pre-heat the oven to gas mark 4, 350°F (180°C).

To begin, toast the pecans by spreading them out on a baking tray and popping them in the oven for 8 minutes. Then, once cool, place them in a processor and grind them down until they look rather like ground almonds.

Now, in a mixing bowl, cream the butter and icing sugar together until light and fluffy, then gradually work in the sifted flours, followed by the ground pecans, bringing the mixture together into a stiff ball. Place the dough in a polythene bag and leave in the fridge to rest for 30 minutes. After that, roll it out to a thickness of ¼ inch (5 mm), then stamp out 16 rounds by placing the cutter on the pastry and giving it a sharp tap, then simply lift the cutter and the piece will drop out. Now arrange the biscuits on the baking trays and lightly prick each one with a fork. Bake for 10-12 minutes, leave on the baking trays for about 10 minutes, then remove to a wire rack to cool completely.

While the shortbreads are cooling, place the raspberries for the purée in a bowl, sprinkle them with the sugar and leave for 30 minutes. After that, purée them in a processor and pass through a nylon sieve to remove the seeds, then place in a serving bowl, cover and chill till needed.

For the raspberry filling, whisk the crème fraîche in a mixing bowl with an electric hand whisk until it becomes really stiff, then add the custard and vanilla extract and whisk again, also until thick. Cover and chill till needed. Just before serving, spread equal quantities of the cream mixture over 8 of the biscuits, then arrange the raspberries on top, not forgetting to reserve 24. Spoon some purée over, then sandwich with the remaining shortbreads. Place 3 raspberries on top of each one, and lightly dust with the icing sugar.
Note: don't be tempted to prepare these too far in advance, because once the filling goes in the shortbreads begin to lose their crunchiness.

Fromage Frais Creams with Red Fruit Compote

In the 'Winter Collection' I made these with Mascarpone, but this low-fat alternative is, I feel, every bit as good as the rich version and the perfect accompaniment to any fruit compote. I like this best made with leaf gelatine, but I've also included instructions for powdered gelatine.

Serves 6

1 lb 12 oz (800 g) 8 per cent fat fromage frais
3 sheets leaf gelatine
5 fl oz (150 ml) semi-skimmed milk
3 oz (75 g) golden caster sugar
1 vanilla pod, split lengthways

For the compote:

8 oz (225 g) fresh plums
8 oz (225 g) fresh cherries
8 oz (225 g) fresh blueberries
8 oz (225 g) fresh strawberries
8 oz (225 g) fresh raspberries
2 oz (50 g) golden caster sugar

You will also need 6 x 6 fl oz (175 ml) mini pudding basins, lightly oiled with a flavourless oil, and an ovenproof baking dish measuring 9 inches (23 cm) square and 2 inches (5 cm) deep.

Pre-heat the oven to gas mark 4, 350°F (180°C).

If you are using leaf gelatine, simply place the sheets in a bowl and cover with cold water, *below left*, then leave them to soak for about 5 minutes, till softened, *below centre*. Meanwhile, place the milk in a saucepan with the sugar and vanilla pod and heat gently for 5 minutes, or until the sugar has dissolved. Then take the pan off the heat and all you do now is squeeze the leaf gelatine in your hands to remove any excess water, then add it to the hot milk, *below right*. Give it all a thorough whisking and leave to cool.

Next, in a large mixing bowl, whisk the fromage frais until smooth, then add the cooled gelatine and milk mixture, removing the vanilla pod, and whisk again really well. Now divide the mixture between the pudding basins, filling them to within ½ inch (1 cm) of the rims. Finally, cover with clingfilm and chill in the fridge for at least 3 hours.

To make the compote, begin by preparing the plums: cut them round their natural line into halves, remove the stones, then cut each half into 4 and place in the ovenproof dish, along with the whole cherries and blueberries. Now sprinkle in the sugar, then place the dish on the centre shelf of the oven without covering and leave it there for 15 minutes. Next stir in the strawberries, halved if large, and return the dish to the oven for 10-15 minutes, or until the fruits are tender and the juices have run out of them. Finally, remove them from the oven and stir the raspberries into the hot juices, then allow it to cool, cover with clingfilm and chill.

To serve the creams, gently ease each one away from the edge of the basin using your little finger, then invert them on to serving dishes and serve with the compote spooned all around.

If you'd prefer to use powdered gelatine instead of leaf, place 3 tablespoons of the milk in a small bowl, then sprinkle the contents of an 11 g sachet over the milk and leave it to stand for 5 minutes. Meanwhile, heat the rest of the milk in a small saucepan, along with the vanilla pod and sugar, until the sugar has dissolved, then remove it from the heat and whisk in the soaked-gelatine mixture. Allow to cool, then just whisk into the fromage frais and continue as for the main recipe.

Coffee Cappuccino Creams with Cream and Sweet Coffee Sauce

If you are a coffee fan, this is the coffee dessert – the best ever! It is based on an old-fashioned recipe for honeycomb mould, which sometimes separates into layers, but sadly it often doesn't. Therefore, I have now given up on layers because, anyway, it tastes absolutely divine. You can make this and serve it in Irish coffee glasses or plain glasses. The contrast of the unsweetened coffee cream mingling with the sweetened sauce and a generous amount of pouring or whipping cream is just gorgeous.

Serves 6
6 heaped teaspoons instant espresso coffee powder
5 fl oz (150 ml) water
1 x 11 g sachet gelatine powder
10 fl oz (275 ml) whole milk
3 large eggs, separated
1 rounded teaspoon cornflour
7 fl oz (200 ml) crème fraîche

For the sauce:
3 heaped teaspoons instant espresso coffee powder
6 oz (175 g) golden granulated sugar
8 fl oz (225 ml) water

To serve:
5 fl oz (150 ml) double cream

You will also need 6 x 7 fl oz (200 ml) serving glasses.

Begin by soaking the gelatine: pour the water into a small bowl, sprinkle in the gelatine and let it soak for 5 minutes. Meanwhile, pour the milk into a medium saucepan and place it over a gentle heat. Then, in a bowl, whisk the egg yolks and cornflour together and, when the milk is very hot and just about to simmer, pour it over the egg-yolk mixture, whisking as you do. Now return the whole lot to the same saucepan, adding the soaked gelatine and coffee powder, then return the pan to the heat and continue to whisk until the custard is thickened and the gelatine and coffee are completely dissolved. Remove the pan from the heat and pour the custard into a large mixing bowl, leave it to cool, then whisk in the crème fraîche.

In another bowl, and using a clean whisk, whisk the egg whites to the soft-peak stage. Now fold 2 tablespoons of the egg whites into the coffee custard to loosen the mixture, then gently fold in the rest. Pour the mixture into the glasses and leave, covered with clingfilm, in a cool place for about 2 hours, then chill in the fridge until needed.

To make the coffee sauce, gently heat the sugar and water together and whisk till all the sugar granules have completely dissolved, then simmer gently for 15 minutes without a lid, until it becomes syrupy. Next, dissolve the coffee in 1 dessertspoon of warm water, stir this into the syrup and transfer it to a serving jug to cool. Meanwhile, whip up the cream to the floppy stage and, when you're ready, serve the coffee creams topped with whipped cream and the coffee syrup poured over.
Note: this recipe contains raw eggs.

8

Fruits for cooking

I think a sub-title for this chapter could be 'How to preserve our heritage.' There is, unfortunately, a price to pay for progress, and while fruits from around the world jetting into our supermarkets daily bring a permanent abundance of choice, it's sad that our own fruit growers are being forced into decline.

I am not against progress; I enjoy having such a wide choice. I feel privileged that I can shop around the world just a few miles from where I live and I love being able to bite into a crunchy fresh apple in June that hasn't gone woolly with storage. It also has to be said that some fruits need the sunshine that's so often elusive in this country. But at the same time I hope that British fruit growers won't ever give up, and we need to encourage them by buying British wherever possible: Kentish cherries, Bramley apples, old-fashioned oval-shaped damsons, Scottish raspberries and countless others. It's important that with all the dazzling choice before us we look at labels and countries of origin and give our fruit growers all the support we can.

On the pages that follow I have tried to give a kind of first-time overall view of various fruits and how to prepare and cook them. This is not, by any means, a comprehensive list, but a look at fruits that are most likely to be used in any day-to-day cooking repertoire.

Apples

It's on the subject of the apple, more than any other fruit, that chefs and cooks often part company. As one of the latter, and being born and bred in England, I am quite definitely a Bramley lover. Chefs, even English ones, are usually educated in French ways, and as the French never had Bramley apples they're not included in classic cuisine. But the Bramley is a star: it has an acidic yet fragrant apple flavour and it cooks to a fluffiness not required in French dishes but very much part of English cooking through the ages – as English as apple pie. That said, there are recipes that require firmer apples to keep their shape, and Cox's and Granny Smiths are both excellent for this purpose.

There are many other varieties of home-grown apples, but in cooking I tend to mostly use these three. They are always widely available and their best season is from the end of August through to March. As the seasons go I tend to cook with apples in the winter months and use other fruits that are more plentiful during the summer. When I first started cooking, seasons were so important and truly dictated the rhythm of cooking through the year, and as I've said elsewhere, I still find this variation makes cooking more interesting.

When it comes to preparing apples for cooking, unless you're going at the speed of lightning, you will need a bowl of lightly salted water, as this will prevent them from browning. First of all you need a small, sharp knife and a potato peeler. Cut each apple in half, then cut one half into quarters using the knife, taking out the core and pips. Now, using the peeler, pare off the skin (if the recipe requires it), then, depending on the recipe, slice or chop the apples and add them to the bowl of water as they are prepared. Use them as quickly as possible, draining in a colander and drying them with a tea cloth first.

Apricots

Here's a fruit that cannot be grown without warm sunshine, so we have to rely on Mediterranean countries for supplies. Picked straight from the tree, an apricot can be delightful to eat raw, warm from the sun, but once they arrive here I feel they need light cooking to bring out the best apricot flavour. The season is short – June to August – but dried apricots are now available all year round and can nearly always be used in apricot recipes.

When it comes to preparing apricots, there's no need to peel them – all you do is cut the apricot around the natural line into two halves, then, holding the half containing the stone in one hand, give a little twist and squeeze as you remove the stone with the other hand. To cook apricots, you can use them in place of plums in the recipe on page 205.

Bananas

A little bit of heaven is a ripe, fragrant, soft-fleshed banana mashed with a fork with just a little brown sugar and piled on to thick slices of buttered crusty wholemeal bread (home-made, see Book One). That and a cup of freshly brewed tea can give anyone renewed strength in the middle of a working day.

When choosing bananas, remember that to be ripe enough to eat the skins must be all yellow with no green bits near the stalk. Also, the riper they are the better they taste – sweeter and more fragrant. A really ripe and ready-to-eat banana will have little brown freckles on its yellow skin, but be warned: ripe and ready means just that, so eat it soon or it might be a little too ripe tomorrow! Remember, too, that bananas come from hot countries and hate the cold, so never, ever put them in the fridge, as the shock of it turns them black. Bananas also tend to discolour if they are exposed to the air, so if you are preparing them for a recipe they should be tossed in lemon juice if they have to wait around. However, when they're submerged and cut off from the air they stay creamy white with no problem. The recipe for Toffee-Fudge Bananas with Toasted Nuts on page 177 is one of the simplest and easiest desserts I know.

Cherries

I remember baskets of Kentish cherries, ripe and red, or 'whites', which were actually pale and creamy with a rosy blush. These have the finest flavour of all cherries and there are still Kentish growers. Because English cherries are in short supply, however, I am grateful to other European countries and the US for sending us a plentiful stock throughout the summer. They are expensive, because cherries are laborious to hand pick, but because the season is relatively short I always make the most of it and seem to eat them practically every day.

What we buy mostly are dessert cherries, but sour cherries, called morello, are brilliant for cooking, with a wonderful, quite unique, concentrated cherry flavour. Because there's a very short supply we only seem to be able to buy the dried here, but bottled ones can be good and morello cherry jam is superb both spread on bread and scones and in a sauce to serve with duck. I have lately discovered that dessert cherries cooked with wine and wine vinegar also make a superb sauce for duck or gammon, so I would serve this in the summer, and then in the winter months make it with dried sour cherries.

Figs

Like apricots, fresh figs ideally need to be eaten picked from the tree, warm from the Mediterranean sunshine, fully ripened and bursting with soft, luscious flesh. If their sweetness is then combined with some thinly sliced Parma or Serrano ham, you would have a feast indeed. Although they are imported throughout most of the year, the best of the European crop (from Turkey and Greece) are at their most luscious in autumn. They should be dark purple, feel soft to the touch when you buy them and their skins should have a soft bloom, which needs to be wiped off with damp kitchen paper. Eat them just as they are, as a topping for sweet galettes (Book One), or arranged in overlapping slices, brushed with honey and baked for 10-12 minutes at gas mark 7, 425°F (220°C). Another very unusual way to serve them is as a starter; see the recipe for Roasted Figs with Gorgonzola and Honey-Vinegar Sauce on page 208.

Lemons

Imagine a world without lemons or a kitchen that didn't always have a lemon tucked away. Can there be a more widely used fruit or absolutely essential ingredient in cooking in the Western world?

Lemons, which are available all year round, contain lots of sharp, acidic juice, but also a fragrant oil that's found in the zest (the coloured outer layer of the skin). In a drink such as a dry Martini or gin and tonic, this pared-off outer skin releases its fragrant oil to give a subtle lemon hint. In cooking, lemon zest is every bit as treasured as the juice, and our heritage of rich fruit Christmas cakes, puddings and mincemeat all contain not only lemon juice and zest but candied lemon peel, giving extra fragrance and flavour. It's always best to use lemons as fresh as possible, but I find extra lemons keep better if they're stored in a polythene bag in the salad drawer of the fridge.

Squeezing

It is said that rolling the lemon with the palm of your hand on a flat surface using a bit of pressure will ensure you get more juice. When my mother made pancakes on Pancake Day she would put plates to warm in the oven and pop the lemon in, too, as this, she said, produced more juice. Either way, I think a wooden lemon squeezer inserted into a half lemon and squeezed and twisted is a wonderfully easy way to extract the juice.

Zesting

If you want finely zested lemon, a grater will do the job, but you need to take care not to include the bitter pith just beneath the zest. Best of all is a lemon zester, which removes only the outer zest and the fragrant oils. A great lemon recipe is the grilled lemon chicken kebabs on page 112.

Limes

Whilst lemon trees grow and thrive in the Mediterranean, they can't survive the hot, steamy humidity of Asian countries – so enter limes, yet another supreme gift of nature. Limes, like lemons, are filled with fragrant acidic juice and the zest contains the same high-flavoured oils. Though limes are a small green lookalike lemon, their flavour is distinctly different. I love limes and always have them in my kitchen. If you want a low-fat salad dressing, look no further – just squeeze lime juice all over and it's remarkable how it offers both its own flavour and at the same time manages to enhance other flavours in the salad. The same applies to the juice, which really enhances the flavour of mango, pawpaw and pineapple.

Mangoes

When you're standing before a ripe, plump mango and you can feel its soft ripeness and smell its quite overwhelming fragrance, that is a time to rejoice. Fast jets now mean everybody can enjoy this most luscious and succulent of fruits, with its dazzling orange-yellow flesh. The fruit itself is fragrant, with a custard flavour. That said, a mango is always rather awkward to prepare, but first you need to check that it's ripe. Colour is not an indication: the skins are variously green, red, yellow-orange or even vaguely purple. As with an avocado you need to hold the fruit in your hand and feel a 'give' of softness when you exert a little pressure. Smell, too, can help you – the riper it is the heavier the perfume.

I love to eat mango on its own with a squeeze of lime, which seems to bring out the flavour of the fruit. Mango salsa in Book One goes beautifully with chicken, and on page 203 you'll find Thai Fish Curry with Mango is quite exquisite.

How to prepare a mango

The best way to start is to place the mango on a flat surface (I often use a dinner plate to catch the juice). Remember there is a large flat stone in the centre, so take a sharp knife, hold the mango in a vertical position, then slice it lengthways either side of the stone, *top right*. Now hold each slice, flesh-side up, and this time, using a small knife, cut a criss-cross pattern into the flesh right down to the skin but being careful not to cut through the skin, *right*. Now you can turn the whole thing inside out and simply cut away the cubes of mango into a bowl, then tip in any juices that are left on the plate.

Slicing the mango

Mangoes can be sliced, but only if they're just ripe and not too soft. This time you need a potato peeler to finely peel off the skin, then hold the mango in one hand and, with a small knife, cut out a slice, *left*, taking the knife down to the stone either side of it, then remove the slice and carry on cutting slices all the way round.

Too ripe

If the mango is too soft and fibrous to chop or slice, cut the cheeks off the mango (as shown on the previous page), then scoop out the flesh and make a purée in the processor with a little lime juice. Lovely as a sauce for something sweet or savoury, or add half its quantity of Greek yoghurt to make a fragrant mango fool.

Oranges

Oranges feature every bit as regularly as lemons in recipes: the famous French classic bigarade (orange and port) sauce served with duck, for instance, and my own favourite classic English sauce, Cumberland, which features orange and lemon, where the juices and finely shredded zest are combined with port and redcurrant jelly. Then there is also, of course, that great British invention, marmalade, which no other country's preserve has ever been able to match. Made with the bitter oranges of Seville that arrive at Christmas, no marmalade made with any other citrus fruit has that tangy intensity of flavour, where the sharpness of the oranges wins hands down over the sugar, totally eliminating that over-sweetness that so often masks the true flavour of the fruit in preserves.

Buying oranges is such a hit and miss affair, and a dry, sour or extra-pithy orange is really not pleasant. So, for eating straight there's only one type of orange that never fails to please, and that's the Spanish navels that arrive in November but disappear at the end of February. They are distinctive in that they have a so-called 'navel', and inside there's a sort of baby fruit attached. I'm not saying other varieties of orange are not good, but with navels you're never disappointed. The good news here is that other countries are now growing them, too, so watch out for navelinas in spring and early summer, and the late-summer version from Argentina.

Peaches and nectarines

Oh to be either in Spain or Italy when the peaches are ripe and fragrant and just about to fall from the trees. The peach, beloved of artists, is a beauteous thing, with its deep-crimson rosy bloom and voluptuous bright-yellow flesh oozing with juice. When we're lucky enough to eat them just like that – ready, ripe and warm from the sun – we need have no thought of recipes. But in this country, where peaches can't be grown on a large scale, we have to suffer tired imports picked too early, so that once the hard flesh becomes soft enough it has often turned woolly, dry and tasteless. Both nectarines and peaches come with white flesh, but the yellow, in my opinion, has more flavour.

However, unripened peaches and their first cousin, nectarines, can be somewhat rescued in cooking, so poaching them in Marsala (*Summer Collection*) is a good idea.

Pineapple

When I first started cooking I was slightly scared of pineapples, not knowing quite how to come at them or where to start with my knife. When I was a child, pineapple came tinned in neat rings packed in syrup. My favourite teacher, Elizabeth David (though only through books), came to my aid and, as always, explained it perfectly, which gave me immense satisfaction as I proudly took the pineapple to the table sprinkled with a little sugar and Kirsch.

First you need to buy a ripe pineapple: look for proud, lively green tufts that don't look too aged or tired. Give one a tug if you can: if it's ripe it should pull off easily. The other thing to look for is the little thorny bits that stick out – they should be brown. The colour of the pineapple itself is not always a guide: some from Central America are very green and others from the Ivory Coast are golden amber. Feel the pineapple at the base: it should give and feel soft if it's ripe, and don't forget to smell its strong pineapple perfume, probably telling you more than anything if it's ready to eat.

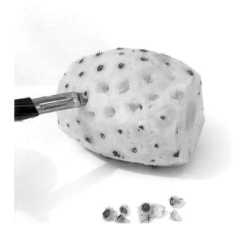

I have now created my own way of dealing with a pineapple. Needless to say, the tough, elusive-looking object needs a really sharp knife. First slice off the leafy top and about ½ inch (1 cm) of the fruit with it – you need to get this as straight as possible. Put it to one side, then cut off the opposite end, which can be discarded. Now stand it upright and slice off the skin vertically in slices, *top right*, going all the way round. What you will now have is a whole peeled pineapple, and what you need to do next is use the tip of a potato peeler to dig out the 'eyes', *centre right*, which are similar to those of a potato. Now slice the pineapple vertically in half, then into quarters. The central core can be a bit tough, so slice this off along the centre of each quarter, *bottom right*, then cut the quarters into slices about ⅓ inch (7 mm) thick. Arrange these in overlapping circles, then sprinkle with a light dusting of sugar and a little Kirsch (rum is also very good) and pop the leafy top in the centre.

Plums, greengages and damsons

Whilst peaches and nectarines may make us think we are disadvantaged living further north, plums and damsons more than adequately make up for it. I have a small Victoria plum tree in my garden in Suffolk, and I love eating them straight from the tree in late summer, giving them a faint squeeze to see which ones are fully ripe, then eating just a few each day for breakfast and lunch until they're all gone. There are several other varieties of home-grown plums, all suitable for cooking or eating raw when fully ripe. Greengages, because of their colour, are deceptive – they can look unripe and forbidding but taste very sweet. I like to cook both greengages and plums in a compote of Marsala wine (see Book One).

Damsons are my favourite member of the plum family. The true damson is small and oval, almost almond-shaped, with dark indigo-purple skin covered in a soft bloom and bright-green sharp-sour flesh that, when cooked with sugar, produces darker, reddish-purple juice. The secret of the damson's utter charm is that because it's a sharp fruit its flavour is not killed by sugar, so damson jam remains perfectly tart and not over-sweet. One of my all-time favourite recipes is for damson chutney: in 20 years I've never been without a little hoard of it stashed away in my cupboard under the stairs. It does wonders for bangers or makes a very sophisticated accompaniment to cold cuts, and I particularly love serving sausages with jacket potatoes and dipping the potato skins in a luscious pile of damson chutney.

Rhubarb

Although it came here originally from Russia, rhubarb is, for me, an extremely English fruit, arriving at a very important time in the calendar – early spring, when there's absolutely no other interesting fruit in season. It really is a curious, wonderfully different fruit – no other comes to us as an elongated stalk. Watching it grow almost secretly under its umbrella of wide green leaves in the garden is fascinating.

As early as March we can buy the tender, pink stalks of forced rhubarb, which have a delicate, youthful flavour. Then in May we begin to see that the rhubarb is a deeper, rosier red. Later on, in June and July, it will be dark crimson, more acid and less sweet, so a little more sugar is needed at this time. Use it in our crumble recipe on page 210, in one-crust pies, or in the Old-Fashioned Rhubarb Trifle on page 206.

When it comes to preparing and cooking rhubarb, first trim off the leaves and cut the stalks into 1 inch (2.5 cm) chunks. I never, ever simmer or boil rhubarb because it tends to mash up, so to keep the pieces intact, it's best to bake it in the oven using 3 oz (75 g) of sugar to each 1 lb 8 oz (700 g) of fruit, pre-heating the oven to gas mark 4, 350°F (180°C). Place it in a shallow dish and give it 30-40 minutes, uncovered. This amount will serve 4 people.

Soft fruits

Blackberries

There is still something very satisfying about blackberrying, although I usually find someone has been there first, plucking off the best ones at the lowest levels! Don't be thwarted – take a walking stick and summon down the upper branches; take some gloves, too, or your hands will be very scratched, and a basket if you're really up for it, or a polythene box if you're not quite so determined!

Either way, wild brambles or blackberries have a character and flavour that the cultivated ones have never captured. It's tricky, though, because if we have a wet summer they will be plump, fleshy and juicy; if we have a dry summer they will be very small and seedy. So, given the vagaries of wild blackberries, the cultivated kind are better than none. Blackberries are absolutely brilliant mixed with apples in a one-crust pie, or why not try them instead of apple in the crumble recipe on page 210?

Blackcurrants

Of all the little sparkly jewels that appear in the height of summer (their season being from June to August), blackcurrants are the richest, with a strong flavour and sharpness that can stand up to sugar. If you like their gutsy, in-your-face flavour there's a French company that makes a range of jams without sugar, using only concentrated fruit juices – its blackcurrant jam packed with fruit is the best I've ever tasted. Good bread, creamy butter and superlative jam makes, for my money, one of the simplest yet most luxurious snacks ever invented.

Blackcurrants make an excellent purée – for six people just take 8 oz (225 g) of currants and 3 oz (75 g) of caster sugar. First remove the stalks from the currants, then sprinkle them with the sugar in a bowl. Leave to stand for 30 minutes, then you can either sieve them directly back into the bowl or, to make the sieving easier, process them first, then sieve into the bowl. Taste to check that you have added enough sugar, then pour into a jug and chill until you're ready to serve.

Blueberries

When I was small my Welsh grandmother used to make tarts with a fruit called bilberry – little berries that grew wild, with purple flesh that yielded dark, deep-red juice. The blueberry is apparently its cousin, and grows wild in North America and Canada, but these are dark indigo-blue outside and inside the flesh is green. The cultivated blueberries we buy here are larger, plump and juicy and very handsome to look at, and they are best and cheapest in the summer.

In America, blueberries are served with buttermilk pancakes for breakfast, in pies and in blueberry muffins (*Summer Collection*). I have used them in the recipe for Fromage Frais Creams with Red Fruit Compote on page 186 – a lovely summery combination.

Raspberries

A truly exquisite soft fruit that needs hardly any adornment. I like them served on a plate spread out in a single layer with a minute sprinkling of sugar, and I eat them just like that as often as I can during the season, which runs from July to October. Treat them more or less like strawberries – no water if possible, and covered if you're forced to keep them in the fridge. Raspberries, like strawberries, also lend themselves to countless recipe ideas. Damaged, over-soft fruits make marvellous tarts, and if you sieve them and add icing sugar to taste you have a wonderful sauce for pouring over ice cream or strawberries.

Redcurrants and whitecurrants

Redcurrant jelly is an absolute must-have as a storecupboard ingredient (see page 16), but I also like the combination of redcurrants mixed with strawberries and raspberries in equal quantities for one of the simplest of desserts. Hand round caster sugar and cream and summer is in every spoonful. Whitecurrants can be used as well for added contrast of colour, and this combination makes a lovely filling for the meringue recipe given in Book One.

To prepare currants, all you do for a hasty separation of currants from stalks is take a bunch in one hand, hold the stalk firmly, then slide the stalk in-between the prongs of a fork held in the other hand. Now pull from top to bottom, sliding them all off in one swift movement.

Strawberries

I think it's true to say that English strawberries are the best in the world, available only in June and July. The season is very short, of course, but my advice is not to think about them at any other time. Our red, ripe strawberries are in quite a different league to the imported varieties that continue to turn up in the winter months. If you want to really enjoy a feast of strawberries, my advice is to drive off somewhere either to pick your own or buy direct from the grower, as they never, ever taste the same over-chilled and irradiated from the supermarket. But if you're forced to buy them there, let your nose be your guide: the plastic boxes have air holes, so make sure the strawberries have a strong, ripe scent, which indicates a good flavour.

Strawberry know-how

To get the most pleasure out of strawberries it's best to know how to treat them before you eat them. This means a bit of TLC, because their sheer beauty can be lost by bad handling.

1) Try to pick your own.

2) Eat them the same day or store in a cool place with the hulls intact.

3) Fridges and strawberries don't like each other. Low temperatures rob them of fragrance and flavour and somehow transfer the flavour to other ingredients in the fridge (uncovered milk or cream can quickly absorb strawberry flavours).

4) Please don't wash them. They tend to absorb water, which makes them mushy, so this also means it's not a good idea to buy them after heavy rain. Just wipe them with damp kitchen paper.

5) Leave the hulls in as long as possible and only remove them an hour or so before eating.

6) If you're forced to put them in the fridge, try sugared strawberries, which involves slicing them in half, sprinkling with caster sugar and storing them in a tightly lidded polythene box. During the storage the juices will mingle with the sugar and form a lovely strawberry-flavoured syrup. Remove from the fridge about an hour before serving.

Exotics

These are not often used in cooking as such but they do make a very splendid fruit salad (see the following page), so I will briefly explain how to deal with them.

Kiwi fruit

You can use a potato peeler here to pare off the skin and slice it, or if you want to eat one whole, slice the top off and scoop the flesh out with a teaspoon, as if you were eating a boiled egg.

Lychees

To prepare this fragrant, juicy little fruit, peel off the papery skin, slice the fruit round the middle, separate it into halves and discard the stone.

Passion fruit

When you buy passion fruit, look for a crinkled skin, which is a sign of ripeness, then just slice the fruit in half and scoop out the edible seeds and all the lovely juicy flesh that surrounds them.

Pawpaw (or papaya)

When ripe a pawpaw should, like an avocado, have some 'give' when you hold it in your hand and exert a little pressure. To prepare it, slice it in half vertically, scoop out the seeds, pare off the skin and slice or chop.

Clockwise from top left: passion fruit, pawpaw, kiwi fruit and lychees

Tropical Fruit Salad in Planter's Punch

Planter's punch, a popular drink throughout the Caribbean, is a delicious combination of rum, orange, lime and pineapple juice, with just a trace of cinnamon and nutmeg. The syrup for this fruit salad is based on exactly the same combination, which makes it very special indeed.

Serves 8

2 bananas, peeled and chopped into
1 inch (2.5 cm) chunks
8 oz (225 g) seedless black
grapes, halved
1 pawpaw, peeled and chopped into
1 inch (2.5 cm) chunks (see page 201)
1 large mango, peeled and chopped
into 1 inch (2.5 cm) chunks (see
page 195)
1 small pineapple, peeled and chopped
into 1 inch (2.5 cm) chunks (see
page 197)
2 oranges, peeled and cut into
segments
8 oz (225 g) lychees, peeled, stoned
and halved (see page 201)
2 kiwi fruit, peeled, halved and
cut into ½ inch (1 cm) slices (see
page 201)
4 passion fruit, halved
1 whole nutmeg

For the syrup:

4 oz (110 g) golden granulated sugar
2 small cinnamon sticks
10 fl oz (275 ml) water
pared zest and juice 2 limes
4 fl oz (120 ml) freshly squeezed
orange juice
4 fl oz (120 ml) pineapple juice
5 fl oz (150 ml) dark rum

Begin by making up the syrup: put the sugar, cinnamon and water in a small saucepan, then add the lime zest. Now, over a gentle flame, heat slowly until all the sugar has dissolved – it will take about 10 minutes. Stir it with a wooden spoon: you should have no sugar crystals left clinging to the spoon when you turn it over. After that, remove it from the heat and allow it to cool.

Add the prepared fruit to a large serving bowl, scooping the seeds from the halved passion fruit using a teaspoon, then strain in the cold syrup, along with the fruit juices, lime juice and rum. Stir well before covering with clingfilm and chilling in the fridge. As you serve the fruit salad, sprinkle a little freshly grated nutmeg over each serving.

Thai Fish Curry with Mango

You won't believe how utterly simple and easy this is, and yet it tastes exotic and wonderful and, what's more, it can all be prepared well in advance and the fish added about 10 minutes before you want to eat it. You can also make this using 1 lb 8 oz (700 g) of raw, peeled tiger prawns, added in place of the fish.

Begin by emptying the coconut milk into the pan or wok and stir while you bring it up to the boil, then reduce the heat to medium and cook until the fat separates from the solids. This will take 20 minutes or so, and you will have about 1 pint (570 ml) left. Now make the curry paste, and all you do is put everything in a food processor or blender and whiz until you have a rather coarse, rough-looking paste and everything is perfectly blended.

Now, over a medium heat, add the curry paste and fish to the pan and, once it has reached simmering point, give it 4 minutes. Finally, add the mango and cook for a further 2 minutes. Serve the curry with the coriander sprinkled over and Thai fragrant rice as an accompaniment. To prepare the curry in advance, make everything up, keeping the paste covered in the fridge, then, 10 minutes before you want to serve, bring the coconut milk back up to the boil, then add the paste, fish and mango as above.

Serves 4 generously
2 lb (900 g) firm fish fillet (Greenland halibut, cod or haddock, for example), skinned and chopped into 1½ inch (4 cm) chunks
1 large mango, peeled and cut into ¾ inch (2 cm) pieces (see page 195)
2 x 400 ml tins coconut milk

For the curry paste:
2 medium red chillies, halved and deseeded
grated zest and juice 1 lime
2 stems lemon grass, roughly chopped
1 inch (2.5 cm) piece fresh root ginger, peeled and sliced
4 cloves garlic, peeled
1 small onion, peeled and quartered
1 teaspoon shrimp paste
3 tablespoons Thai fish sauce

To garnish:
3 tablespoons chopped fresh coriander leaves

You will also need a deep frying pan with a diameter of 10 inches (25.5 cm), or a wok.

Plum and Cinnamon Oat Slices

This is really an all-fruit recipe – it's exceptionally good with plums, but I love it with fresh or dried no-soak apricots, or apples, raspberries and blueberries; in fact you can add whatever is in season. It's wonderful served either warm as a dessert with cream, or cold with ice cream, instead of cake with tea. It's also a great recipe for children to make, as it's so easy.

Start by cutting all the plums in half, around and through their natural line, give a little twist to separate the halves and remove the stones, then cut them into thin slices. Now place them in a bowl and toss them around with the cinnamon. Next mix the flour and porridge oats together with the salt in a mixing bowl, then melt the butter and sugar in a small saucepan over a fairly gentle heat, stirring from time to time until the butter has melted. Now mix the melted butter and sugar with the oat mixture, starting with a wooden spoon but finishing off with your hands so you end up with a lump of dough. Now halve the dough and press one half of the mixture into the baking tin, pressing it firmly all over the base with your hands like a wall-to-wall carpet. Next scatter the plums evenly over the surface, then top with the remaining oat mixture, again pressing down firmly.

Now place the tin on the centre shelf of the oven and bake for 25-30 minutes, or a bit longer if you like the top really crispy. Then remove the tin from the oven and allow to cool for about 10 minutes before marking into 15 squares – to do this make 2 cuts lengthways, then 4 cuts widthways, and don't worry if they're not all even. Unless you want to serve these warm, leave to cool completely in the tin.

Note: if you want to serve this as a dessert, it can be made in a round 9 inch (23 cm) springform tin, in which case it can be cut into 8-10 wedges and served warm from the oven.

Makes 15
1 lb (450 g) fresh plums
1 rounded teaspoon ground cinnamon
10 oz (275 g) organic plain wholemeal flour
5 oz (150 g) organic porridge oats
1 teaspoon salt
8 oz (225 g) butter
4 oz (110 g) light brown soft sugar

You will also need a non-stick baking tin measuring 10 x 6 inches (25.5 x 15 cm) and 1 inch (2.5 cm) deep, lightly greased.

Pre-heat the oven to gas mark 6, 400°F (200°C).

Opposite, top: Apricot and Cinnamon Oat Slice; bottom: Plum and Cinnamon Oat Slice

Old-Fashioned Rhubarb Trifle

Old-fashioned because when I was a child – a very long time ago – I used to love jelly trifles, and my mother would always make one for my birthday. This is a much more adult version, and the sharp, fragrant acidity of the rhubarb makes it a very light and refreshing dessert for spring and early summer.

Serves 6

1 lb 8 oz (700 g) fresh rhubarb
4 oz (110 g) golden caster sugar
grated zest and juice 1 orange
2 oz (50 g) pecans
6 trifle sponges
3 tablespoons marmalade
4 fl oz (120 ml) sercial Madeira
about 10 fl oz (275 ml) freshly
squeezed orange juice
1 x 11 g sachet gelatine powder
12 oz (350 g) fresh custard
7 oz (200 g) Greek yoghurt

To serve:

a little pouring cream (optional)

You will also need an ovenproof baking dish measuring 7½ inches (19 cm) square and 2 inches (5 cm) deep, and 6 individual serving bowls or 1 large trifle bowl with a capacity of 3½ pints (2 litres).

Pre-heat the oven to gas mark 4, 350°F (180°C).

To prepare the rhubarb, cut it into 1 inch (2.5 cm) chunks and add these to the baking dish. Then sprinkle in the caster sugar, together with the zest and juice of the orange. Now pop the whole lot in the oven without covering and let it cook for 30-40 minutes, until the rhubarb is tender but still retains its shape. At the same time, place the pecans in the oven and put a timer on for 7 minutes to toast them lightly, then you can either leave them whole or chop them roughly.

While the rhubarb is cooking, slice the trifle sponges in half lengthways, spread each half with the marmalade, then reform them and cut each one into 3 little sandwiches. Now arrange them either in the individual serving bowls or the large trifle bowl. Then make a few stabs in the sponges and sprinkle the Madeira carefully over them, then leave it all aside so it can soak in.

When the rhubarb is cooked and has become completely cold, taste it – if it is a bit sharp, add a little more sugar. Take a draining spoon and carefully remove the chunks of rhubarb, placing them in and amongst the sponges. Now pour all the juices from the dish into a measuring jug and make this up to 18 fl oz (510 ml) with the orange juice.

Next, pour 8 fl oz (225 ml) of this into a small saucepan, scatter the gelatine over, whisk it and leave it to soak for 5 minutes. Then place the pan over a gentle heat and whisk everything until all the gelatine has completely dissolved – about 2 minutes – then return this to the remaining juice in the jug and give it all another good whisk. Now pour it over the sponges and rhubarb. When it is completely cold, cover it with clingfilm and leave in the fridge till completely set. The last thing you need to do is whisk the custard and Greek yoghurt together in a mixing bowl, then spoon this mixture over the set jelly.

Now cover with clingfilm again and chill until you're ready to serve. Don't forget to sprinkle the toasted pecan nuts over just before serving, and, although it doesn't strictly need it, a little chilled pouring cream is a nice addition.

Roasted Figs with Gorgonzola and Honey-Vinegar Sauce

This may sound like an unlikely combination but it's simply brilliant – a first course that's fast, unusual and absolutely no trouble to prepare.

Serves 4 as a starter
12 ripe figs
6 oz (175 g) Gorgonzola Piccante, chopped into ¼ inch (5 mm) dice
salt and freshly milled black pepper

For the sauce:
2 tablespoons Greek honey
2 tablespoons red wine vinegar

You will also need a baking tray measuring 10 x 14 inches (25.5 x 35 cm), oiled.

Pre-heat the grill to its highest setting.

All you do is wipe and halve the figs, then place them, cut-side up, on the baking tray. Season with salt and freshly milled black pepper, then pop them under the grill for 5-6 minutes, until they're soft and just bubbling slightly. When the figs are ready, remove the baking tray from the grill and divide the cheese equally between them, gently pressing it down to squash it in a bit. Then pop them back under the grill for about 2 minutes, until the cheese is bubbling and faintly golden brown.

Meanwhile, make the sauce by combining the honey and vinegar together, then serve the figs with the sauce poured over.

Spiced Oranges in Port

This is a great Christmas recipe because you can make it ahead, it keeps well and can be used to accompany cold cuts of poultry, game or pork and it is especially good served with cooked ham, hot or cold.

First you need to dry-roast the coriander seeds and cardamom pods, and to do this place them in a small frying pan or saucepan over a medium heat and stir and toss them around for 1-2 minutes, or until they begin to look toasted and start to jump in the pan, then lightly crush them in a pestle and mortar. Now arrange the orange wedges in the base of the casserole, skin-side down, then sprinkle the spices on top (the pods of the cardamom seeds can go in as well). Next add the rest of the ingredients, then, over a gentle heat, slowly bring everything up to simmering point. Put the lid on and pop the casserole in the oven on a low shelf and leave it there for 3 hours, by which time the orange skins will be meltingly tender. When the oranges have cooled, store them in a jar or a lidded polythene box in the fridge for a couple of days to allow the flavours to develop.

Serves 6-8
2 navel oranges, each cut into 16 wedges, skin left on
6 fl oz (175 ml) tawny port
1 teaspoon coriander seeds
6 cardamom pods
4 whole cloves
1 inch (2.5 cm) piece fresh root ginger, peeled and cut into thin slices
½ cinnamon stick
4 oz (110 g) light brown soft sugar
4 fl oz (120 ml) water

You will also need a lidded flameproof casserole with a diameter of 8 inches (20 cm) and a capacity of 4 pints (2.25 litres).

Pre-heat the oven to gas mark 1, 275°F (140°C).

Apple and Almond Crumble

This is another moveable feast because absolutely any fruit can be used. I love it with peaches or apricots in summer, in spring it's good with rhubarb, and in autumn I use half blackberries and half apples. Whatever fruit you use, though, the great thing about the topping is that it bakes to a lovely short, crumbly crispness that is almost crunchy.

Serves 6-8
1 lb 8 oz (700 g) Bramley apples
8 oz (225 g) Cox's apples
1 oz (25 g) light brown soft sugar
1 teaspoon ground cinnamon
¼ teaspoon ground cloves

For the crumble:
4 oz (110 g) whole almonds, skin on
3 oz (75 g) chilled butter, cut into small dice
6 oz (175 g) self-raising flour, sifted
2 teaspoons ground cinnamon
4 oz (110 g) demerara sugar

To serve:
custard or pouring cream

You will also need either an oval ovenproof baking dish measuring 7½ x 11 inches (19 x 28 cm) and 1¾ inches (4.5 cm) deep, or a round ovenproof baking dish with a diameter of 9½ inches (24 cm) and 1¾ inches (4.5 cm) deep.

Pre-heat the oven to gas mark 6, 400°F (200°C).

Begin by preparing the apples. I always find the best way to do this is to cut them first in quarters, then pare off the peel with a potato peeler and slice out the cores. Now cut them into thickish slices and toss them in a bowl with the sugar, cinnamon and ground cloves, then place them in the baking dish and put to one side.

Next make the crumble, which couldn't be simpler, as it is all made in a processor. All you do is place the butter, sifted flour, cinnamon and sugar in the processor and give it a whiz till it resembles crumbs. Next add the almonds and process again, not too fast, until they are fairly finely chopped and there are still a few chunky bits. If you don't have a processor, in a large bowl, rub the butter into the sifted flour until it resembles crumbs, then stir in the cinnamon, sugar and almonds, which should be fairly finely chopped by hand. Now simply sprinkle the crumble mixture all over the apples, spreading it right up to the edges of the dish, and, using the flat of your hands, press it down quite firmly all over; the more tightly it is packed together the crisper it will be. Then finish off by lightly running a fork all over the surface.

Now bake the crumble on the centre shelf of the oven for 35-40 minutes, by which time the apples will be soft and the topping golden brown and crisp. Leave it to rest for 10-15 minutes before serving, then serve it warm with custard or pouring cream.

Key Lime Pie

This is a very famous recipe from Florida, where a certain special variety of limes called Key limes are used. Their season is short and there aren't enough grown to export; however, the pie tastes just as good with other varieties of lime in this authentic American recipe.

Serves 8-10
For the base:
3½ oz (95 g) butter
6 oz (175 g) digestive biscuits
2 oz (50 g) Grape-Nuts

For the filling:
1 tablespoon grated lime zest
(zest 3 limes)
5 fl oz (150 ml) lime juice
(juice 4-5 large limes)
3 large egg yolks
14 oz (400 g) condensed milk

To finish:
a little crème fraîche
lime slices

You will also need a loose-based flan tin with a diameter of 9 inches (23 cm), 1 inch (2.5 cm) deep, and a solid baking sheet.

Pre-heat the oven to gas mark 4, 350°F (180°C).

Traditional Key lime pie has always had a crumb crust, and I have discovered recently that the addition of Grape-Nuts breakfast cereal gives the whole thing extra crunch. So begin by placing the butter in a pan over the lowest heat to melt, then crush the digestive biscuits. The easiest way to do this is to lay them out flat in a polythene bag and crush them with a rolling pin, rolling over using a lot of pressure. Now empty the contents of the bag into a bowl and mix in the Grape-Nuts, then add the melted butter and mix well. Next place the butter-crumb mixture in the flan tin and, using your hands, press it down evenly and firmly all over the base and up the sides of the tin. Then place it on the baking sheet and bake on the centre shelf of the oven for 10-12 minutes, or until crisp and golden brown.

While that's happening, place the egg yolks and lime zest in a bowl and, using an electric hand mixer, whisk them for about 2 minutes, or until the egg has thickened, then add the condensed milk and whisk for another 4 minutes. Finally, add the lime juice and give it another quick whisk, then pour the whole lot on to the baked crust and return it to the oven for another 20 minutes, or until it feels just set when you lightly press the centre with your little finger. Now remove it from the oven and, when it's completely cold, cover it with clingfilm and chill until needed. Serve cut in slices with crème fraîche and a twist of lime for decoration.

9

Cheese in the kitchen

Cheese with 'L' plates is how I want to introduce this chapter, because for a beginner, getting to grips with cheese as a universal subject can be a little fearsome. That said, though, cheese for me will always be one of nature's supreme culinary gifts, for the same magic ingredient the world over originally preserved the excess milk yields of four species (cows, goats, sheep and, to a small degree, buffalo) and transformed them into such a vast eclectic miscellany of textures and flavours, national and regional.

All of these are governed by varying climatic conditions, the types of grazing or feeding, with mountain air, sea breezes, highlands and marshlands all playing their part – and not forgetting the wealth of human skill and creativity that goes not just into the making of the cheese but into its careful ripening and maturing.

In a very short space of time – just 30 years – we have all moved into a vast new world of cheese. I can remember when there was only a handful of British cheeses to choose from, but now we're witnessing something akin to a cheese revolution. There are now not only countless excellent British regional cheesemakers, but a good number of exceptional Irish cheeses available, too. All this has taken place alongside a multiplicity of imported varieties. So to say we're spoilt for choice would be something of an understatement!

Cheese – the ultimate fast feast

What else can provide, all by itself, an instant but interesting, complete nourishing meal without any cooking? One 15th-century writer reverently described it as being part of the Trinity of the Table, along with good bread and fine wine. Another revered combination, equally sublime but perhaps more British, would be the partnership of good, sharp cheese with real ale, crusty home-baked bread and home-made chutney (or the Irish version, with Guinness or Murphy's and home-baked soda bread).

Without bread, cheese has a wonderful affinity with crackers, oatcakes or digestive biscuits, the last adding a touch of sweetness to a sharp, assertive cheese. Or, as my Yorkshire grandparents taught me, the combination of the same with some rich, dark, brandied fruitcake makes a lovely sharp and sweet contrast – great at Christmas with a glass of port.

The milder, lactic cheeses, such as Cotherstone or Lancashire, are great with crisp, sharp apples, while blue cheeses seem to have an affinity with crunchy celery and fresh-shelled walnuts. In Italy, Pecorino Romano is often served with ripe, fragrant pears, and in Spain they serve thin slices of their famous Manchego with a sweet paste made of quince.

Cheese for eating (the five families)

For a beginner, the easiest way to get a knowledge of cheese is to place them into five groups, or families.

1) Squidgy and creamy

These are called soft-paste cheeses and are distinctive in that they have floury, unwashed rinds. The most famous of these are Camembert, Brie and Coulommiers, all from Normandy. Now there is strong competition from Scotland in their version, called Bonchester, and another beautiful cheese called Cooleeney from Ireland. Other popular squidgy-creamy cheeses are Brie de Meaux, Reblochon, Emlett (sheep) and Tymsboro (goat).

2) Medium-soft

These are slightly firmer than the previous group, but still have a soft texture, and they undergo a washing process that keeps the rind moist and helps to encourage fermentation. Pont l'Evêque is from Normandy, whilst Taleggio is from Italy. Other cheeses I would include in this group include Livarot, also from Normandy, and Durrus and Milleen, both of which are from Ireland.

3) Hard and not so hard

This family includes pressed, uncooked cheeses, where the curds are drained and bandaged in a cheese cloth, placed in moulds and then kept under pressure for up to 24 hours. The hardest of these are Pecorino Romano, Grana Padano and the world-famous Parmesan (Parmigiano Reggiano). Pecorino is a sheep's cheese very much like Parmesan, but has a coarser, sharper flavour.

Then comes the less-hard group, including Cheddar, Leicester, Double Gloucester and Cheshire, as well as the hard but crumbly varieties, such as Lancashire, Cotherstone and Feta.

Finally, there are the cheeses with holes, which have undergone a sort of cooking process before being put into moulds and pressed as above. During the maturing period fermentation occurs internally, and this creates the little air pockets, or holes, that distinguish this type of cheese, of which the most famous are Gruyère and Emmenthal.

4) The blues

What happens here is the cheese is injected with a harmless penicillin mould while the cheese is being made. This lies quite dormant during the maturation process, but then later on needles are inserted to allow air in, activating the mould, which then spreads itself in tiny blueish-green veins throughout the cheese during the rest of the maturing period. Three countries claim to have the finest blue cheese: from France, Roquefort, from Italy, Gorgonzola, and from England, Stilton, all great cheeses indeed, although I would say that Cashel Blue from Ireland is another great blue.

Other examples are Shropshire Blue, Bleu de Bresse and Dolcelatte (a milder Gorgonzola).

5) Goats' cheese

These can be like any of the groups above, from a soft, spreadable young cheese with a mild flavour, to a well-matured, strong, zesty, very goaty-flavoured one. For eating I like the strong-flavoured French Crottins de Chavignol, the English Chabis, or Mine Gabhar, which is Welsh. The log-shaped Chèvre, dusted in ashes, is a medium-matured softer goats' cheese. For a fresh farmhouse goats' cheese with a milder flavour that also grills very well, Perroche is superb. But because the quantity of goats' cheese made on farms fluctuates with the seasons, it is often in short supply. There are farm-made soft-rind goats' cheeses labelled Welsh or Somerset, which are fine for cooking.

Fresh soft curd cheeses

This is the unfermented fresh cheese collection – all are made from skimmed, semi-skimmed, whole milk or cream. Because these are not strictly in the same cheese class as those just mentioned, information about these is in the dairy chapter (page 172), where I think they sit more happily.

How to serve a good cheese board

Keep it simple is my philosophy on this one, and what I would do is choose one cheese from each of the following groups: one soft, squidgy cheese (Camembert, for example), one hard cheese (unpasteurised Cheddar), one blue cheese (Cashel Blue), one medium-soft (Taleggio) and one goats' cheese (Crottin). A cheese board sample is photographed left. Simply pick any five cheeses, using the lists to guide you as to what you would prefer.

Pasteurised or unpasteurised?

Pasteurised is a word that causes much debate both within the world of cheesemaking and amongst consumers and cheese lovers everywhere. In cheesemaking the skill is directed towards the flavour and aroma of the finished cheese. This is derived from the animal that has given its milk and the plant oils it has digested. We have all experienced that particular taste and smell, which we are at a loss to describe other than it's like tasting the farm or the countryside. Every good cheese, like every fine wine, has its own unique and special earthiness, which is linked to its equally unique and special environment.

Thus if raw, untreated milk is used to make the cheese, all that's described above is left intact and unimpaired. What pasteurisation (heat-treating the milk) does is destroy any harmful microorganisms, which may be a good thing when the traditional care and skill of the cheesemaker has not been adhered to, but the bad thing is it can destroy much of the flavour-enriching microorganisms at the same time. So it is argued that pasteurised cheese can never have the distinctive and unique flavour that will satisfy a true cheese lover. I would say that in my own experience I have found this to be absolutely true, and I would always go that extra mile for an unpasteurised Camembert or Cheddar. However, there is a new generation of skillful and clever cheesemakers who are making excellent cheeses with pasteurised milk, so in the end, let your palate be your guide.

Cheese for cooking

Some cheeses are best simply for eating as they are; others are good to eat and also respond extremely well in cooking; others are best kept just for cooking, and below I have put cooking cheeses into three categories.

Strong and assertive

Stilton	Strong unpasteurised Cheddar
Gorgonzola	Parmesan (Parmigiano Reggiano)
Pecorino	Crottin
Roquefort	

Cheesy but subtle

Gruyère	Medium Cheddar
Feta	Lancashire
Fontina	Brie
Medium goats' cheese	

Subtle and creamy

Mozzarella	Taleggio
Ricotta	Mild goats' cheese

Good melting cheeses

This group melts in a flash, so is excellent for cooking, and includes Fontina, Gruyère, Mozzarella and smoked Mozzarella (Scamorza).

How to store cheese

This is a question there is no absolute definitive answer to. I have heard of suitable cool places: a spare bedroom (no heating on), garages, garden sheds and car boots, but it all depends on the weather. I was once storing and ripening a Camembert in my garage, and the weather turned warm when I was away and my mother was looking after the house. I got a call that said something like, 'I think there's something dead in your garage.'

Storing cheese in the fridge at too low a temperature means the flavour can be impaired, but if the weather is hot, sweaty cheese is hardly preferable.

The real answer to this question is to buy your cheese from a reliable supplier (see page 251). You will then receive it in good condition so it's ready to eat, so the very best thing to do is eat it a.s.a.p., otherwise store the cheese, wrapped carefully – with no cracks or bits showing – in either waxed paper or greaseproof or parchment paper, sealed with adhesive tape or an elastic band. If the weather is cool, any of the places mentioned above is suitable, if not then place it in the lowest part of the refrigerator. Clingfilm is not recommended, but I do keep my Parmesan in a polythene bag tied at the top in a cheese box in the fridge, and it keeps very well.

Welsh Rabbit with Sage and Onions

Rarebit or rabbit? I like the latter, which (so the story goes) is what the hunter had for his supper when the rabbits had escaped his gun.

Serves 4 for lunch or as a starter or 2 as a main course

4 large, thick slices from a good-quality white sandwich loaf
1 dessertspoon chopped fresh sage
1 rounded dessertspoon grated onion
8 oz (225 g) mature Cheddar, grated
1 rounded teaspoon mustard powder
4 tablespoons brown ale
1 large egg, beaten
1 teaspoon Worcestershire sauce
a pinch cayenne pepper

You will also need a grill pan or baking tray lined with foil.

Pre-heat the grill to its highest setting.

Begin by mixing all the ingredients together, apart from the bread and cayenne pepper. Now place the bread under the grill and toast it on both sides till crisp and golden, then remove it to a toast rack for 3 minutes to get really crisp. After that, divide the cheese mixture into 4, spread it over the toast – right to the edges so they don't get burnt – then sprinkle each one with a light dusting of cayenne pepper. Then back they go under the grill, 3 inches (7.5 cm) from the heat, until the cheese is golden brown and bubbling, which will take 4-5 minutes. Serve it just as it is or with some salad leaves and a sharp dressing.

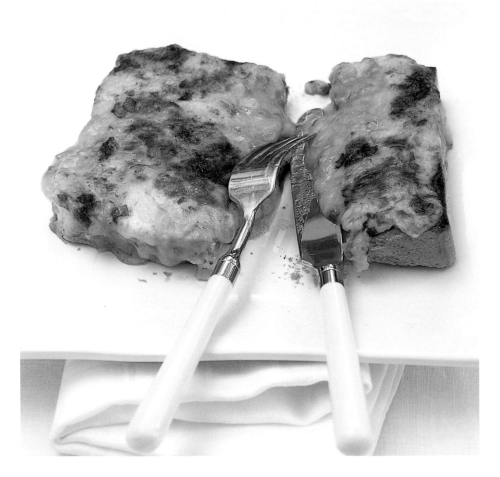

Crumpet Pizza

Well, a crumpet pizza does make sense if you think about it – soft, squidgy bread that gets lightly toasted for just a bit of crunch, then all those wonderful holes so that the cheese and other ingredients can melt right down into it. And because crumpets are quite small, the fillings get piled up very high and it all becomes rather lovely.

All you do is lightly toast the crumpets on each side (they can be quite close to the heat at this stage) – they need to be lightly golden, which takes about 1 minute on each side. Then remove them to a baking sheet and all you do is pile up the Gorgonzola and Mozzarella on each crumpet, then sprinkle with the chopped walnuts and, finally, place the sage leaves – first dipped in the olive oil – on top. Now back they go under the hot grill, but this time 5 inches (13 cm) from the heat source, for 5 minutes, by which time the cheeses will have melted, the walnuts toasted and the sage become crisp. Then you can serve them absolutely immediately.

You can get really creative and make up loads more ideas of your own. Obviously the whole thing can be very easily adapted to whatever happens to be available.

Serves 4 as a snack or 2 as a main course

4 crumpets

6 oz (175 g) Gorgonzola, cubed

2 oz (50 g) Mozzarella, cubed

2 oz (50 g) chopped walnuts

12 medium-sized fresh sage leaves

1 tablespoon olive oil

Pre-heat the grill to its highest setting.

Mexican Enchiladas with Cheese

What are enchiladas? Well, they're Mexican wheat-flour pancakes that can be spread with some spicy salsa and stuffed with almost anything you have handy – in this case cheese – and then baked. An excellent light lunch dish served with a salad.

Serves 4 for lunch or as a starter or 2 as a main course

For the salsa:
1 x 400 g tin chopped tomatoes
1 medium green chilli (the fat, squat variety that isn't too fiery)
1 medium red onion, peeled and finely chopped
2 heaped tablespoons chopped fresh coriander leaves, plus a little extra to garnish
juice 1 lime
salt and freshly milled black pepper

For the enchiladas:
4 large flour tortillas
4 oz (110 g) Wensleydale, grated
5 oz (150 g) Mozzarella, grated (a block of Mozzarella is best for this)
7 fl oz (200 ml) half-fat crème fraîche

You will also need an ovenproof baking dish measuring 9 inches (23 cm) square and 2 inches (5 cm) deep, lightly oiled, and a frying pan.

Pre-heat the oven to gas mark 4, 350°F (180°C).

Begin by making the salsa: first tip the tomatoes into a sieve over a bowl to let the excess liquid drain away. Next remove the stalk from the chilli, cut it in half, remove and discard the seeds, chop the flesh very finely and place it in a bowl. Then add half the chopped onion, the drained tomatoes, chopped coriander leaves and lime juice, and season well with salt and pepper. Now give everything a thorough mixing.

Meanwhile, mix the two cheeses together in a bowl. Next put the frying pan over a high flame to pre-heat and, when it's hot, dry-fry each of the tortillas for 6 seconds on each side. Place one tortilla on a flat surface and spread a tablespoon of salsa over it, but not quite to the edges, sprinkle over a heaped tablespoon of the cheese mixture, then follow this with a tablespoon of the crème fraîche. Then roll the tortilla up and place it in the baking dish with the sealed-side down. Repeat this with the others, then spread the remaining crème fraîche on top of the tortillas in the dish and sprinkle the rest of the salsa over the top, followed by the remaining cheeses and red onion. Now place the dish on a high shelf of the oven for 25-30 minutes, garnish with the extra coriander and serve absolutely immediately – if you keep them waiting they can become a bit soggy.

Toasted Goats' Cheese with Blackened Sherry-Vinegar Onions

Toasted goats' cheese became very fashionable in the 1990s, and not surprisingly, as it's still a supremely good way to enjoy good goats' cheese just on the point of melting. The blackened onions make a great accompaniment – lots of lovely gutsy flavour.

Serves 4

2 x 100 g soft-rind goats' cheeses, such as Welsh or Somerset (or 4 crottins)
3 fl oz (75 ml) sherry vinegar
1 lb (450 g) large, mild Spanish onions (about 3)
1 oz (25 g) molasses sugar
2 tablespoons extra virgin olive oil
1 small curly lettuce
2 oz (50 g) rocket, stalks removed
salt and freshly milled black pepper

For the vinaigrette:
1 clove garlic, peeled
1 rounded teaspoon Maldon sea salt
1 rounded teaspoon mustard powder
1 dessertspoon balsamic vinegar
1 dessertspoon sherry vinegar
5 tablespoons extra virgin olive oil
freshly milled black pepper

You will also need a baking tray measuring 10 x 14 inches (25.5 x 35 cm) for the onions, and a smaller, solid baking tray, lightly oiled, for the goats' cheese.

Pre-heat the oven to gas mark 8, 450°F (230°C).

Begin this by roasting the onions: first you need to mix the sugar and vinegar together in a large bowl and give it a good whisk, then leave it to one side for 10 minutes or so for the sugar to dissolve. Meanwhile, peel the onions, then, leaving the root intact, cut each one into 8 sections through the root, so in half first and then each half into 4. Then add the onions and oil to the vinegar and sugar mixture and toss them around so they get a good coating. After that, spread them out on the baking tray, pouring the rest of the dressing over and season well. Now place them on a high shelf in the oven and cook for 15 minutes; after that turn them over and give them another 15 minutes. Towards the end of the cooking time, check them and remove and set aside any that are in danger of over-blackening. Continue to cook the rest till they are all fairly dark, then remove them from the oven and set aside – they're not meant to be served hot.

When you are ready to serve the salad, pre-heat the grill to its highest setting for at least 10 minutes. Then make the vinaigrette dressing by first crushing the garlic and salt to a creamy paste in a pestle and mortar, then work in the mustard. Now switch to a whisk and add the vinegars and oil, then season with freshly milled black pepper. Next slice each goats' cheese in half so you have 4 rounds, season these with freshly milled black pepper. Now place them on the oiled baking tray and grill them 3 inches (7.5 cm) from the heat for 5-7 minutes, until they are brown on top and soft (if you use the smaller crottins these take only 3-4 minutes).

While they're grilling, arrange some lettuce leaves on each serving plate and divide and scatter the rocket between them. Then, when the cheese is ready, place one in the middle of each plate, scatter the onion all round and, finally, drizzle the vinaigrette dressing over each salad. Needless to say, lots of crusty bread should be available.

Pasta with Four Cheeses

I know you can see only three cheeses in the smaller picture below, but there is a hidden one, because Torta Gorgonzola is in fact made from layers of two cheeses, Gorgonzola and Mascarpone, as you can see from the main picture. Add to that Ricotta and some Pecorino and you have a five-star recipe – including the best-quality pasta, of course!

Serves 2

8 oz (225 g) dried pasta (penne, for example)
2 oz (50 g) Ricotta
3 oz (75 g) Torta Gorgonzola, diced
1 oz (25 g) Pecorino Romano, finely grated, plus a little extra to serve
2 tablespoons snipped fresh chives
Maldon sea salt

You need to start this by measuring out the cheeses on a plate to have them at the ready, then cook the pasta in plenty of boiling salted water for 1 minute less than the full cooking time (if you're using Martelli or other good-quality pasta this would be 11 minutes) – but you need to know your pasta, so see Book One. As soon as it's ready, drain the pasta in a colander and immediately return it to the saucepan so that it still has quite a bit of moisture clinging to it. Now quickly add the chives, Ricotta, Torta Gorgonzola and Pecorino, and stir till the cheese begins to melt. Serve it in hot bowls with the extra Pecorino on the table to sprinkle over.
Note: if you can't find Torta Gorgonzola, there is a very similar layered cheese called Torta di Dolcelatte, which you could use instead.

Cauliflower Soup with Roquefort

This is a truly sublime soup, as the cauliflower and Roquefort seem to meld together so well, but I have also tried it with mature Cheddar, and I'm sure it would be good with any cheese you happen to have handy. More good news – it takes little more than 40 minutes to make.

The stock for this is very simply made with all the cauliflower trimmings. All you do is trim the cauliflower into small florets and then take the stalk bits, including the green stems, and place these trimmings in a medium-sized saucepan. Then add the water, bay leaves and some salt, bring it up to the boil and simmer for 20 minutes with a lid.

Meanwhile, take another large saucepan with a well-fitting lid, melt the butter in it over a gentle heat, then add the onion, celery, leek and potato, cover and let the vegetables gently sweat for 15 minutes. Keep the heat very low, then, when the stock is ready, strain it into the pan to join the vegetables, adding the bay leaves as well but throwing out the rest. Now add the cauliflower florets, bring it all back up to simmering point and simmer very gently for 20-25 minutes, until the cauliflower is completely tender, this time without a lid.

After that, remove the bay leaves, then place the contents of the saucepan in a food processor or liquidiser and process until the soup is smooth and creamy. Next return it to the saucepan, stir in the crème fraîche and cheese and keep stirring until the cheese has melted and the soup is hot but not boiling. Check the seasoning, then serve in hot bowls, garnished with the chives.

Serves 4-6

1 medium, good-sized cauliflower (about 1 lb 4 oz/570 g)
2 oz (50 g) Roquefort, crumbled into small pieces
2½ pints (1.5 litres) water
2 bay leaves
1 oz (25 g) butter
1 medium onion, peeled and chopped
2 sticks celery, chopped
1 large leek, trimmed, washed and chopped
4 oz (110 g) potato, peeled and chopped into dice
2 tablespoons half-fat crème fraîche
salt and freshly milled black pepper

To serve:
1 tablespoon snipped fresh chives

Caramelised Balsamic and Red-Onion Tarts with Goats' Cheese

The long, slow cooking of red onions and balsamic vinegar gives a lovely sweet, concentrated, caramel consistency. These are then spooned into crispy cheese-pastry cases and topped with goats' cheese and thyme. Serve as a special first course with some balsamic-dressed salad leaves.

Makes 8

For the pastry:

3 oz (75 g) butter, at room temperature

6 oz (175 g) plain flour, plus a little extra for rolling

2 oz (50 g) mature Cheddar, grated

½ teaspoon mustard powder

a pinch cayenne pepper

a little cold water

1 large egg, beaten, for brushing

For the filling:

6 tablespoons balsamic vinegar

2 lb (900 g) red onions, peeled and very finely sliced

2 x 100 g soft-rind goats' cheeses, such as Welsh or Somerset, top and bottom rinds removed and discarded, each sliced into 4 rounds

1 oz (25 g) butter

1 dessertspoon chopped fresh thyme

8 sprigs fresh thyme

a little olive oil

cayenne pepper, for sprinkling

salt and freshly milled black pepper

You will also need 8 mini flan tins, each with a base diameter of 4¼ inches (11 cm), ¾ inches (2 cm) deep, greased, and a 6 inch (15 cm) plate to cut around.

Pre-heat the oven to gas mark 4, 350°F (180°C).

First make the pastry by rubbing the butter lightly into the flour, then add the cheese, mustard and cayenne, plus just enough cold water to make a smooth dough – 1-2 tablespoons. Then place the dough in a polythene bag to rest in the refrigerator for 20 minutes. After that, roll it out as thinly as possible and use the plate as a guide to cut out 8 rounds. Line the greased flan tins with the pastry and lightly prick the bases with a fork, then place on a baking sheet and cook on the centre shelf of the oven for 15-20 minutes, or until the pastry is cooked through but not coloured. Then allow the pastry cases to cool on a wire rack and store them in an airtight container until they are needed.

To make the filling, melt the butter in a heavy-based medium-sized saucepan, stir in the onions, balsamic vinegar and chopped thyme, season and let everything cook very gently without a lid, stirring often, for about 30 minutes, until the mixture has reduced down, taken on a lovely glazed appearance and all the excess liquid has evaporated. Then let the mixture cool until you are ready to make the tarts.

To bake the tarts, brush a little beaten egg over each pastry case and pop them back in the oven – same temperature as before – for 5 minutes: this helps to provide a seal for the pastry and stops it from becoming soggy. Now spoon the onion mixture into the cases and top each one with a slice of goats' cheese and a sprig of thyme that has first been dipped in the olive oil. Finally, sprinkle with a little cayenne pepper and bake for 20 minutes.

Cheese and Herb Fritters with Sweet-Pepper Marmalade

If you want to serve a meal without meat or fish, this is just the thing. It's also a great recipe for using up odd bits of cheese, which can be varied as long as the total amount ends up being 12 oz (350 g) for four people or 6 oz (175 g) for two. The sweet-pepper marmalade is an amazingly good accompaniment and keeps well, so can be made in advance.

Begin this by sifting the 2 oz (50 g) of flour and cayenne pepper into a large bowl and season with salt and black pepper, then make a well in the centre and break the eggs into it. Now gradually whisk in the eggs, incorporating any bits of flour from the edge of the bowl as you do so. Next whisk in the milk until you have a smooth batter, then gently stir in the grated cheeses and herbs. Now cover the bowl and leave it to stand in a cool place for about an hour, as this allows all the flavours to develop.

While that's happening you can make the sweet-pepper marmalade. First heat the oil in a saucepan over a medium heat and, when it's hot, add the onion and peppers. Cook them, tossing them around from time to time, until golden and tinged brown – about 10 minutes – then add the garlic and cook for another minute. Now add the sugar, cider vinegar and cider, stir and bring everything back up to simmering point. Then season with salt and freshly milled black pepper, turn the heat down to its lowest setting and simmer gently, uncovered, for 1¼ hours, or until the liquid has almost evaporated and you have a thick, marmalade consistency.

When you're ready to cook the fritters, take 1 tablespoon of the mixture at a time and make 12 rounds, flatten them gently to about 2½ inches (6 cm) in diameter, then lightly dust each one with the seasoned flour. Next, heat the oil over a highish heat in the frying pan and, when it's shimmering hot, cook half the fritters over a medium heat for 45-60 seconds each side, or until golden brown and crispy. Then carefully lift them out of the pan to drain on crumpled greaseproof or kitchen paper. Keep the first batch warm while you cook the second, then serve with the sweet-pepper marmalade. A green salad would make a good accompaniment.

Serves 4

4 oz (110 g) Feta, finely grated
4 oz (110 g) Gruyère, finely grated
4 oz (110 g) mature Cheddar, finely grated
3 heaped tablespoons chopped mixed herbs (basil, thyme, oregano and parsley, for example)
2 oz (50 g) plain flour, plus 1 slightly rounded dessertspoon seasoned flour
2 good pinches cayenne pepper
2 large eggs
2 tablespoons milk
3 tablespoons olive oil
salt and freshly milled black pepper

For the sweet-pepper marmalade:
2 large red peppers, deseeded, thinly sliced into lengths, then cut into 1 inch (2.5 cm) pieces
1 tablespoon olive oil
1 medium onion, peeled and finely chopped
2 cloves garlic, peeled and crushed
2 tablespoons dark brown soft sugar
3 tablespoons cider vinegar
8 fl oz (225 ml) medium cider
salt and freshly milled black pepper

You will also need a frying pan with a diameter of 10 inches (25.5 cm).

Semolina Gnocchi with Gorgonzola

In Book One we made potato gnocchi, but this is another quite different version, made with semolina instead of potato. They are equally charming, with crisp, baked edges, and are light and fluffy on the inside. Remember, though, that the mixture needs to be prepared the day before you want to serve the gnocchi.

Serves 3-4

5 oz (150 g) coarse semolina
2 oz (50 g) Gorgonzola Piccante, chopped into small dice
10 fl oz (275 ml) milk
10 fl oz (275 ml) water
freshly grated nutmeg
2½ oz (60 g) Parmesan (Parmigiano Reggiano), finely grated
2 large eggs
2 oz (50 g) Ricotta
salt and freshly milled black pepper

You will also need a non-stick baking tin measuring 6 x 10 inches (15 x 25.5 cm), 1 inch (2.5 cm) deep, lined with silicone paper (parchment), a 2 inch (5 cm) pastry cutter and an ovenproof baking dish measuring 7½ inches (19 cm) square and 2 inches (5 cm) deep, lightly buttered.

First of all you'll need a large saucepan, and into that put the milk and water, along with a good grating of nutmeg, 1 teaspoon of salt and some freshly milled black pepper. Then sprinkle in the semolina and, over a medium heat and stirring constantly with a wooden spoon, bring it all up to the boil. Let the mixture simmer gently for about 4 minutes, still stirring, until it is thick enough to stand the spoon up in, then remove the pan from the heat and beat in 2 oz (50 g) of the Parmesan and the eggs. Now adjust the seasoning, then pour the mixture into the prepared tin and spread it out evenly with a spatula. When it's absolutely cold, cover the tin with clingfilm and leave it in the fridge overnight to firm up.

When you are ready to cook the gnocchi, pre-heat the oven to gas mark 6, 400°F (200°C). Turn the cheese and semolina mixture out on to a board and peel away the silicone paper, then cut the mixture into 2 inch (5 cm) rounds with the pastry cutter, reshape the trimmings and cut out more rounds until the mixture is all used up. I quite like rounds, but if you prefer you can cut out squares or triangles – it makes no difference. Place them slightly overlapping in the baking dish, then dot with the Ricotta and sprinkle over the Gorgonzola, followed by the rest of the Parmesan. Bake on a high shelf of the oven for 30 minutes, until the gnocchi are golden brown and the cheese is bubbling.

Begin by adding the semolina to the milk and water mixture in the pan

Bring to the boil, then simmer till you can stand the spoon upright in the mixture

Next beat in the grated Parmesan and eggs, then taste to check the seasoning

Spread the mixture out in the tin and, once cold, cover and refrigerate overnight

Turn the mixture out, peel the base paper away and stamp the gnocchi out

Lay them in the dish, add the remaining cheeses and bake until golden brown

Curd Cheesecake with Greek Yoghurt, Honey and Pistachios

Well, the title says it all, and you can imagine what a brilliant combination of flavours and textures this is. It's quite simply one of the best cheesecakes ever, and perfect for parties, as it's quite large. It's also extremely good topped with summer fruits, in which case add 2 oz (50 g) of caster sugar to the curd cheese and top with 1 lb (450 g) of any mixture of soft fruit, then dust with icing sugar before serving. Don't forget that cheesecakes are best left in the warmth of the oven to get cold, as this stops them from cracking, so you need to think ahead.

First of all make the cheesecake base: first melt the butter in a saucepan over a very low heat, then spread the biscuits out flat in a polythene bag and crush them firmly with a rolling pin. Next tip the crumbs into a bowl, along with the chopped pistachios. Now add the Grape-Nuts and melted butter and mix everything together, then spread the mixture over the base of the tin, pressing it down very firmly, and pop it on the baking sheet and into the oven for 20 minutes.

Now, in another bowl, combine the curd cheese, eggs and vanilla and beat with an electric hand whisk until the mixture is smooth and velvety. Then pour this into the tin, on top of the crumbs, smooth the top and place it back on the baking sheet on the centre shelf of the oven for 30 minutes, then turn the oven off and let the cheesecake get quite cold in the oven. After that it should be covered and chilled for at least 2 hours, or preferably overnight.

To serve, unmould the cheesecake, spread the surface with the yoghurt first, then drizzle with the honey and scatter the pistachios over. Serve with extra honey at the table to spoon over.

Serves 10-12
1 lb 8 oz (700 g) curd cheese
2 oz (50 g) shelled unsalted pistachios, roughly chopped
3 oz (75 g) butter
6 oz (175 g) sweet oat biscuits
1 oz (25 g) Grape-Nuts cereal
3 large eggs, beaten
2 teaspoons vanilla extract

To finish:
7 oz (200 g) Greek yoghurt
3 tablespoons Greek honey, plus a little extra to serve
about 1 oz (25 g) shelled unsalted pistachios, roughly chopped

You will also need a springform tin with a diameter of 9 inches (23 cm), and a solid baking sheet.

Pre-heat the oven to gas mark 2, 300°F (150°C).

10
Proper chocolate

Evocations of the chocolate of my childhood have flooded my mind while pondering this introduction. Even when I was very small I much preferred the dark, sophisticated adult-tasting chocolate to the over-sweet milky version. I had a favourite brand – no longer available, unfortunately – called Nestlé Superfine, which was always given to me on birthdays.

Sometimes it was a straight chocolate bar; sometimes it contained clusters of dark, highly roasted almonds. Either way it was always an enormous treat, not only to be anticipated but to be savoured right down to the very last square. Those were the days of sweet rationing in the early years after the war, and I sometimes think it's sad that the specialness of chocolate has faded. Now it's available everywhere from kiosks, tobacconists and vending machines and so has become just an ordinary everyday item. Worse than that, the mass marketing of chocolate has brought an inevitable downgrading in quality, and the nation's increasing addiction to sugar and sugar substitutes has meant that chocolate is not always eaten for itself but as a backdrop, more to satisfy a craving for sweetness, so much so that if you're addicted to sweet substances like diet cola and so on the true glory of chocolate will probably escape you. What, then, is the true glory?

To discover it we need to consider how much *actual* chocolate is in a chocolate bar. It is a moot point. Close examination of the packaging will reveal that it can be as high as 75 or as low as 20 per cent. For chocolate lovers – and particularly for the cook – these variations need explaining.

What is chocolate?

Chocolate comes from the cocoa bean, the fruit of the cacao tree, which grows in Africa, South America and the West Indies, and the beans vary in quality and flavour. After roasting and crushing, the beans become a thick paste called chocolate mass, and this is composed of cocoa solids and cocoa butter, which is chocolate's natural oil. Cocoa solids, once they are crushed again and sieved, become cocoa powder. For chocolate, however, cocoa butter is essential, as this is what gives it its melting qualities, and the higher the proportion, the better the chocolate. We need not concern ourselves here with the complexities of how the beans are transformed into the silky-textured ingredient known as chocolate; what we do need to know is how much actual cocoa the chocolate contains. My advice is not to worry about technical words such as cocoa mass, cocoa butter or cocoa solids, but to look fairly and squarely at the word cocoa on the packet. How much does it have? Manufacturers usually use the words 'cocoa solids', and we need 75 per cent if we want an intensely chocolatey flavour, and if we are cooking with it and adding it to other ingredients (which will dilute it somewhat), it's essential to get the highest-possible cocoa-solid content.

What is *not* chocolate?

If only 20 per cent of the essential component, cocoa solids, is present in a chocolate bar, this means 80 per cent of it comprises something else. This can be vegetable fat or butterfat, emulsifiers, milk solids, flavourings and, worst of all, sugar – so much of it that the small quantity of cocoa solid is killed. The reason for this is that mass marketing is always about price. Real chocolate costs more money, so the higher the cocoa content, the higher the price. But here we are concerned with how to cook, and with chocolate that means getting the best you can afford.

How to buy chocolate

Thankfully people are rediscovering real chocolate and, for eating, it is even possible for the connoisseur to buy chocolate made from single-estate cocoa plantations, each with their own distinctive characteristics. These will be clearly marked 75 per cent cocoa solids and you will find just three ingredients listed: cocoa, sugar and cocoa butter. For cooking it's now easy to buy 75 per cent cocoa-solid chocolate, which will contain an emulsifier called lecithin and, sometimes, a flavouring such as vanilla.

Milk and white chocolates

With milk chocolate, the chocolate's intense flavour is purposely diluted to produce a creamier taste. This is achieved by adding whole milk solids, sometimes in equal quantity to the cocoa solids. White chocolate is not actually chocolate at all. It is made from milk solids, sugar and fat, with a little cocoa butter added, and has a bland, over-sweet taste. Neither are ideal for cooking as such, but are useful for coating or topping (see page 248).

Listen to the snap

We had great fun, while filming the television series, demonstrating how to tell good chocolate from not-so-good. The secret is in the snap. When you break off a piece of good-quality chocolate it makes a sharp, quite definite 'snap'. With a lesser chocolate it is just a dull break – if you hear anything at all. We found the sensitive microphone picked up the snap superbly, so that none of us could be in any doubt ever again.

Cooking with chocolate

I have learnt how to deal with chocolate the hard way, as I have, more often than I care to remember, ended up with a claggy lump fit only for the bin. The outcome of these disasters is that I now know the solution to the problem of melting chocolate: that is to follow the instructions below to the letter and never rush it! I know it's a bore, but believe me, you have to wait.

How to melt chocolate

Here you'll need a large heatproof bowl to sit over a saucepan containing a couple of inches of barely simmering water, making sure the base of the bowl doesn't touch the water. Break up the chocolate, add the pieces to the bowl and, keeping the heat at its lowest, leave them to melt – it will take 5-10 minutes to become smooth and glossy (though the time will vary depending on the amount of chocolate – individual timings are given in each recipe). Then remove it from the heat, give it a good stir and it's ready.

   A list of quality mail-order chocolate suppliers is given on page 251.

A Very Chocolatey Mousse

This was the chocolate recipe of the 1960s, but it has now, sadly, been eclipsed by other eras and their equally fashionable recipes. So time for a revival, I think, because it's certainly one of the simplest but nicest chocolate desserts of all.

Serves 6

7 oz (200 g) dark chocolate (75 per cent cocoa solids), broken into pieces
4 fl oz (120 ml) warm water
3 large eggs, separated
1½ oz (40 g) golden caster sugar

To serve:
a little whipped cream (optional)

You will also need 6 ramekins, each with a capacity of 5 fl oz (150 ml), or 6 individual serving glasses.

First of all place the broken-up chocolate and warm water in a large heatproof bowl, which should be sitting over a saucepan of barely simmering water, making sure the bowl doesn't touch the water. Then, keeping the heat at its lowest, allow the chocolate to melt slowly – it should take about 6 minutes. Now remove it from the heat and give it a good stir until it's smooth and glossy, then let the chocolate cool for 2-3 minutes before stirring in the egg yolks. Then give it another good mix with a wooden spoon.

Next, in a clean bowl, whisk the egg whites to the soft-peak stage, then whisk in the sugar, about a third at a time, then whisk again until the whites are glossy. Now, using a metal spoon, fold a tablespoon of the egg whites into the chocolate mixture to loosen it, then carefully fold in the rest. You need to have patience here – it needs gentle folding and cutting movements so that you retain all the precious air, which makes the mousse light. Next divide the mousse between the ramekins or glasses and chill for at least 2 hours, covered with clingfilm. I think it's also good to serve the mousse with a blob of softly whipped cream on top.
Note: this recipe contains raw eggs.

Chocolate-Crunch Torte with Pistachios and Sour Cherries

This is the easiest chocolate recipe ever invented – I first made a more basic version on children's television. Since then it's got much more sophisticated, but the joy of its simplicity and the fact that no cooking is required make it a real winner for busy people.

Begin this the day before by soaking the dried cherries and raisins in the rum overnight. When you are ready to make the torte, place the broken-up chocolate and butter in a large heatproof bowl, which should be sitting over a saucepan of barely simmering water, making sure the bowl doesn't touch the water. Then, keeping the heat at its lowest, allow the chocolate to melt – it should take about 6 minutes to become smooth and glossy. Now remove the bowl from the pan, give the chocolate a good stir and let it cool for 2-3 minutes. Next, fold in the whipped cream, followed by the soaked fruits in rum, the pistachios and chopped biscuits, and give it all a good mix. Finally, spoon it into the cake tin as evenly as possible, cover with clingfilm and chill for a minimum of 4 hours. To serve, dust the surface with a little cocoa powder, cut the torte into wedges, then serve with crème fraîche, whipped cream or pouring cream.

Serves 12

8 oz (225 g) dark chocolate (75 per cent cocoa solids), broken into pieces
4 oz (110 g) unsalted pistachio nuts, roughly chopped
2 oz (50 g) dried sour cherries
2 oz (50 g) raisins
3 tablespoons rum
2 oz (50 g) butter
5 fl oz (150 ml) double cream, lightly whipped
8 oz (225 g) sweet oat biscuits, roughly chopped

To serve:
a little cocoa powder, to dust
crème fraîche, whipped cream or pouring cream

You will also need a loose-based cake tin with a diameter of 8 inches (20 cm), 1½ inches (4 cm) deep, lightly greased with a flavourless oil.

Melting Chocolate Puddings

This, I suspect, could be the *chocolate recipe for the beginning of the 21st century – very light, very chocolatey individual baked puddings that have a melted fudge-chocolate sauce inside that oozes out as you put your spoon in. My thanks to Galton Blackiston and everyone at Morston Hall in Norfolk for giving me their recipe.*

Serves 8
7 oz (200 g) dark chocolate (75 per cent cocoa solids), broken into pieces
7 oz (200 g) butter, diced
2 tablespoons brandy
4 oz (110 g) golden caster sugar
4 large eggs, plus 4 large egg yolks
1½ teaspoons vanilla extract
2½ oz (60 g) plain flour

To serve:
a little pouring or whipped cream

You will also need 8 mini pudding basins, each with a capacity of 6 fl oz (175 ml), generously brushed with melted butter.

First of all place the broken-up chocolate, along with the butter and brandy, in a large heatproof bowl, which should be sitting over a saucepan of barely simmering water, making sure the bowl doesn't touch the water. Then, keeping the heat at its lowest, allow the chocolate and butter to melt slowly; it should take 6-7 minutes. Then remove it from the heat and give it a good stir until it's smooth and glossy.

While the chocolate is melting, place the sugar, whole eggs, yolks and vanilla extract in a large mixing bowl, place it on a tea towel to steady it, then whisk on a high speed with an electric hand whisk until the mixture has doubled in volume – this will take between 5 and 10 minutes, depending on the power of your whisk. What you need to end up with is a thick, mousse-like mixture that, when you stop the motor and lift the whisk, leaves a trail like a piece of ribbon (*see below left*).

Now you need to pour the melted-chocolate mixture around the edge of the bowl (it's easier to fold it in from the edges) and then sift the flour over the mixture. Using a large metal spoon, carefully but thoroughly fold everything together. Patience is needed here; don't be tempted to hurry it, as careful folding and cutting movements are needed, and this will take 3-4 minutes.

Now divide the mixture between the pudding basins (it should come to just below the top of each one) and line them up on a baking tray. If you like, the puddings can now be covered with clingfilm and kept in the fridge or freezer until you need them.

When you're ready to bake the puddings, pre-heat the oven to gas mark 6, 400°F (200°C). Remove the clingfilm and bake on the centre shelf of the oven for 14 minutes if they have been chilled first, but only 12 if not; after that time the puddings should have risen and feel fairly firm to the touch, although the insides will still be melting. Leave to stand for 1 minute before sliding a palette knife around each pudding and turning out on to individual serving plates. If you're cooking these puddings from frozen, give them about 15 minutes' cooking time and allow them to stand for 2 minutes before turning out. Serve absolutely immediately, with some chilled cream to pour over.

As the puddings cool, the melted chocolate inside continues to set, so they can, if you like, be served cold instead as a fudgey-centred chocolate cake with whipped cream.
Note: this recipe contains partially cooked eggs.

Cheat's Chocolate Trifle

This one's either for people who don't like to cook or for devoted cooks who nonetheless need something really speedy. First you need to zip round the supermarket to collect the ingredients, then, after the cherries have soaked, this is all made in moments.

Serves 8

3 double-chocolate-chip American-style muffins

7 oz (200 g) dark chocolate (75 per cent cocoa solids)

1 x 680 g jar pitted morello cherries, drained and soaked overnight in 3 fl oz (75 ml) dark rum

2 tablespoons morello cherry jam or conserve

9 oz (250 g) Mascarpone

14 oz (400 g) fresh custard

10 fl oz (275 ml) whipping cream

You will also need a trifle bowl or serving dish with a capacity of 4 pints (2.25 litres).

You need to start this recipe the day before you want to serve it, and all you do at this stage is soak the drained cherries overnight in the rum. The next day, begin by slicing the muffins horizontally in half, then spread each slice with some jam and weld the slices back together to their original muffin shape. Now cut each one vertically into 4 pieces approximately ¾ inch (2 cm) wide, and lay these all around the base of the trifle bowl or serving dish. Now take a skewer and stab them to make holes, then strain off the rum the cherries have been soaking in and sprinkle it all over the muffins, scattering the cherries on top.

Now, reserving 2 oz (50 g) of the chocolate for decoration, break the rest up into squares. Place the broken-up chocolate in a large heatproof bowl, which should be sitting over a saucepan of barely simmering water, making sure the bowl doesn't touch the water. Then, keeping the heat at its lowest, allow the chocolate to melt slowly – it should take about 5 minutes to become smooth and glossy. Remove the bowl from the pan and give it a good stir, then let the chocolate cool for 2-3 minutes.

While that's happening, put the Mascarpone in a bowl and beat to soften it, then add the custard and whisk them together. Next whisk in the cooled melted chocolate, then pour the whole lot over the soaked muffins and cherries. Now whip the cream to the floppy stage, then carefully spoon this over the trifle, spreading it out with a palette knife. Lastly chop the rest of the chocolate (using a piece of foil to protect it from the heat of your fingers as you steady it), shredding it very finely. Sprinkle the shreds over the surface of the trifle, cover with clingfilm and chill until needed.

Chocolate and Prune Brownies

I never much cared for the flavour of orange and chocolate or raspberries and chocolate, but prunes and chocolate are, for me, a heavenly partnership. Plus, if, for a special occasion, you soak the prunes in Armagnac, so much the better. Brownies can be served warm as a dessert or just eaten cold as they are.

Begin this the night before you are going to make the brownies by soaking the chopped prunes in the Armagnac. The next day, begin by pre-heating the oven to gas mark 4, 350°F (180°C), then chop the almonds roughly, place them on a baking sheet and toast them in the oven for 8 minutes. Please use a timer here, or you'll be throwing burnt nuts away all day.

While the almonds are toasting, put the chocolate and butter together in a heatproof bowl fitted over a saucepan of barely simmering water, making sure the bowl doesn't touch the water. Allow the chocolate to melt – 4-5 minutes – remove it from the heat, then beat till smooth. Next, stir in the other ingredients, including the prunes and Armagnac, until well blended. Now spread the mixture into the prepared tin and bake on the centre shelf for 30 minutes, or until slightly springy in the centre, then leave it to cool for 10 minutes before cutting into squares and transferring to a wire rack.

Makes 15

2 oz (50 g) dark chocolate (75 per cent cocoa solids), broken into pieces
2 oz (50 g) pitted pruneaux d'Agen, chopped and soaked overnight in
2 fl oz (55 ml) Armagnac
2 oz (50 g) skin-on almonds
4 oz (110 g) butter
2 large eggs, beaten
8 oz (225 g) demerara sugar
2 oz (50 g) plain flour
1 teaspoon baking powder
¼ teaspoon salt

You will also need a non-stick baking tin measuring 10 x 6 inches (25.5 x 15 cm) and 1 inch (2.5 cm) deep, lightly greased and lined with silicone paper (parchment).

Chocolate, Prune and Armagnac Cake

This is the very lightest chocolate cake of all, the reason being that no flour is used – it's simply made with eggs and cocoa powder. It's very fragile, almost soufflé-like, but once you've tried it you'll never want any other kind. Don't forget to start this a couple of days ahead if possible by heating the prunes with the Armagnac and leaving them to soak up all the delicious flavour.

Serves 8

For the cakes:
6 large eggs, separated
5 oz (150 g) golden caster sugar
2 oz (50 g) cocoa powder, sifted

For the filling:
14 oz (400 g) pitted pruneaux d'Agen, soaked overnight (or longer if possible) in
4 fl oz (120 ml) Armagnac (see the introduction)
1 tablespoon crème fraîche

To finish:
5 oz (150 g) dark chocolate (75 per cent cocoa solids), broken into pieces
1 tablespoon crème fraîche

You will also need 2 x 8 inch (20 cm) loose-based sandwich tins, 1½ inches (4 cm) deep, the bases and sides well oiled and the bases lined with silicone paper (parchment).

Pre-heat the oven to gas mark 4, 350°F (180°C).

Start off by first placing the egg whites in a large, clean, grease-free bowl. Put the yolks in another bowl, along with the sugar, and whisk them until they just begin to turn pale and thicken – be careful not to thicken them too much; they need approximately 3 minutes' whisking. After that, gently fold in the sifted cocoa powder.

Next, with a spanking-clean whisk, beat the egg whites until stiff but not too dry. Now, using a metal spoon, fold a heaped tablespoon of the egg white into the chocolate mixture to loosen it up a little, then carefully and gently fold in the rest of the egg white, slowly and patiently trying not to lose any air. Now divide the mixture equally between the prepared sandwich tins and bake near the centre of the oven for 15 minutes. They won't appear to be cooked exactly, just set and slightly puffy and springy in the centre, so when they're taken out of the oven they will shrink (but that's normal, so don't panic). Leave the cakes to cool in their tins, then slide a palette knife around the edges, gently invert them on to a board and carefully strip off the base papers.

To make the filling for the cake, first of all set aside 10-12 of the largest prunes, then place the rest, plus any remaining soaking liquid, in a processor, along with the crème fraîche, and whiz to a purée. After that, transfer the purée straight from the processor on to one half of the cake, placed carefully on to a plate first, then spread the purée out and place the other half of the cake on top.

Now all you need is the chocolate covering. For this place the broken-up pieces of chocolate in a large heatproof bowl, which should be sitting over a saucepan of barely simmering water, making sure the bowl doesn't touch the water. Then, keeping the heat at its lowest, allow the chocolate to melt slowly – it should take about 5 minutes to become smooth and glossy. Then remove it from the heat and give it a good stir, then let the chocolate cool for 2-3 minutes.

Now take each one of the reserved prunes and dip it into the melted chocolate so that half of each one gets covered. As you do this place them on a sheet of parchment paper to set. Next, stir the crème fraîche into the chocolate, then use this mixture to cover the surface of the cake. Spread it over carefully with a palette knife, making ridges with the knife as you go. Now decorate the cake with the chocolate prunes. Cover the whole thing with an upturned, suitably sized bowl or polythene cake container, and keep it in the fridge until about an hour before you need it.

Chocolate Crème Brûlées

Serves 6

5 oz (150 g) dark chocolate (75 per cent cocoa solids), broken into pieces

1 pint (570 ml) whipping cream

6 large egg yolks

2 oz (50 g) golden caster sugar

1 rounded teaspoon cornflour

For the caramel:

6 oz (175 g) white granulated sugar

You will also need 6 ramekins, each with a base diameter of 2½ inches (6 cm), a top diameter of 3 inches (7.5 cm), and 2 inches (5 cm) deep.

What chocolate mousse was to the 1960s, crème brûlée has been to the 1990s, as it seems to have been on almost every restaurant menu. It's truly a great British classic that easily lends itself to variations like this one – a smooth, velvety chocolate custard topped with a very crunchy caramel. Because of the vagaries of domestic grills, I've done a cheat's version of the caramel topping, or there's an alternative using a cook's blow torch.

Start the crème brûlées the day before you want to serve them. Place the broken-up chocolate, along with 5 fl oz (150 ml) of the cream, in a large heatproof bowl sitting over a saucepan of barely simmering water, making sure the bowl doesn't touch the water. Then, keeping the heat at its lowest, allow the chocolate to melt slowly – it should take 5-6 minutes. Remove it from the heat and give it a good stir until it's smooth and glossy, then remove the bowl from the pan and let the mixture cool for 2-3 minutes.

After that, whisk the egg yolks, caster sugar and cornflour together in a separate bowl for about 2 minutes, or until they are thick and creamy.

Now, in a separate pan, heat the remaining cream just up to simmering point and pour it over the egg-yolk mixture, whisking as you pour. Return the whole lot to the pan and continue to stir over a gentle heat until it thickens – this will take 2-3 minutes. Next, whisk the melted chocolate and cream together until completely smooth, add a little of the custard mixture to it and continue to whisk it in. After that, add the remaining custard, whisking until everything is really smooth. Then divide the custard between the ramekins, making sure you leave a ½ inch (1 cm) space at the top for the caramel. Now leave them to cool, cover the pots with clingfilm and chill overnight in the fridge.

A few hours before serving the brûlées, make the caramel. To do this, put the granulated sugar in a small saucepan, place it over a medium heat and leave it like that, keeping an eye on it. When the sugar begins to melt around the edges, *opposite, top*, and just starts to turn liquid – which will take 4-6 minutes – give the pan a good shake and leave it again to melt until it's about a quarter melted. Now, using a wooden spoon, give it a gentle stir, *opposite, centre*, and then continue to cook until the sugar has transformed from crystals to liquid and is the right colour – amber or like dark runny honey, *opposite, bottom*. Keep stirring gently until you're sure all the sugar has dissolved. The whole thing should take 10-15 minutes.

Now remove the pan from the heat, remove the clingfilm and pour the caramel over the custards, covering the surface of each one. Tilt the ramekins gently from side to side to get an even, thin covering of caramel, then leave them for a few minutes for the caramel to harden, and cover them loosely with foil (don't use clingfilm, or the moisture from the brûlées will soften the caramel). Return them to the fridge until needed.

Chocolate Mini Muffins with Toasted Hazelnuts

These were invented specifically for children to make for the 1997 Comic Relief campaign with red cherries on top. This is a more adult version, but children can still make them using chocolate drops for melting and cherries instead of nuts.

Makes 24

2 oz (50 g) dark chocolate (75 per cent cocoa solids), roughly chopped
5 oz (150 g) plain flour
2 tablespoons cocoa powder
1 dessertspoon baking powder
¼ teaspoon salt
1 large egg, lightly beaten
1½ oz (40 g) golden caster sugar
4 fl oz (120 ml) milk
2 oz (50 g) butter, melted and cooled slightly

For the topping:
2 oz (50 g) hazelnuts, roughly chopped
3 oz (75 g) dark chocolate (75 per cent cocoa solids), broken into pieces

You will also need 2 x 12-hole mini-muffin tins, well greased or lined with mini-muffin paper cases.

Pre-heat the oven to gas mark 6, 400°F (200°C).

You need to begin this recipe by toasting the hazelnuts for the topping. To do this, place the chopped nuts on a baking sheet and toast them in the pre-heated oven for 5 minutes; it's important to use a timer here.

Next, for the muffins, start off by sifting the flour, cocoa powder, baking powder and salt into a large bowl. Then, in a separate bowl, mix together the egg, sugar, milk and melted butter. Now return the dry ingredients to the sieve and sift them straight on to the egg mixture (this double sifting is essential because there won't be much mixing going on). What you need to do now is take a large spoon and fold the dry ingredients into the wet ones – quickly, in about 15 seconds. Don't be tempted to beat or stir, and don't be alarmed by the rather unattractive, uneven appearance of the mixture: this, in fact, is what will ensure that the muffins stay light. Now fold the chopped chocolate into the mixture – again with a minimum of stirring; just a quick folding in.

Divide the mixture between the muffin cups, about 1 heaped teaspoon in each, and bake on a high shelf of the pre-heated oven for 10 minutes, until well risen. Then remove the muffins from the oven and cool in the tins for 5 minutes before transferring them to a cooling tray.

While they're cooling, make the topping. To do this, place the broken-up chocolate in a small heatproof bowl, which should be sitting over a saucepan of barely simmering water, making sure the bowl doesn't touch the water. Then, keeping the heat at its lowest, allow the chocolate to melt slowly – it should take about 3 minutes to melt and become smooth and glossy. Then remove it from the heat and give it a good stir, then let the chocolate cool for 2-3 minutes.

Then, when the muffins are cool enough to handle, spoon a little melted chocolate on to each one, then place it back on the cooling tray and scatter the hazelnuts over the top of each muffin.

Suppliers and stockists

Mail-order kitchen equipment suppliers in the UK are as follows:

Lakeland Limited
Alexandra Buildings
Windermere
Cumbria
LA23 1BQ

Telephone: 015394 88100
Fax: 015394 88300

David Mellor
4 Sloane Square
London SW1W 8EE

Telephone: 0207 730 4259
Fax: 0207 730 7240

Divertimenti
45-47 Wigmore Street
London W1H 9LE

Telephone: 0207 935 0689
Website: www.divertimenti.co.uk

For information on the availability of equipment or ingredients in this book, send an A4 sae to:
How To Cook Book Two, 20 Upper Ground, London SE1 9PD.

My choice of quality food suppliers are:

For chicken:

Label Rouge chickens are available from Sainsbury's and Waitrose.

For Kelly's Old Fashioned Original Chicken and a list of their stockists, contact:

Kelly's
Springate Farm
Bicknacre Road
Danbury
Essex CM3 4EP

Telephone: 01245 223 581
Fax: 01245 226 124
Website: www.kelly-turkeys.com

For British cheeses:

Neal's Yard Dairy Mail Order
6 Park Street
Borough Market
London SE1 9AB

Telephone: 0207 407 1800
Fax: 0207 378 0400

For British and continental cheeses:

Paxton and Whitfield Ltd
93 Jermyn Street
London SW1Y 6JE

Telephone: 0207 930 0259
Fax: 0207 321 0621
Website: www.cheesemongers.co.uk

Jeroboams
96 Holland Park Avenue
London W11 3RB

Telephone: 0207 727 9359
Fax: 0207 792 3672

For Jeroboams' mail-order service:
Telephone: 0207 727 9792
Fax: 0207 792 3672

For single-estate chocolate:

Grivan Products Company Ltd
Unit 5
Deptford Trading Estate
Blackhorse Road
London SE8 5HY

Telephone: 0208 692 6993
Fax: 0208 691 2053

Index